# ENCOUNTERING GOD'S WORD

Beginning  biblical studies

Edited by Philip Duce & Daniel Strange

APOLLOS

APOLLOS (an imprint of Inter-Varsity Press)
*38 De Montfort Street, Leicester LE1 7GP, England*
*Email: ivp@uccf.org.uk*
*Website: www.ivpbooks.com*

*First published 2003*

**British Library Cataloguing in Publication Data**
A catalogue record for this book is available from the British Library.

ISBN 0–85111–792–9

Set in Monotype Garamond 11/13pt
Typeset in Great Britain by Servis Filmsetting Ltd, Manchester
Printed and bound in Great Britain by Creative Print and Design (Wales),
Ebbw Vale

*Inter-Varsity Press is the publishing division of the Universities and Colleges Christian
Fellowship (formerly the Inter-Varsity Fellowship), a student movement linking Christian
Unions in universities and colleges throughout Great Britain, and a member movement of the
International Fellowship of Evangelical Students. For more information about local and
national activities write to UCCF, 38 De Montfort Street, Leicester LE1 7GP, email us at
email@uccf.org.uk, or visit the UCCF website at www.uccf.org.uk.*

# CONTENTS

# FOREWORD

When religious and theological students begin their academic study of the Bible, very often they take up the challenge of these courses because they have become Christians and want to know their Bible better. Of course, they may have been warned that academic study of the Bible can be dangerous to their spiritual health, but most students, in my experience, adopt Peter's stance: 'Even if all fall away on account of you, I never will' (Matthew 26:33). Once they enter this academic world, however, they find themselves in a strange domain full of learned writers of whom they have never heard, bristling with arguments and evidence they have no skill or knowledge to evaluate, and sometimes suffused with a none-too-subtle arrogance that is brusque and dismissive of 'fundamentalist' beliefs. Typically, students are then inclined to respond in one of three ways: they may lurch towards academic respectability at the cost of the faith they once held dear; they may create two hermetically sealed chambers in their brains, one for academic thought and the other for worship, with as little communication as possible between the two, leaving themselves exposed to massive epistemological dissonance that will later produce poisonous fruit; or they may slowly learn to engage our culture, our world of contemporary biblical scholarship, discovering on the way that there are alternative bibliographies, alternative ways of looking at things, a long and deep tradition of orthodoxy that cannot be dismissed as cavalierly as some contemporaries think. These latter students will discover that no-one is wrong all the time, and no-one is right all the time, and there are tried-and-tested reasons and means for bringing everything back to the gospel, to the lordship of Jesus, to the test of Scripture.

This little book will help students who opt for the third response; indeed, it may encourage some students to pursue that path who would otherwise never attempt it.

Those who read this book will find it particularly helpful if they do not bring false expectations to the task. This is not so much a book of 'answers' to tough critical questions (though it provides a few) – other books do that sort of thing better. Rather, this is a book that orients you to the study of the Old and New Testaments, by encouraging you to think of what is involved in such study, of some principles of biblical interpretation, of some of the relationships between 'objective' study and 'faith' (where *both* words need defining!), of larger Christian commitments that must be part of faithful study of the Bible. On the one hand, it is characterized by sufficient rigour and integrity that it avoids mere sloganeering; on the other, it is written sensibly, simply, straightfor-wardly, and is pitched at those who are starting out in their journey. And it will prove helpful not only to the students themselves, but to pastors, parents and friends of these students who need to catch at least a glimpse of the terrain the student is about to traverse.

D. A. Carson
Trinity Evangelical Divinity School

# EDITORS' PREFACE

*'This is the one I esteem: he who is humble and contrite in spirit, and trembles at my word.' Isaiah 66:2b*

Whatever fashionable new entries appear in the Top Ten chart of 'theological challenges to faith', for *evangelical* students beginning university and college courses in theology and biblical studies the Number One invariably involves questions of authority and epistemology, and these questions ultimately come back to one's doctrine of Scripture. It is not hard to understand why this is the case. There is 'nothing new under the sun' (Ecclesiastes 1:9), and throughout the history of the church much doctrinal debate and disagreement has boiled down to questions of authority and mankind's reaction to God's Word. Indeed, this is what went on at the dawn of world history in the garden of Eden, when Adam and Eve questioned God; and it is what goes on today in many lecture theatres and seminar rooms when the Bible is placed under the microscope of the academy. Many scholars who might be described as members of the 'theological élite' neither presuppose nor cherish those things which define our faith: central here is the lordship of the triune God, with its necessary corollary that God's words are infallible, authoritative, sufficient, self-authenticating, perspicuous, final, and the source for all 'God-talk'. Clothed in terms like 'scientific study' or 'neutrality' (where faith commitments have to be put aside), there can be a discourse of disguise where a particular worldview is

simply assumed and never questioned, and where evangelical presuppositions are either rejected out of hand or simply ignored.

In our experience, many evangelical students are living in the
shock and aftermath of a cycle of personal spiritual earthquakes,
as different tectonic plates of ultimate authority continually collide
with one another. When this happens, the impact on the evangelical student can often result in confusion and a gradual, downward
cycle of doubt, disengagement and despair. For us, the real tragedy
of the situation is that many students do not see what is going on
'behind the scenes' with respect to presuppositions and assumptions, and so are not able to brace themselves for impact, let alone
try and build something constructive. One aim of this volume is to
help students to engage with such assumptions and presuppositions, and to develop a framework for an intellectually rigorous
approach to biblical studies that also presupposes a 'high' view of
Scripture.

However, even with appropriate presuppositions in place, and
even in evangelical institutions, more tough questions arise in our
studies. For example, can, or should, the Bible be subjected to
'critical' study at all? How do the Old and New Testaments relate
to each other? What are the principles for properly evangelical
exegesis and hermeneutics? How do I know that the Bible is the
Word of God written?

This volume provides introductory surveys of key topics and
issues, along with orientation and guidance, for those beginning
academic study of the Bible in universities and theological colleges. The essays are not replacements for, or duplicates of,
material in standard introductory textbooks. Rather, the intention
is to complement set texts and lecture courses. The contributors
are all younger scholars, whose own experiences as students and
subsequently in teaching, research and ministry enable them to
provide fresh, up-to-date perspectives and advice.

This is the third volume resulting from collaboration between
the Religious and Theological Studies Fellowship and Inter-Varsity
Press. We are grateful to the authors for writing the essays in the
midst of other pressing demands, to Don Carson for kindly agree-
ing to provide the Foreword, and, once again, to Elizabeth Fraser
for her assistance in the RTSF office.

Overall, we hope the essays in this volume will provide a healthy, solid and stable foundation from which students can see the immense privilege we have in encountering God's Word in the context of academic studies, and that in this encounter we are transformed *by* it as we meet the living, triune God *in* it.

Philip Duce
Daniel Strange
May 2003

# 1. BEGINNING TO STUDY THE OLD TESTAMENT

## Peter J. Williams

*Peter Williams* is currently lecturer at Aberdeen University. He was formerly Research Fellow at Tyndale House, Cambridge. His PhD from Cambridge University was on the Syriac translation of 1 Kings.

## Preparing to study

The Old Testament (OT) is a sizeable body of writings, the composition of which, according to people of the most diverse persuasions, took a very long time. The history of that extended period of composition is itself complex, which makes study difficult. The matter is complicated further by the fact that the OT is written in a couple of dead languages (Hebrew and a bit of Aramaic). To cap it all, the account of the origins of the OT given by many contemporary scholars is quite different from the account the OT seems to give of its own origins. So it is hardly surprising that someone beginning OT study should feel lost.

Because of this a student choosing modules for a religious studies course might well be tempted to avoid OT study altogether. However, it would be rather ironic for any Christian student to avoid studying the OT, so often cited by Jesus. Moreover, the OT is itself a foundation for all other disciplines within Christian theology. No-one can develop a serious understanding of the New Testament without the backdrop of the Old, nor can any biblical or systematic theology afford to ignore the material of the OT. For anyone wanting to develop a serious theological outlook the study of the OT is unavoidable. The question, then, is not *whether* to study the OT but *when* and *how*.[1]

Answering the *when* question first, it is important to remember that a confused mind presented with a complicated issue is unlikely to obtain greater clarity than that with which it started. Someone approaching in-depth study of the OT will therefore greatly benefit from prior familiarity with the OT subject matter, and a clear mind about it. To put it briefly: it is helpful to have read the OT, preferably several times, before beginning an OT paper. This may seem like a high demand, but given that to read the whole OT out loud in English takes less than fifty hours, the demand is not really so high. Yet it might seem that to become familiar with the OT before studying it formally defeats the object of study. After all, the main motivation for a student taking an OT paper is usually precisely to become familiar with the OT. But at a practical level this does not work. Most lecturers would deeply love their students to immerse themselves in the primary text (in this case the OT), but also need to test that students are working. To do this they have to set essays, and essays require arguments which in turn require the reading of secondary literature. Again, in order to test that students are working (and in order to make sure that those who have read the primary text before the course do not get off too lightly) lecturers will normally set for reading a quantity of secondary literature that will fill all the available time. Filling all available time is generally not hard, because often not

---

1. This introduction is specifically aimed at those studying the OT as undergraduates in a university context. It is written for self-consciously Christian students, though I hope that other readers may benefit from it too. Because it is only an introduction I have chosen to focus on a general approach, and usually to refrain from giving specific solutions to debated issues. Needless to say, my self-restraint here should not be mistaken for agnosticism. I am simply trying to lay a foundation for further study. I am grateful to James Palmer, to two readers, and to my wife Kathryn for comments on earlier drafts.

much time is available for an essay anyway! There is similar pressure from the student's side to read secondary rather than primary literature. There is no doubt that fifteen well-spent minutes cribbing from secondary literature will in general help a student ask cleverer sounding questions than fifteen minutes spent on the primary sources. There is also no doubt that those who pursue such a short-sighted approach over a long period are liable gradually to lose touch with the text they are supposed to be studying. Most contemporary scholarly writing will only be of minor historical interest within a generation, whereas the primary text will live on. So it is *vital* to read the text first. Anyone who has already started an OT paper without having read the OT through should endeavour to read the whole at the first available opportunity (such as a holiday week).

This necessity (I do not think *necessity* is too strong a word) of familiarity with the biblical text prior to engaging in academic study of it is in line with how we learn best. Essay topics will inevitably invite students to assess critically their own assumptions and views, as well as those of others. Students with good reasons for believing what they believe should not be anxious about such probing; it is, rather, an opportunity to develop mentally. However, in order to evaluate properly the views of authors in the bibliography it is necessary not only to evaluate the strength of the arguments they use, but also to know whether there are additional relevant contrary arguments which they do not consider. How can you critically assess any writer if you have a blank mind to start with?

So the question of when to study the OT is answered simply: *study the OT when you have a firm outline in your mind of its contents and a basic familiarity with its text.*

The next question is *how* to study, including what order to study things in. I would like here to advise strongly that someone beginning OT study should consider prioritizing study of Hebrew. Not everyone finds languages equally easy or attractive, and not everyone is given the opportunity to learn Hebrew. However, this is one of the first questions you need to ask: are you going to learn Hebrew and study the OT in its original language, or are you going to study it all in translation? Here there is something analogous to

the contrast above between studying primary and secondary literature. Progress with any language will seem incredibly slow at first,
and much quicker comprehension of what is going on will be
achieved if the same time is spent reading the English translation
of the Bible. You need to weigh the effort of learning Hebrew
against the length of a course in OT. If the course is three years or
more, then you should learn Hebrew.

The advantages of tackling original languages in Bible study are
several, but only for those who persevere for the reward:

1. In the long run you can save time reading secondary literature.
   It is still necessary and profitable, for instance, to read
   commentaries on books of the Bible, but you no longer need
   to rely on these as the major way of finding out the meaning
   of words.
2. You can critically evaluate commentaries. A surprising number
   of commentaries are written by people who do not have a good
   grasp of Hebrew. Familiarity with the original languages will
   help you recognize which commentators are more worth
   reading and which less.
3. Many parts of the Bible use specific items of vocabulary as
   linking words, in wordplay, or in other similar devices. You will
   be able to recognize these easily if you know the language.
4. All academic disciplines are subject to fashions to one degree or
   another. It is possible to become immersed in the theories that
   prevail while one is a student, only to find that they have become
   outdated within a generation. Language skills are less affected by
   fashion.

If you do decide to take up the challenge of Hebrew, you
should take it up sooner rather than later. You should begin learning, and then, by seeking to use the Hebrew text at every
opportunity, all subsequent study can revise your Hebrew. If you
do not, then you need to get used to consulting a variety of translations of the Bible, and to learn to suspect suggestions made in
commentaries about the original language that cannot be verified
in at least one other source (see Deuteronomy 19:15).

## A Christian approach to the Old Testament

### Presuppositions

Before proceeding further it is necessary to look at the presuppositions of study. It is impossible to study without presuppositions, and to admit to having presuppositions is not to admit to having an incurable disease of brain-bias. Presuppositions can be modified, and often need to be, but no-one is without them. So the question is not whether one has presuppositions or not, but whether one has good presuppositions or not, and whether they are held in the right way. This is an explicitly Christian introduction to OT study, and its approach is moulded by the beliefs that God is truthful and that the Bible is speech from God. These statements need both elaboration and defence and space here permits neither. Nevertheless, I hope that the rest of this chapter at least provides a little of both.

A Christian approach to the OT is different right from the moment you open a Bible. Though physically we may be over the text and we take in things from it by the exertion of our faculties over it, yet often its contents probe and challenge us deeper than we it. When we read that 'The fear of Yahweh is the beginning of knowledge' (Proverbs 1:7) we are faced with a choice. Either it is true, in which case the way to be knowing, even about the statement itself, is to adopt a reverent attitude before Yahweh, the God of the OT, or we can reject the statement without having entered into the state exhorted by the verse. There is no possible position of abstract consideration of the truth of this statement: you either adopt the attitude it exhorts and fear Yahweh, or you reject its claims in both thought and experience. While the Yahweh-fearing cannot claim objectivity, neither can the person who has rejected the statement without ever entering into the state exhorted. It can be argued that religious writings outside the Christian faith also exhort followers to engage with them by a similar trick of insisting that personal experience is the only test. But the point here is simple: according to claims within the OT it is not possible to consider Yahweh in a dispassionate way. Involvement with the God of the OT means more than mental assent, but life, desires and everything. So a student considering study of the OT needs to be involved beyond the mental level. Prayer and obedience need to integrate with study if we are going to have any claim that our approach is Christian.

But there is surely a problem here. If the student is involved in this way in study, will this not lead inevitably to being uncritical, and to religious bias clouding judgment? Not necessarily. Arguably those who are explicitly aware of their biases will be more able to prevent them from clouding their judgment than those who deny that they have such biases. Moreover, as one studies the OT one is also often studying the supposed basis for beliefs. Students may find with time and study that certain starting assumptions they have are not supported in the way they thought, and this can lead to modifications of belief. The key thing here is that change is made after due reflection and after one has sought at appropriate length for explanations within the paradigm within which one is working. A leaking roof in an individual's worldview does not necessitate abandoning the building. Christian students encountering faith problems should be familiar enough with their own tradition and broader Christian heritage to know whether there are ways of plugging the epistemological roof.

Most university and college courses aim to teach students to think critically by setting a number of written assignments which require evaluation of contrary arguments. In order to maximize the intellectual exercise, assignments are generally set in areas of controversy. Over the course of a year's study a student may look at literally dozens of such controversial issues under the inevitable time pressures that accompany these assignments. Such courses are not, however, designed so that students reach closure on an issue. That is, it is not expected that students will have reached the definitive answer by the time they complete their essays. The exercise is to *start* people thinking about issues. This is important in terms of how students regard conclusions they came to at the end of their essays. They should not be viewed as definitive results, and students need to be ready to revise their views with subsequent study. It also means that a student needs to be ready for more questions to be opened than are closed. It generally takes much less time to ask a question than to give a coherent answer. This may mean that at the end of a year there are a lot of open questions, and in OT studies some of these will inevitably touch on matters of faith. It needs to be recognized up front that the number of such questions that lie open bears relatively little relationship to whether the questions are soluble or not, and very much relationship to the general way that people are taught to think in the academic system. Thus it is entirely plausible that someone could end up with much greater mental confusion after a course than reflected by the uncertainties of the subject. This is not anyone's fault, but simply a product of a learning system, which beside this disadvantage has many advantages. Returning to our house analogy, everyone wants to live in a habitable house; if there are too many unresolved issues in someone's mind, then it may be like a house with a large number of leaks. There is no reason to believe that any of the leaks cannot be plugged, and there is absolutely no reason to doubt the soundness of the basic structure of the building, but the leaks may well make someone want to move out. To speak plainly, unanswered questions in large quantities make people want to shift their paradigm of general belief. However, unanswered questions in large quantities can result from two quite different sources: (1) from the inadequacy of the general paradigm being used; (2) from a problem-centred method of learning. It is important to distinguish these two. The only way this can be done is by going out of your way to look for answers to the problems that arise, and to do so persistently. It is only after trying this that one should consider a major paradigm shift.

Related to this it is important to come to a proper assessment of the certainty of the knowledge that has been acquired during any particular course. Even a relatively certain conclusion in an undergraduate essay may scarcely be a conclusion that one could never imagine being reversed under any circumstance. Humans need to admit the provisional and limited nature of their knowledge. This is difficult in an academic environment where essays are generally a means of showing off knowledge to a tutor, and where admitting ignorance is hard.

### Alert reading

Feeding on his or her own tradition while undertaking a broadly secular course should lead the Christian student to read a wide

variety of literature. At a university or college, students of the OT
will inevitably be challenged to read books by those who do not
share their view of the OT. To interact with this literature is an
important part of the intellectual training the course provides.
However, if a course is set from a secular viewpoint it is likely that
Christian students will find that the course leaves little time for
them to get to know their own heritage. Of course, on many
topics it may be that the approach the student finds most helpful is
not written from a Christian point of view. It may be more helpful
because it provokes that student, or simply because it is a fairer
treatment of a subject. However, students need to beware of
knowing much that has been said from non-Christian points of
view and yet knowing little of what has been written from a
Christian point of view. To overcome this practical hurdle requires
a student to be organized and to arrange time to read Christian
approaches on the same issue. Because of limitations of time
during a course it may even be beneficial if a student reads such
approaches before beginning the course, but since advance
warning of essay topics is often not given this is difficult.

So *what* is read is important. Yet it is also important to know *how*
to read. Frequently the best book on a subject is not a Christian
book. Most often there simply is no ideal book on a subject from
any standpoint, but several from which the relevant information
needs to be gleaned. For this reason it is necessary to develop the
ability to evaluate secondary literature critically, to separate information and data that an author gives from their paradigmatic
trappings, and to develop a sense of what needs to be double-
checked.

Sometimes scholars are kind enough to state their world view.
Consider the following quotation from the well-published OT
scholar Philip R. Davies in an essay entitled 'Whose History? Whose
Israel? Whose Bible? Biblical Histories, Ancient and Modern'.[2]

---

2. In Lester L. Grabbe (ed.), *Can a 'History of Israel' Be Written?* (Journal for
   the Study of the Old Testament Supplement Series 245; Sheffield:
   Sheffield Academic Press, 1997), pp. 104–122. Quotation from
   pp. 116–117.

The belief in a single transcendental being who can comprehend, indeed controls, all history is precisely a biblical belief: it is one of the major tenets of biblical historiography . . . When I claim, then, that there is no 'objective' history I am implying a world-view incompatible with that of the biblical writings (except perhaps Qoheleth) for whom history was defined by divine deeds . . .

In the ensuing context Davies criticizes other scholars who have indicated that they are atheist or agnostic for adopting the Bible's framework that there is a definitive view of the past, and thus for having a 'theistic' approach to history.[3] The conclusion of the essay that a good historian needs 'to remain sceptical, minimalist and negative' gives us insight into his approach and will not entice many students with a faith commitment. Unfortunately, Davies' candour is rare. This means that a student needs to be aware both of wider agendas that can influence the work of scholars and of how a Christian approach may lead to different conclusions.

### Historical issues

One of the first issues that any student of the OT is faced with is the issue of historicity, or the question 'Did it happen?' Here one needs to be up front about the importance of a historical basis for the Christian faith,[4] and about the fact that the church's consensus up until the time of the Enlightenment was that the OT was true history.[5] There were, of course, many for whom literal historicity

---

3. Davies, 'Whose History?' p. 117 n. 19. Davies even criticizes Karl Marx's view of history as 'theistic'.

4. See e.g. the argument of Paul in 1 Corinthians 15:1–19.

5. N. P. Lemche, *The Israelites in History and Tradition* (London: SPCK, 1998), p. 2, holds rather bizarrely that 'the historical reading of the Bible is a comparative newcomer in comparison to such venerable procedures as allegorical understanding or typological interpretation . . .' He manages to maintain this by stressing that exclusively historical interpretations only developed more recently.

was not the major concern. A prominent church father, Origen (c. 185–254), was one of a number who stressed the primacy of the allegorical interpretation of Scripture. But this should not be taken to mean that he denied the general historicity of Scripture. Nor were considerations of the OT's historicity without qualification. Martin Luther, for instance, who accepted the book of Job as history, held that Job's speeches in the book were not records of his actual words, but a creative expression by the author of Job's thoughts.[6] Luther thus maintained the historical nature of biblical books, but also that truth can be presented in a variety of literary genres.

### It is literature too

'Genre' has been a much-used word recently as a number of scholars have stressed the *literary* nature of the OT.[7] Their approach maintains that many parts of the Bible contain literary structures showing careful composition. The relevance of this to the issue of history in the OT has been to shift the focus of investigation of certain texts from their historicity to their literary nature. Authors with this literary approach vary on a spectrum from those who use the literary nature of a work to deny its historical nature through to those who accept the historical nature of the work but choose to focus on literary structures.[8] Some such approaches to a text are called 'synchronic' because they seek to view the text without

---

6. Theodore G. Tappert (ed.), *Luther's Works.* Vol. 54: *Table Talk* (Philadelphia: Fortress, 1967), pp. 79–80.

7. Robert Alter, *The Art of Biblical Narrative* (London: Allen & Unwin, 1981); Robert Alter and Frank Kermode (eds.), *The Literary Guide to the Bible* (London: Collins, 1987); Adele Berlin, *Poetics and Interpretation of Biblical Narrative* (Bible and Literature Series 9; Sheffield: Almond, 1983); Shimon Bar-Efrat, *Narrative Art in the Bible* (Bible and Literature Series 17; Journal for the Study of the Old Testament Supplement Series 70; Sheffield: Almond, 1989).

8. This latter category includes many of the authors in Leland Ryken and Tremper Longman III (eds.), *A Complete Literary Guide to the Bible* (Grand Rapids: Zondervan, 1993).

regard to temporal distinction in origin, and thus interpret the whole without considering historical development. The synchronic approaches are contrasted with the diachronic ones, which look at the development of texts through time.[9] Whatever approach ultimately is taken, it must be justified on a basis other than widespread use. It is important that texts are allowed to speak for themselves and that a serious attempt is made to understand the focus and themes of a text as a whole. This said, no student can afford simply to ignore historical questions.

Recognizing a literary focus may even alter one's view of the history to which a narrative refers. Thus King Jeroboam II of Israel receives relatively little treatment in the biblical narrative, much less than King Ahab, though there can be little doubt that in terms of his political achievements Jeroboam was by far the more significant.[10] The emphasis of the biblical text thus differs from what would be given by a modern historian. The same mismatch between thematic biblical emphasis and generally applied quantitative criteria for importance is present with regard to the Babylonian exile. According to Jeremiah 52:29 the number of captives taken by Nebuchadnezzar king of Babylon at the time of the destruction of Jerusalem in 587/586 BC was 832. Thus one of the most significant events in the whole OT, round which Jeremiah and Ezekiel focus their narratives, which is the precondition for a book like Lamentations, and which is the culmination of the books of Kings (or arguably Genesis to Kings), is the deportation of a relatively small number of people. By contrast a much more significant military event just over a century earlier is passed over in these

_____

9. Quite closely related to synchronic approaches is the 'canonical' approach, developed especially by Brevard S. Childs. See his *Introduction to the Old Testament as Scripture* (London: SCM, 1979). See also the evaluation of this, with qualifications, by Paul R. Noble, *The Canonical Approach: A Critical Reconstruction of the Hermeneutics of Brevard S. Childs* (Biblical Interpretation Series 15; Leiden: E. J. Brill, 1995).

10. Jeroboam II is treated in the short passage 2 Kings 14:23–29, whereas Ahab is treated from 1 Kings 16:29 – 22:40, though some of this is taken up with the figure Elijah.

words: 'In the fourteenth year of King Hezekiah, Sennacherib king of Assyria came up against all the fortified cities of Judah and seized them (2 Kings 18:13).'[11] If Sennacherib's own account of this expedition is to believed, he took 200,150 captives at this time.

The average student with a general familiarity with the OT, but who had not studied it formally, would be quite surprised to know that there is no document outside the Bible that records Nebuchadnezzar's capture of Jerusalem and taking of the people captive in 587/586 BC. This might even cause the student to conclude that the Bible's narrative could not be relied on historically at this point. However, this would be because the student had confused narrative or theological importance with the sort of importance that would cause a foreign historian to record the events about the fall of Jerusalem. Besides, it would be to ignore the fact that the records of the other interested party, Nebuchadnezzar, no longer survive for the relevant period, the last surviving chronicle of his reign referring to 594/593 BC.

All this means that it is very important to read the biblical narrative with the utmost care to ensure that one is not attributing significance to an event recorded, which it does not actually have. This could be to attribute a wrong international importance to a narrative, or wrong archaeological significance to an event. It is necessary for the biblical narrative to be carefully examined in a literary way before one can properly assess its historical implications.

### Fact or fiction?

When the narrative of the OT is considered as a whole it is obvious that there is generally more agreement about the historical nature of records recounting events towards the end of the OT period than about those that report earlier events. Though some would assign the whole OT to the category of story with no his-

---

11. I am of course exaggerating the case slightly. Jeremiah 52:28–30 and
    2 Kings 24 – 25 attest more than one deportation at the time of the
    Babylonian exile, involving more than 832 people.

torical basis,[12] most believe that narrative books such as Ezra and Nehemiah are substantially historical,[13] and that books relating to earlier periods have successively less historical substance until one reaches zero some time before the opening of the Bible in Genesis. Among scholars the cut-off point varies greatly: some deny a basis for the Bible's picture of Solomon's splendour, more deny any historical basis for the exodus, and only a minority accept that if there were patriarchs, they did anything like what is attributed to them in the Bible.[14]

Thus, broadly speaking, the more remote an event is from the present the more likely it is that its historicity will be doubted, disputed or denied by scholars. This difference between nearer and more remote events is, of course, what would be expected if the biblical authors wrote basically towards the end of the period that the Bible is about, and possessed no superhuman insight into the more remote periods. In that model, writers of Bible books were able to describe with moderate accuracy the time in which they lived and even preserve a certain amount of information about the time shortly before them. For more distant events they only had tradition, which was liable to corruption, and a certain level of imagination. Sometimes it is even said that in Bible times writers did not have a sense of history as we do now.[15] However, differences in emphasis and historiography should not be taken to indicate a fundamental discontinuity between the approach to history then and now. Denial of a sense of continuity between attitudes to history then and now has particularly arisen within a postmodern view,

---

12. This is generally the approach of Lemche in *Israelites*.

13. Speaking of Ezra and Nehemiah, David J. A. Clines says, 'From these books we learn virtually all we know about the history of the post-exilic community.' See his *Ezra, Nehemiah, Esther* (Grand Rapids: Eerdmans, 1984), p. 14.

14. Cyrus H. Gordon and Gary A. Rendsburg, *The Bible and the Ancient Near East* (4th edn.; New York: W. W. Norton, 1997), represent a more maximalist trend towards viewing the Bible as historical while working within a secular framework.

15. Thus Lemche, *Israelites*, p. 2.

which as part of a wider philosophical scheme refuses to acknowledge continuity between thought of the present and of the past.

However, the question of the historicity of earlier parts of the
Bible needs also to be seen from another perspective. What was
more remote from biblical writers is also more remote from us,
and when considering the biblical period greater uncertainties
attach to modern scholarly reconstructions of earlier as opposed
to later stages in that period. While the chronology of events in
the fifth century BC is generally fixed to within a year, the chronology of a millennium before is open to wider dispute, with three
quite different chronologies, for example, of the first dynasty of
Babylon, varying by about 120 years, and related uncertainties
sometimes of around 64 years in Egyptian dating.[16] It is true that
one particular chronology of Egypt, the 'Low Chronology', is
more widely accepted, but it is important for a student to appreciate the various levels of uncertainty in the study of different
periods. The gaps in our information about the history of the
period around 1,000 BC when, according to the Bible, David was
king are very much greater than those around the time when
Nehemiah was governor of Judah in the fifth century BC.

A further complication is the issue of antisupernaturalism (or
naturalism) in historical investigation. It is possible, even common,

---

16. Paul Åström (ed.), *High, Middle or Low? Acts of an International Colloquium on
    Absolute Chronology Held at the University of Gothenburg 20th–22nd August 1987,
    Parts 1–3* (Gothenburg: Paul Åströms Förlag, 1987–9). Very much on the
    fringe of scholarship, a small group has proposed ultra-low chronologies
    that reduce parts of the Egyptian low chronology by several centuries
    during the Third Intermediate Period (normally around 1069–664 BC).
    Proponents claim that such schemes are alternative paradigms into which
    conventional data can be arranged to provide striking confirmation of
    biblical narratives. See Peter James et al., *Centuries of Darkness: A Challenge
    to the Conventional Chronology of Old World Archaeology* (London: Pimlico,
    1992), and the journalistic David Rohl, *A Test of Time: The Bible – From
    Myth to History* (London: Century, 1995). Several scholars reply to the
    former book in the review feature in the *Cambridge Archaeological Journal* 1.2
    (1991), pp. 227–253.

for historians studying ancient texts to discount the possibility of narrated miracles, and to assume that only natural processes have been involved in the past. If processes other than natural ones have been at work, then this naturalistic method will lead to historical distortion. For instance, in Deuteronomy 29:5 Moses points out to the Israelites how during forty years of wandering in the desert their sandals had not worn out. The narrative plainly appeals to something outside ordinary processes, and there is the implication that if one sought for the usual evidence for sandal-wear it would not be there. There is the claim, then, of event without usual evidence. If a scholar, therefore, were to argue that the wanderings did not happen on the ground of lack of evidence of wear on sandals, it would be an illegitimate argument. On the other hand, if a scholar were to argue that the wanderings did not happen on the ground of lack of evidence for bodies that perished in the desert, it would be a legitimate *type* of argument, because there is a legitimate expectation of evidence in this case.[17]

Of course, scholars often do not come to the view that they should not make allowance for miraculous or non-natural events on the basis of mere prejudice. Often they first come to an opinion that the genre or date of literature in the Bible is not such as we can expect to give us reliable information about non-natural processes

---

17. One scholar who proposed a host of practical objections to the Exodus narrative was the nineteenth-century figure John William Colenso, whose objections were particularly shocking at that time because he was Bishop of Natal. See his *The Pentateuch and Book of Joshua Critically Examined*, vol. I (London: Longman, Roberts & Green, 1862). Not all his arguments are equally compelling, and several are predicated on an overly pedantic reading of the text. An example of a rather obtuse objection is that he rejects the historicity of the numbers of Levites given in the Pentateuch, since they are counted in the first census in the book of Numbers as 22,000 males, and in the second thirty-eight years later as 23,000 males (p. 110). His objection, based on population growth statistics in England from 1851 to 1861, is that they should have grown more (as he estimates starting from 22,000 to 48,471 thirty-eight years later). However, many of his objections are more substantial.

in the past. Nevertheless, the issue of naturalistic presuppositions in scholarly discussion is one that a Christian needs to address. A student must assess independently the likelihood that any statement about ancient history, particularly in regard to the history within the Bible, has been established on a basis that he or she may want to question. This is not to encourage a dismissive attitude to the work of others, but merely to encourage an awareness of the theory-laden nature of people's observations. Nowhere do the conditions of remoteness and of naturalistic presupposition come more to the fore than in consideration of the highly disputed first eleven chapters of Genesis.[18] The issue is too complicated to address here, but any solution reached with these chapters must be able to be consistently applied in method to other parts of the OT, and within a coherent Christian theology.[19]

But the pillars of scholarly consensus on the subject of OT history have not only recently been examined for assigning too great a level of certainty to scholarly reconstruction and naturalistic assumptions; recently scholarly consensus on the OT has been questioned from a new approach that is hyperconservative in terms of sources admitted to discussion of history. Proponents of this approach have often been labelled 'minimalists'.[20] Lemche is a leading proponent of such a view and denies that the OT can be

---

18. After a long absence the possibility of constructing theories of origins outside naturalistic assumptions is now firmly back on the agenda; see William A. Dembski, *The Design Inference* (Cambridge: Cambridge University Press, 1998), and Dembski, *Intelligent Design* (Downers Grove: IVP, 1999).

19. For an outline of the interaction between science and faith see Philip Duce, *Reading the Mind of God* (Leicester: Apollos, 1998). An approach that seeks to address some of the scientific issues but without the usual positivistic trappings of a Christian apologist is Leonard Brand, *Faith, Reason and Earth History: A Paradigm of Earth and Biological Origins by Intelligent Design* (Berrien Springs, MI: Andrews University, 1997). A fresh approach to the issue of origins can be found in Kurt P. Wise, *Faith, Form, and Time* (Nashville: Broadman & Holman, 2002).

20. Scholars associated with this group include Niels Peter Lemche and Thomas L. Thompson, both of Copenhagen, and Philip R. Davies of

viewed in any way as historical in the classic sense of the word.[21] Lemche clearly sees his approach as having advantages for a Christian viewpoint:

> This new trend [i.e. the trend of which Lemche is a part] seems to be liberating the Bible from the tyranny of having to be historically accurate in the most minute detail in order to remain a Bible for Christians and Jews.[22]

Lemche goes on to make a trenchant critique of the assumptions behind much OT study. Drawing on a variety of socio-anthropological discussions Lemche claims that OT scholars have too often tried to view historical Israel with presupposed concepts of ethnicity and nationality that can be shown to be invalid. Nevertheless, the 'minimalist' critique of consensus historiography is not merely sociological. Lemche seeks to support his view with an examination of ancient documents seeking to establish that there is virtually no evidence for regarding the biblical narrative as a reliable source of historical information.[23]

### When enemies are friends

Perhaps the easiest thing for a Christian student to do when faced with Lemche's approach is to look for an instant refutation. Plenty of responses will be found both within mainstream scholarship and from explicitly Christian scholarship, which are firmly aligned in their opposition to minimalism. The lesson here is to see that

---

Sheffield. Lemche and Thompson prefer the term 'maximalist' for themselves, but this is in part due to a rhetorical technique used by the Copenhagen scholars whereby they subvert accepted meanings of terms. See *Biblical Archaeology Review* 23. 4 (July/August 1997), p. 28.

21. Lemche, *Israelites*, p. 1.

22. Ibid. T. L. Thompson's critique of much of the academic consensus in historiography is likewise framed in rather religious terms. See his *The Historicity of the Patriarchal Narratives: The Quest for the Historical Abraham* (Beihefte zur Zeitschrift für die alttestamentliche Wissenschaft 133; Berlin: De Gruyter, 1974), pp. 326–330.

23. Lemche, *Israelites*, pp. 35–64.

the interplay between data and paradigm is extremely complex. Those with a common general outlook may disagree over data at the same time as those without a common outlook agree over it.

In order to consider the dynamics here we will look at a specific issue in OT history, namely the relationship between the biblical figure Shishak and an Egyptian Pharaoh called Shoshenk.

The Bible tells us that in the fifth year of Rehoboam's reign King Shishak of Egypt came up against Jerusalem and took away a large amount of treasure from both the temple and the royal palace (1 Kings 14:25–26). Shishak's name in the Bible, especially in a consonantal form in which it occurs, *šwšq*, is naturally compared with the Pharaoh Shoshenk (low Egyptian chronology 945–924 BC) who invaded Palestine and recorded his invasion on a temple gate at Karnak in Egypt. The establishment of a time link, a *synchronism*, between the Bible and the Egyptian record has had important consequences in scholarship. First of all, it provides the earliest agreed record of an event recorded in the Bible that is also recorded in another document. Secondly, by the addition of the reigns of the kings of Judah within the Bible, the event can be given a date.[24] This in turn is used to fix dates in Egyptian history, which otherwise would not be able to be calculated to the precision of a year. Shishak's/Shoshenk's invasion is calculated to c. 926 or 925 BC.

This striking agreement between the Bible and an Egyptian record has been called into question by some of those with more minimalist leanings. Garbini criticizes the standard reconstruction for arbitrary manipulation of Egyptian chronology in order to achieve an agreement with the Bible.[25] He argues that if

---

24. Of course, it is necessary to count the reigns of the kings of Judah back from a fixed date. For a number of dates in OT history after 853 BC Assyrian documents are compared with biblical ones to provide chronological anchors.

25. Giovanni Garbini, *History and Ideology in Ancient Israel* (tr. John Bowden; London: SCM, 1988), pp. 29–30. There are important differences between Garbini and some other minimalists. See James Barr, *History and Ideology in the Old Testament: Biblical Studies at the End of a Millennium* (Oxford: Oxford University Press), pp. 91–92.

Egypt were given its most natural chronology without biblical interference, it would be seen that the campaign of Shoshenk did not take place during Rehoboam's reign, but during the reign of his predecessor, Solomon. The Bible has moved it in order not to take away from the glory of Solomon's reign. A different critique of the synchronism is made by Lemche.[26] He argues that there is a strong distinction between the Egyptian and biblical texts. Whereas the biblical text records that Shishak came up against Jerusalem (1 Kings 14:25),[27] the Egyptian record lists a large number of towns captured during Shoshenk's campaign, but gives no indication that he visited Jerusalem, or even came near it. Lemche concludes that the biblical account of Shishak's campaign to Jerusalem has been made up by a later writer on the basis of a memory of a campaign by Shoshenk in Palestine generally. The detail that Rehoboam handed over gold to get rid of Shoshenk was made up on the basis of the way Hezekiah in 701 BC handed over gold to buy off the Assyrian Sennacherib.[28]

So far there appears to be a spectrum of opinion with minimalists at one end. A critical consensus stands between them and maximalists, among whom are a number of explicitly Christian scholars. A Christian student with a natural proclivity towards maximalism may be tempted to proceed at once to a critique of minimalism, perhaps even using arguments supplied from within an academic consensus to which they do not ordinarily belong. The problem is that this simple spectrum view does not reflect the whole truth, for this match between Egyptian history and the Bible has also been challenged from a quite different angle. As noticed previously (note 16) there has been a small, even more 'maximalist', trend in recent writing, which has been prepared to question more radically the foundations of Egyptian chronology. It has not succeeded in making any significant dent in the

---

26. Lemche, *Israelites*, pp. 55–57.

27. And we might add that according to 2 Chronicles 12:4 he captured all the fortified cities in Judah. For these see 2 Chronicles 11:5–12.

28. Lemche, *Israelites*, pp. 57, 187.

consensus, but it has been most interesting to note some striking parallels between the writings of minimalists and these strong maximalists. Thus Bimson has challenged the equation between Shoshenk and the biblical Shishak.[29] A key point in his argument is the geographical mismatch between the description of the campaign in the Bible and that in Karnak. Thus a scholar who has a very positive view of the historicity of biblical material is found to be using arguments with considerable affinity to those of one with a very negative view of biblical historicity.[30] This illustrates how important it is to reject a spectrum view of modern scholarly literature. Almost all scholars have a large familiarity with material related to the OT, but their analysis can also be influenced by their wider paradigm, or even world view. It is important, therefore, to understand a scholar's work as a whole and to attempt to separate as far as possible information given from the interpretation put on it. Those who are positive towards the historicity of a narrative should not rule out the possibility that a minimalist's critique of a scholar arguing for a more positive view of historicity is correct. Sometimes a scholar occupying middle ground can be more guilty of mixing methodologies than a scholar at the extreme. This said, there is a lot of strength in the

---

29. John J. Bimson, 'Shoshenk and Shishak: A Case of Mistaken Identity?' *Journal of the Ancient Chronology Forum* 6 (1992/1993), pp. 19–32. However, in the *New Bible Commentary: Twenty-First Century Edition*, ed. D. A. Carson, R. T. France, J. A. Motyer and G. J. Wenham (Leicester: IVP, 1994), p. 355, Bimson identifies Shoshenk with Shishak. This may not be a revision of his earlier opinion, but rather a curtailment of discussion for a popular audience. Bimson became known for his book *Redating the Exodus and Conquest* (Journal for the Study of the Old Testament Supplement Series 5; Sheffield: JSOT Press, 1978), which argued that the Exodus was essentially historical.

30. This sort of crossover is common. The minimalist T. L. Thompson finds himself approving Bimson's critique of W. F. Albright's widely accepted chronology. See Thompson, *Early History of the Israelite People: From the Written and Archaeological Sources* (Leiden: E. J. Brill, 1992), pp. 24–25.

central ground. Despite critiques of Egyptian chronology the present consensus can be seen to provide considerable historical confirmation of the biblical account. The Egyptologist K. A. Kitchen, for instance, observes the vast amount of gold available in the pharaoh's coffers at a time directly after Shoshenk's raid.[31] It is not far-fetched to suppose that some of this is the gold that, according to the Bible, Rehoboam inherited from his fabulously rich father and surrendered to Shishak. But the records are mute, and coincidences like this may not provide incontrovertible proof of the correctness of a paradigm. So where does that leave us? A range of competent scholars come to quite different views of biblical historicity. Why do they do so? It is hard to deny that the results have at least as much to do with presuppositions as with data. Presuppositions can work at the highest level of one's view of life as a whole, but can also provide smaller paradigms within which data are observed and ordered. A student needs to be aware of the interplay of data and interpretation, to avoid an approach that too readily claims historical confirmation of the Bible, and to see the paradigm-myopia of so many claims of dis-proof of the historicity of the Bible. A proper critique of minimalism needs first to understand what is right within mini-malism.

There are, of course, many problems with minimalism. To bolster its case minimalism has resorted to charges of archaeo-logical forgery;[32] it is constantly having to push the interpretation

---

31. Kitchen, 'Where Did Solomon's Gold Go?' *Biblical Archaeology Review* 15.3 (May/June 1989), p. 30.

32. Lemche's readiness even to raise the possibility that a properly excavated inscription mentioning the 'House of David', or another inscription mentioning kings of the Philistine city Ekron, are fakes shows a lack of judgment. He retracted the latter opinion in a footnote. However, before examination for him to have raised the possibility of forgery, with its implied slur on the behaviour of others, is one of the more disingenuous traits of Lemche's behaviour. See *Biblical Archaeology Review* 23.4 (July/August 1997), pp. 36–38, and Lemche, *Israelites*, p. 182 n. 38.

of data to the limits (and beyond).[33] Moreover, its negative pre-suppositions are never given full justification.[34]

The most natural reading of quite a few sources is that they provide confirmation of the historicity of some of the events and persons within the biblical narrative. The seal impressions of a number of figures in the Bible have been found: King Ahaz, King Hezekiah, Jerahmeel the king's son (Jeremiah 36:26), Baruch son of Neriah (Jeremiah's scribe, in whose handwriting the book of Jeremiah would have been written), and Gemariah son of Shaphan (Jeremiah 36:12).[35] The Mesha stele and Sennacherib's annals provide, respectively, contrasting accounts of Mesha's engagement with Israel, the subject of 2 Kings 3 and of Sennacherib's siege of Jerusalem in 2 Kings 18 – 20.[36] When adequate account is made of the difference of perspective of these enemy kings the outline of the biblical narratives receives broad confirmation. These documents, however, are a long way from providing confirmation of the historicity of the Bible as a whole. In the writer's opinion both attempts to prove the historicity of the Bible by external

---

33. This was certainly done by John Rogerson and Philip R. Davies in denying that the inscription commemorating the completion of the Siloam tunnel was from before the Babylonian exile. See Rogerson and Davies, 'Was the Siloam Tunnel Built by Hezekiah?' *Biblical Archaeologist* 59 (1996), pp. 138–149, with a strong rebuttal in the multi-authored review feature 'Defusing Pseudo-Scholarship: The Siloam Inscription Ain't Hasmonean', *Biblical Archaeology Review* 23.2 (March/April 1997), pp. 41–50, 68.

34. Take Lemche's statement about the biblical writers: 'Everything narrated by them may in principle be historical, but the biblical text cannot in advance be accepted as a historical source or documentation; it has in every single case to prove its status as a historical source' (*Israelites*, p. 29).

35. See, e.g., Hershel Shanks, 'Fingerprint of Jeremiah's Scribe', *Biblical Archaeology Review* 22.2 (March/April 1996), pp. 36–38.

36. The Mesha stele, also known as the 'Moabite Stone', may provide some of the earliest references outside the Bible to the dynasty of David. See André Lemaire, '"House of David" Restored in Moabite Inscription', *Biblical Archaeology Review* 20.3 (May/June 1994), pp. 30–37.

'confirmation' and attempts to disprove its historicity have failed largely due to faulty paradigms. For this reason, students in seeking to adopt positions consistent with the nature of Scripture as God's Word need to distance discussion of detail somewhat from paradigms.

## Compositional issues

A second basic question a student encounters beside the question 'Did it happen?' is 'Who wrote it?' Here is asked not the theological question of divine authorship, but who or what type of human author or authors a particular work or section had. As with questions of history, questions of authorship are complicated for several reasons:

1. Much of the OT is anonymous. This is the case for short books like Ruth, and for massive works like Job and Chronicles. Where there are authorship attributions they are widely disputed by scholars.[37]
2. Many OT scholars hold that the OT contains few large units with unified authorship. This is the case not only for classic examples such as the Pentateuch, which has been divided between four strands called J, E, D and P, and Isaiah, which has been divided into First, Second and Third Isaiah, plus redactors, but even for so short a book as Obadiah, the twenty-one verses of which have been divided even by a moderate commentator between up to four authors.[38]

---

37. A contrast to the general trend among scholars has been M. D. Goulder's series *Studies in the Psalter* (Journal for the Study of the Old Testament Supplement Series; Sheffield: Sheffield Academic [earlier JSOT] Press, 1982– ). Goulder takes the titles of the psalms seriously as authorship attributions and reconstructs hypothetical historical situations in which groups of psalms were sung or composed.
38. Hans Walter Wolff, *Obadiah and Jonah: A Commentary* (tr. Margaret Kohl; Minneapolis: Augsburg, 1986), pp. 21–22.

3. Parallel passages in the OT give clear support to the view that
   books may involve reuse of pre-existing material. Most obviously, the song in 1 Chronicles 16 is composed of parts of
   Psalms 96, 105 and 106.

The result of these factors is that it is necessary sometimes for a
student to consider the possibility of multiple authorship of biblical texts, though there is also a confusing array of opinions on
authorship of the biblical text. It is often not enough to have read
a biblical text and to have considered its argument. Students will
regularly be required to interact with quite complicated views of
the origins of books or passages. This as well as sometimes posing
theological problems is also often a significant factor in reducing
an individual's enjoyment of OT studies. In some circles appreciation of complex literary theories seems to be a precondition for
appreciation of the literature itself.

A Christian approach to the OT cannot, however, reject out
of hand questions of human authorship. Whereas in Islam the
Qur'an is viewed as God's word as opposed to the word of
humans, Christianity knows no such dichotomy with regard to the
Bible. An appreciation of human authorship can therefore contribute to the understanding of individual texts, even though a
student should also avoid the opposite error of so focusing on
human authorship that divine authorship is ignored. The issue is
not therefore *per se* unity of human authorship, but what criteria
may be used for deciding authorship. It is at precisely this point
that the movement within OT studies towards the multiplication
of human authors for individual works is seen to be problematic.
Often schemes of multiple authorship are built upon the foundation of seeing conflict within texts. Sometimes texts within a single
book of the Bible are seen as so opposed that the possibility of
any coherent divine purpose within them is rejected. Usually,
however, it is not that texts are opposed to each other, but that
they are read within schemes that oppose them to each other.
What follows here is a consideration of criteria used for division
of authorship. The focus is on criteria rather than on the authorship of individual books in order to illustrate the principles that
should be applied to specific cases.

## Monolithic writers

A frequent assumption in examining OT texts is that the authors expressed simple thoughts only. This is rarely articulated, though it seems to lie behind many comments. In brief, authors are seen as only expressing unambiguous, stark views, rarely being able to appreciate two sides of an argument. Where there is tension in a text it is not the result of an author genuinely seeing that there was strength in quite different perspectives, but in a redactor or later tradent inheriting a text that differed from his own view and that he modified towards his view.

To give a concrete example, Julius Wellhausen (1844–1918), the brilliant German scholar who in many ways is still the father of modern OT studies, seems to make simplistic assumptions about the bias of authors throughout his classic *Prolegomena to the History of Israel*. Consider the description of Jacob's wives: Rachel as beautiful and Leah as less attractive (Genesis 29:17). Since Rachel was the mother of Joseph and Benjamin and Joseph produced the two tribes Ephraim and Manasseh, the story recording the relative beauty of the matriarchs of Israel clearly originated among Joseph tribes.[39] The problem with this view is that it maintains that the author's personal biases are obvious in the narrative. The scholar's picture of the author has preceded his analysis of the text. Reconstructing authorship within a Wellhausenian view is not particularly difficult. If a narrative is positive about a particular place, then it has usually been composed to assert the importance of that place by its devotees. Tribal biases likewise reveal themselves simply. When genuine tensions appear in a narrative, then the tension is used to support theories of multiple authorship. On the whole this approach has far too simple a view of an author's motivation. Evidence needs first to be brought forward, for instance, that authors only praised the tribes to which they belonged.

Another similar model is applied with regard to the authorship of prophetic oracles. Throughout a number of prophetic works, such as Micah and Isaiah 1 – 12, there is an intermingling of positive and

---

39. Wellhausen, *Prolegomena to the History of Israel* (Edinburgh: A. & C. Black, 1885), pp. 324–325.

negative oracles, or, as they are sometimes called, oracles of 'weal' and 'woe'. Both of these types of oracles seem to have the people of God as their main focus. Critics often assign positive and negative oracles that lie adjacent to one another in the text to different authors or editors.[40] Thus Micah is viewed as composed of a wide array of material spanning centuries,[41] and Isaiah 1 – 12 is similarly divided.[42] Again the grounds for such division of authorship are open to question. Few scholars are willing to deny that Isaiah had a son called Shear-Jashub, which means 'a remnant shall return' (Isaiah 7:3). This biographical detail shows that the positive message of a returned remnant could go back to Isaiah's own time, when it must have stood alongside his oracles of doom. The message of a remnant is, however, two edged. It implies destruction for Israel, but not complete destruction. It is a sure sign that prophets were able to think in balanced terms.[43] The only difference between the widely held view, which allows Isaiah to have had a son called 'Shear-Jashub' but otherwise says that he preached judgment, and the view that allows him to have uttered significant positive oracles throughout his ministry is one of quantity not quality.

---

40. H. G. M. Williamson warns against too monolithic a view of Isaiah as merely a prophet of doom. See *The Book Called Isaiah: Deutero-Isaiah's Role in Composition and Redaction* (Oxford: Clarendon, 1994), p. 103, esp. n. 26.

41. Jan A. Wagenaar, *Judgment and Salvation: The Composition and Redaction of Micah 2 – 5* (Supplements to Vetus Testamentum 85; Leiden: E. J. Brill, 2001).

42. Against some modern trends in splitting up Isaiah 1 – 12 see C. H. W. Brekelmans, 'Deuteronomistic Influence in Isaiah 1 – 12', in Jacques Vermeylen (ed.), *The Book of Isaiah/Le Livre d'Isaïe* (Leuven: Peeters, 1989), pp. 167–176. See also the discussion of positive elements in Amos in G. F. Hasel, *Understanding the Book of Amos: Basic Issues in Current Interpretations* (Grand Rapids: Baker, 1991), pp. 105–109.

43. A fine treatment of the concept of remnant is by G. F. Hasel, *The Remnant: The History and Theology of the Remnant Idea from Genesis to Isaiah* (Andrews University Monographs 5; 2nd edn.; Berrien Springs, MI: Andrews University, 1974).

### Can prophets predict?

A further issue that affects assessments of authorship is the question of the nature of prophecy. Biblical prophecy is widely viewed in popular circles as straight prediction, but this is not the full story. When Matthew's Gospel says that through Jesus' stay in Egypt and his departure from there Hosea's saying 'Out of Egypt I called my son' was fulfilled,[44] it is clear that simple prediction is not in mind. Matthew evidently sees fulfilment in this case as some sort of correspondence to the original statement, but not the original statement as asserting that a specific future event will happen. No doubt the nature of prophecies vary, and Matthew's use of Hosea does not deny the possibility of prediction, though it does mean that prophecy needs to be viewed more widely than as mere prediction.

A Christian approach to the OT is, however, not at all opposed to the notion of direct prediction of the future within prophecy. Here it is in stark contrast to a naturalistic approach that cannot allow miraculous prediction. The two approaches may not differ in every case with regard to the dating of prophetic utterances, and a mediating position is sometimes seen to be that of the scholar who rejects the *a priori* assumption that predictive prophecy cannot happen, but believes that *prima facie* long-term projections are a literary device written after the event.[45] But contemporary critical scholarship has little place for long-term predictive prophecies. However, many scholars hold that while long-term prophecy is not present in the Bible, the prophets did often correctly predict events that took place *shortly* after they spoke, which could be foreseen by natural human intuition. This view is typically taken with a book like Habakkuk, and is sometimes even assumed in argument without a commentator feeling any need to justify it.

Habakkuk chapter 1 deals with the invasion of Judah by the Chaldeans (i.e. Babylonians; Habakkuk 1:6). Mason tries to date the

---

44. Hosea 11:1 in Matthew 2:15.

45. Thus John E. Goldingay, *Daniel* (Word Biblical Commentary 30; Word: Milton Keynes, 1991), pp. xxxix–xl.

oracle about the Chaldeans to around 612 BC.[46] His reason for this seems to be that it is at that time that the Babylonians, with the Medes, captured Nineveh, capital of Assyria, and thus showed themselves to be major players on the international stage. The unexpressed idea seems to be that by 612 BC Habakkuk would have been able with normal human insight to foresee the Babylonians as eventual conquerors of Judah too. The problem here is that Habakkuk himself prefaces his announcement about the Chaldeans as something so amazing that his audience would not believe it if they were told (Habakkuk 1:5). The scenario that Habakkuk could foresee a short way by clever insight and yet his audience be completely amazed by the same idea is hard to believe. However, Mason's reasoning here is fairly standard. Another commentator, Roberts, expresses himself differently, preferring merely to say that the oracle in Habakkuk 1:5–6 must predate 605 BC, by which time the Babylonian threat could cause no surprise to Habakkuk's audience.[47] Roberts rejects an earlier date for the beginning of Habakkuk's ministry, for instance that of Fohrer of between 626 and 622 BC,[48] saying, 'It is difficult to square the description of the Chaldeans in 1:6–10 with such an early date . . .'[49] Clearly it is considered that only short-term prediction is possible, despite the fact that prediction beyond the normal is such an important part in the biblical presentation of prophets.[50] A student needs to be aware of the presuppositions that have led scholars to place prophetic oracles so close to their fulfilment and should, when other factors allow, feel free to consider earlier dates for oracles.

Such dating considerations in turn affect evaluations of the unity

46. Rex Mason, *Zephaniah, Habakkuk, Joel* (OT Guides; Sheffield: JSOT Press, 1994), p. 82.

47. J. J. M. Roberts, *Nahum, Habakkuk, and Zephaniah: A Commentary* (Old Testament Library; Louisville: Westminster/John Knox, 1991), pp. 82–83.

48. Georg Fohrer, *Introduction to the Old Testament* (tr. David Green; London: SPCK, 1970), p. 455.

49. Roberts, *Nahum, Habakkuk, and Zephaniah*, p. 83.

50. John F. A. Sawyer, *Prophecy and the Biblical Prophets* (rev. edn.; Oxford: Oxford University Press, 1993), pp. 17–18.

of a book. As noted earlier, a wide range of scholars view Isaiah to be composed of units from different periods, with three substantial units called First, Second and Third Isaiah, authors whose work is held to be found within chapters 1 – 39, 40 – 55, and 56 – 66.[51] Much of the material in these three sections is thus assigned to the latter end of the eighth century BC, to the late exilic period (i.e. some time before 538 BC), and to the post-exilic period, respectively. This is only a simplistic scheme: most scholars hold that the book is composed of more than three elements, and has received editorial additions at a number of stages, though specific schemes of scholars are often mutually incompatible. Methods used to reach divisions in the book of Isaiah have not always obtained reliable results. Bernhard Duhm (1847–1928), who originally proposed the entity Third Isaiah, assigned parts of the book (e.g. chs. 24 – 27) to the second century BC, and units within that to yet later dates, such as 25:9–11, which he assigned to the time of Alexander Jannaeus (103–76 BC).[52] These views have been proven false by the discovery of the Dead Sea Scrolls and a copy of the book of Isaiah dating to the second century BC. The student therefore has good reason to demand a high degree of proof from those who claim to be able to isolate separate authorial units within the book.

The issue of the historical background of the book of Isaiah has continued to be the object of a complex debate.[53] There has

51. Only a relatively small number of authors maintain that Isaiah son of Amoz (mentioned in 1:1; 2:1; 13:1) wrote the whole book. These include J. N. Oswalt, *The Book of Isaiah, Volumes 1 and 2* (New International Commentary on Old Testament; Grand Rapids: Eerdmans, 1986, 1998), and Motyer (see bibliography). The same position is maintained by Richard L. Schultz, author of *The Search for Quotation: Verbal Parallels in the Prophets* (Journal for the Study of the Old Testament Supplement Series 180; Sheffield: Sheffield Academic Press, 1999).

52. Bernhard Duhm, *Das Buch Jesaia* (4th edn.; Vandenhoeck & Ruprecht: Göttingen, 1922), p. 172.

53. Williamson, *Book Called Isaiah*, seeks to avoid multiplying hypotheses in relation to the book by ascribing a more significant role in composition and editing to the figure he identifies as Second Isaiah.

been a clear tension running through scholarship between an observation of an overall unity to the book and a desire to place each of its oracles at a date close to the historical background it is perceived to have.[54] Sometimes stress on the unity of the book may cause a scholar to avoid ascribing any of the book to Isaiah son of Amoz, as is witnessed by Watts's comment that 'If the claim for eighth-century authorship is eliminated, no strong reason remains to deny unity to the book.'[55] Watts, along with many other scholars, would reject the notion that the claim that part or all of the book of Isaiah must have been composed after the lifetime of Isaiah is founded upon a prejudice against long-range prophecy, and would seek to establish the division on grounds of literary style and the best historical background to the book or its parts. However, scholars often use reconstructed historical background to date prophetic writings in a single direction: a book is seen as a unit coming from the latest historical period considered to be the background of one of its parts.

### How many authors?

The movement in Isaianic studies towards an emphasis on literary unity is paralleled throughout biblical studies. In traditional critical scholarship the material of the Pentateuch was assigned to four basic sources: J, after the name for God that originally identified it in Genesis, namely *Yahweh* (formerly Jehovah); E, after the name for God that marked it in Genesis, namely *Elohim*; D for *Deuteronomic* material; and P for *Priestly* material. This traditional assignment of the Pentateuch to four sources, called the Documentary Hypothesis, tends to receive less emphasis now than it did once. The reasons for this are various:

---

54. A central argument for assigning much of chapters 40 – 55 to the late exilic period is the mention of Cyrus in 44:28 – 45:1, as well as the wider Babylonian background.

55. John D. W. Watts, 'Isaiah', in Watson E. Mills and Richard F. Wilson (eds.), *Mercer Commentary on the Bible* (Macon, GA: Mercer University, 1995), p. 566.

1. The general movement emphasizing literary artistry in composition has sometimes denied the source-critical approach, but often simply replaced it.
2. The wider move in society from modernism to postmodernism has involved increased doubt about scholarly ability to reconstruct history, including literary history. Related to this, though not strictly as a postmodern movement,[56] a number of scholars have adopted a hyperconservative view of what literary evidence may be used to reconstruct history. This in turn has led to rejection of the Documentary Hypothesis crystallized by Wellhausen.[57]
3. Though no replacement has been created for the Documentary Hypothesis it has received a vast amount of attention, but has not led to consensus on more than a broad outline. Scholars have turned from further investigation, therefore, partly through boredom.

The fading popularity, at least in English-speaking scholarship, of the Documentary Hypothesis, has clearly not taken place for reasons of high merit.[58] Moreover, at least in some minds, the emphasis on the literary aspects of biblical literature is accompanied by a belief that this literature cannot be used for reconstruction of the history of the period it purports to describe. Since the relationship between biblical literature and history is important for a Christian it will be necessary to assess literary arguments carefully.

## Ethical issues

Alongside such questions as 'Did it happen?' and 'Who wrote it?' students of the OT often have to ask the question 'Is it good?' This is a question of ethics – of rights and wrongs. Here the Christian is not bound to justify every event in the Bible. The Bible

---

56. Barr, *History and Ideology*, p. 157.
57. Lemche, *Israelites*, pp. 26–27.
58. This is also the conclusion of Barr, *History and Ideology*, pp. 17–18.

records many things without approval. Nevertheless, there must
be a level at which the Bible is promoting ethics that are right. But
despite the large amount of narrative in the OT there is relatively
little explicit in biblical narratives about the rights and wrongs of
particular human actions. There are notable exceptions to this. For
instance, after David's adultery with Bathsheba and murder of her
husband Uriah, the text comments that 'the thing David had done
was bad in the eyes of the LORD' (2 Samuel 11:27, my tr.). The narrative of the ensuing chapters in 2 Samuel 12 – 20 seems almost to
centre on the portrayal of the tragic effects of these misde-
meanours on David's family and kingdom. Yet the second half of
2 Samuel is more obvious than most OT texts in its evaluation of
rights and wrongs. The narratives of Genesis about the patriarchs
Abraham, Isaac and Jacob seem harder to assess. Was the polygamy of Jacob something the writer viewed as good (a sign of
God's great blessing upon him) as neutral or as bad? Is it possible
that the writer did not mind something but that we should
because, for some reason, we have a higher ethical standard now?
How did biblical writers view Rahab's lying (Joshua 2:4–5), and can
we mimic it? Were the men of Sodom in Genesis 19 viewed as
particularly sinful because of their homosexual practices, their
violence or their lack of hospitality, or a combination of these?

   In approaching such questions of narrative ethics it is important
to read texts closely. Approval and disapproval may not be marked
explicitly and the wider context needs to be considered. Thus to take
the issue of Jacob's polygamy, there are a number of indications that
his practice was not ideal. In the wider narrative, the perfect situation
portrayed in Genesis 2 was of a couple, and bigamy is first intro-
duced in the context of a figure who is viewed negatively (Lamech in
Genesis 4:19–24). All those whom God saves on the ark have a
single partner, humans and animals (7:2)! Abraham took his second
wife when he doubted God's promise, and there was subsequently
domestic strife (21:8–13). Jacob ends up with two wives, Leah and
Rachel, as a result of his father-in-law's trick (29:22–23). However,
Jacob is hardly innocent, since Laban's substitute of the older sibling
for the younger seems only to be the just reward for Jacob's earlier lie
to his father Isaac, when he had pretended to be his own older
sibling (27:19). Rivalry between the two wives ensues and Jacob gets

two more wives, the handmaids of Leah and Rachel, specifically to beget children as part of this rivalry. The existence of a plurality of wives also allows favouritism to develop towards particular children (37:3), which in turn provokes strife between Joseph and his brothers. Thus taking a broader view of the narrative, Jacob's polygamy is seen as highly problematic, even if God's goodness towards Jacob despite his errors is a yet more important theme in Genesis.[59]

A similar approach could be taken with the issue of homosexual practice in Genesis 19. There is little doubt that the inhabitants of Sodom are implicitly criticized both for violence and for lack of hospitality. Yet it is hard within the wider narrative and context of the OT to claim that this passage contains no critique of homosexual practice.[60] An OT narrative brings home ethical teaching, almost invariably avoiding explicit comment, by portraying sets of events in such a way that an insightful reader will see a connection (e.g. of cause and effect, crime and punishment, or promise and fulfilment) between them.

### Is genocide ever fair?

A peculiar problem within the OT is the conquest of Canaan by the Israelites. The Israelites are enjoined to destroy the inhabitants of the land of Canaan completely and to show them no mercy (Deuteronomy 7:1–6, especially v. 2). Here the problem for a Christian reading of the OT is that these commands, having come from God, must necessarily be right. Yet, living as we do after a century that has seen atrocious genocide, the command to the Israelites to leave nothing alive (Deuteronomy 20:16) seems particularly hard. The destruction includes humans of every age and animals. The narrative naturally raises the question of how an

---

59. A recent discussion of the ethical force of biblical narrative is Gordon J. Wenham, *Story as Torah: Reading the Old Testament Ethically* (Edinburgh: T. & T. Clark, 2000).

60. As is maintained by V. P. Furnish, 'What Does the Bible Say about Homosexuality?' in Sally B. Geis and Donald E. Messer (eds.), *Caught in the Crossfire: Helping Christians Debate Homosexuality* (Nashville: Abingdon, 1994), pp. 59–60.

interpreter is to view this as God's Word and why if a divine
mandate could be given to genocide at that time it might not also
be given now.

Although generally I have avoided discussing specific issues, the
size of this ethical problem so outweighs others in the OT that if
it can be seen to be of a different quality from modern mass
slaughter, other ethical problems will not be seen as so much
beyond the reaches of a solution. Here, I am not within such a
brief discussion, trying to solve a problem that ultimately may lie
beyond human solution. I am merely seeking to demonstrate that
the problem is not one that definitely has no ultimate solution.

The problem must be approached within the broader framework
of the OT narrative. As indicated earlier, the historicity of the narrative generally is widely questioned, and many commentators will
maintain that the killing of the Hittites, Girgashites, Amorites,
Canaanites, Perizzites, Hivites and Jebusites (Deuteronomy 7:1,
though lists vary) never really took place and that some of these
peoples never even existed. To maintain that the narrative is unhistor-
ical does not, however, solve the problem. The exhortation to destroy
is not made more or less ethical by whether it was carried out or not.
But regardless of views of the narrative's historicity, the command
must be viewed within its wider biblical context. Back in Genesis 15
God had already promised to Abram that he would be given the land
of these various nations (vv. 18–21). However, the promise is given a
very special delay of 400 years (vv. 13–16) because 'the sin of the
Amorites is not yet full' (v. 16, my tr.). The 'Amorites' here clearly
stand for all the peoples in the land, and the text makes explicit that
God will not hand over the land until the people in it are bad enough
for him to do so. Furthermore, according to Leviticus 18 (vv. 3, 21,
24–25) those who inhabited the land before the Israelite conquest
had the practice of sacrificing their own children. Now these texts
containing the Bible's negative evaluation of the inhabitants of the
land may be rejected as untrue by modern interpreters, but it is difficult to justify divorcing these texts from the command to kill those
peoples. The biblical texts must be judged together rather than in
isolation from each other. Taken this way, the ethics in the narrative
are distinct from modern conflict situations involving genocide where
it is scarcely possible to argue that the party being destroyed is more

wicked than other nations. The negative evaluation of the Amorites, however, cannot be seen as mere Israelite nationalistic propaganda, since such propaganda would inevitably set up a comparison between the Amorites and the Israelites. The context, moreover, in Deuteronomy specifically states that the Israelites were not good, being 'stiff-necked', and the Bible sets this within a further statement of the connection between the wickedness of the land's inhabitants and their destruction (Deuteronomy 9:4–6). The destruction of the people is, therefore, closely connected with evil behaviour. Within the biblical narrative adults earned their own destruction.

Nevertheless, this observation does not solve the ethical dilemma. The command of total destruction includes children and animals for whom the issue of guilt cannot be invoked in the same way as with the adults. One could say that because of close kinship ties any children spared by the Israelites would no doubt have avenged the death of their parents. Pragmatically speaking, this would necessitate destruction of Amorite children in order not to perpetuate conflict. But a pragmatic justification for the killing will not suffice. However, on the premise that the wicked acts of the land's adult inhabitants required their death (a premise many would dispute), the death of their children could be seen as something the inhabitants themselves had caused. This could be regarded as not so far removed from the ethics applied in modern liberal societies. UN sanctions imposed on Iraq after the Gulf War in 1991 were justified by successive Western governments, even though by them innocent Iraqi people, including children, suffered. Such governments held Saddam Hussein personally responsible for the problems caused to his people by the sanctions.[61] This ethic was not perfect because, among other things, it ignored ways in which Western societies themselves contributed historically to the problems of Iraq. The Bible, however, presents us with a situation in which the Amorites did evil without any others having contributed to their problems. To that extent the ethics of the biblical narrative are certainly not inferior to those applied by

61. This seems to be the thrust of the statement by the United States Department of State found at http://usinfo.state.gov/regional/nea/iraq /iraq99.htm.

modern liberal governments, and probably rather better in that those who judged the Amorites had not contributed to the problems of their society – rather a contrast with what Britain and the US could say of themselves as they seek to resolve issues in Iraq in 2003.

There are differences in each situation, and the parallels are not exact, but it has too often been stated in indignant and self-righteous terms that the Bible here represents a primitive ethic that should have no place in a modern society. We need to remove any plank from our own eye before we have a right to criticize further.[62]

### Psalms of hate?

But in making decisions about rights and wrongs in narrative, we are not merely making assessments of the past. The question inevitably arises as to the normative nature of the ethics involved. When is an example in the OT to be followed and when avoided? This question arises not only with narrative but also with prayers. A well-known case is the so-called imprecatory psalms.[63] These psalms often contain prayers for judgment to fall on the enemies of the psalmist (e.g. Psalms 58:6–11; 83; 109). How should Christians who have been taught by Jesus to love and pray (good) for their enemies (Matthew 5:43–45) evaluate these psalms?

Again here it is instructive to take the most extreme case. This is probably the ending of Psalm 137.[64] The psalm that begins with the famous words 'By the rivers of Babylon – there we sat down and wept' ends with the following prayer:

> Remember, LORD, against the Edomites the day of Jerusalem,
>     how they said, 'Raze it, raze it, to its foundations!'
> O daughter Babylon, to be devastated!

---

62. Much can be gained from a rather different discussion in Peter C. Craigie, *The Problem of War in the Old Testament* (Grand Rapids: Eerdmans, 1978).

63. The imprecatory psalms are not a particularly natural group, since they represent a variety of types of psalm, but are grouped together by moderns because of the common ethical problems they pose.

64. If so, Psalm 109 is in close second place.

> Happy shall the one be who repays to you what you have done to us.
> Happy shall the one be who takes your children
> and dashes them against the rock! (vv. 7–9, my tr.)

Following my method elsewhere, I will not seek to justify the ethics of this passage, but rather endeavour to show that its ethics should not be rejected out of hand as incapable of being part of God's Word. The context is important: it is a lament over the destruction of Jerusalem by the Babylonians in 587/586 during which the Edomites also seem to have joined in (Obadiah 10–14). The important thing to note in this text is that it is not a simple prayer of hatred. In verse 7 the psalmist asks God to remember against the Edomites what they have done. That is, there is a call for a punishment equal to their crime, not greater, not less. The same emphasis on equal punishment is brought out in the next verse, where a blessing is pronounced on the one who *repays* them for their crime. The nature of the repayment is then explained in verse 9 as smashing children against the rock. Since the focus is on exact repayment, there is the implication that the Babylonians had smashed the children of the people of Judah against the rock.[65] Thus, rather than being an expression of wanton cruelty against innocents, the psalm is seeking to remember the full extent of Babylonian cruelty. To a modern reader's mind it may seem that the psalmist does not care about the fate of the children. However, it could be argued that the benediction pronounced by the psalmist precisely is motivated by the psalmist's concern about the fate of children, namely the children of the people of Judah. Ultimately, there is no evidence that Israelites sought vengeance personally for their own loss at the time of Jerusalem's captivity. They did not form terrorist organizations which brought forward their cause by attacking children, and the benediction was not a bounty or reward. The psalm may, however, express the goodness of a situation where justice is done,

---

65. Perhaps a further confirmation of this principle of exact retaliation is that Isaiah 13:16–18, announcing judgment on the Babylonians carried out by the Medes, states that the Medes will smash the Babylonians' children mercilessly before their eyes.

and where the perpetrator of a wrong receives an exact retribution. The Babylonians would themselves be the responsible ones for any pain suffered by their children. If this is correct, the focus of the psalm is on the effect of the punishment on the Babylonian adults, and it is in the effect on them, not the necessarily accompanying effect on the Babylonian children, that the blessedness of the punishment is held to lie.

It is not here argued that this analysis solves all the moral problems of this imprecatory psalm, but it is maintained that the psalm is not *initiating* violence or causing hatred.[66] Unlike modern conflicts where the will to do harm to the enemy is endless, a feature of all imprecatory psalms is that they contain, at least implicitly, a limitation of the *lex talionis*, or law of 'an eye for an eye and a tooth for a tooth' (Exodus 21:24 etc.). Nowhere is it prayed that the enemy might, as it were, lose two teeth in revenge for a single tooth of the supplicant.

The New Testament (NT), while setting the highest possible example of Jesus, who did not pray for revenge (Luke 23:34), does not reject the idea that it is legitimate to pray for injustice done to oneself to be requited (Revelation 6:9–11).


## Interpretation

### Coherence or contradiction?
One of the areas where a Christian approach can differ most from those taken by other scholars is in the issue of harmony within biblical writings. If biblical writings are genuinely expressions of a coherent divine mind, then they must cohere at the level of what they communicate, even if ultimately the nature of the coherence

---

66. A useful treatment of the same issue is found in C. S. Lewis, *Reflections on the Psalms* (London: Geoffrey Bles, 1958), pp. 20–33, though I cannot agree with all of Lewis's emphases. Further insights on Psalm 137 and psalms of revenge generally are in Erich Zenger, *A God of Vengeance? Understanding the Psalms of Divine Wrath* (tr. Linda M. Maloney; Louisville: Westminster/John Knox, 1996), especially pp. 47–50, 90–91.

is beyond mortal comprehension. Thus while there is no problem
in the admission that contrary statements appear in the Bible,[67]
these are seen as linguistic codes for a message which at a deeper
level is coherent. Contradiction is a perfectly legitimate method of
communication,[68] one frequently used by humans, but which
when found in the Bible is used to deny coherence. However, the
issue of coherence in the Bible is one that must be explored
beyond the level of mere contrary statements, which can easily be
seen to have slightly different referents.

One of the attractions, however, of secular academic methods is
that, according to them, the interpreter is not bound to see a coherence between two different texts. This 'liberates' the interpreter
from the constraint of fitting together incoherent texts and is held
to be fairer to the text. The appeal thus of secular critical methods
is that by them the interpreter is being *more* faithful to the Bible than
within a framework 'constrained' by seeking to find a deep harmony
between passages in Scripture. This view is a strong element moti-
vating people to abandon a classical view of Scripture's coherence
derived from the Bible's statements about God's Word.

Nevertheless, this appeal needs to be examined to see whether it
is all that it seems. In fact, much modern research on how language works indicates the importance of unexpressed elements in
the context of a text for its correct understanding.[69] The proper
interpretation of texts, therefore, can require a wide context.
Historical-critical scholars can, however, by their focus on the true

---

67. Cf., e.g., 'I repent that I have made Saul king' (1 Samuel 15:11) with 'The
    Glory of Israel does not lie or repent' (1 Samuel 15:29); or 'They feared
    the LORD' (2 Kings 17:33; cf. 17:41) with 'they do not fear the LORD'
    (2 Kings 17:34). If these statements were treated in isolation they could
    easily be ascribed to different levels in the compositional process.
    However, why should they not come from a single author?

68. Witness the opening of Charles Dickens's classic 1859 *Tale of Two Cities*,
    'It was the best of times, it was the worst of times . . .'

69. This is at the heart of the linguistic discipline of pragmatics. A useful
    introduction to pragmatics is Stephen C. Levinson, *Pragmatics* (Cambridge
    Textbooks in Linguistics; Cambridge: Cambridge University Press, 1983).

meaning of small units of text be in danger of treating small isolated texts as self-interpreting. It is important to see clearly that fairness to a text does not necessitate viewing it in isolation. What is the natural reading of a text in isolation may be a distortion of its meaning, while what is a less natural reading of a text in isolation, but one motivated by reading it in a wider context, may be the correct one.

An example of this are passages in the prophets that seem to express prophetic disapproval of the OT sacrificial system and festivals (e.g. Isaiah 1:11–14). It would be possible to treat these statements as an isolated unit by some hypothetical author who believed that animal sacrifices should not be offered to God. However, viewing the verses within a wider context allows another interpretation.[70]

But there is a danger here. It is possible so to qualify the interpretation of a text by a wider context that one drowns out the message of the individual text. An interpreter can bring a text into false harmony with another text. This must be avoided, while one should also be wary of historical-critical approaches that use the identification of incompatibly divergent voices within Scripture as a foundation upon which to build a history of OT religion. Proponents of this method can seek to discover divergent voices within the OT, since such divergences are the building blocks to write a 'critical' history; that is, one not dependent on an uncritical acceptance of scriptural statements. The way to avoid misinterpretation seems to be to read texts as a whole and simultaneously with regard to the detail they contain. Detail can modify one's interpretation of the whole, as can the whole modify one's interpretation of the detail.

The interpreter of Scripture also needs to be aware of the ramifications of positions taken on issues of interpretation. While coming to a view that two biblical texts cannot express truth about a coherent reality may appear like the best solution to an interpretative problem, it makes it hard to view both texts as coming from a single divine author. A student should expect a corpus as rich and diverse as the OT to present a balance of statements on a number

---

70. Sawyer, *Prophecy and the Biblical Prophets*, pp. 21–24.

of subjects and should not quickly conclude that a variety of statements indicates a variety of theologies in the OT, if by 'a variety of
theologies' is meant incompatible rather than merely complementary theologies.

It might be urged that to encourage students to be patient in recognizing unity within Scripture will lead to an uncritical approach.
There are, however, many parallels for this within other academic
disciplines. For example, while a popular perception of science is
that it proceeds from evidence to understanding to belief, this is
very often not the case. Invariably students of quantum mechanics
believe it before they understand it, often even believing it although
they never expect to understand it. The order is as in Anselm's
saying *credo ut intellegam*, 'I believe in order that I may understand.'
For Anselm, as for Augustine before him, belief preceded understanding. This is a frequent human order, because without the
belief that something makes sense it is often difficult to summon
the patience to see how it makes sense. If students believed
quantum mechanics to be incoherent and to have no correspondence to the universe, they would certainly not have the patience to
study it as intensely as if they believed that it was one of physics'
great unifying theories with wide explanatory powers. There is, of
course, a danger with *credo ut intellegam*, since it can be used to justify
continuing to believe in something unworthy of belief. However,
the principle of patient positive study of Scripture to find unity is
not something that should be lightly abandoned.

### Use of background

As mentioned above, context is important for the interpretation of
text. Yet the context in which a text is to be interpreted is not
merely written text, but also its whole cultural context. This is
obvious for texts other than the Bible, but is more problematic for
the OT. At one level it is fairly obvious that background information is needed for correct interpretation of the OT. For instance,
if a Hebrew word occurs only once in the whole OT, then information from outside the Bible may be useful in identifying its
meaning. This information could include occurrences of the word
in later Hebrew documents, what early authorities said the word
meant, or the meaning of connected words in languages close to

Hebrew (such as Aramaic). Thus information outside the Bible is used for biblical interpretation. However, the context of the occurrence itself must be given priority in deciding meaning. Background information must never be used to negate context.

Information outside the Bible is similarly needed for correct identification of many locations mentioned within the Bible.[71] However, caution is needed in the use of extrabiblical information in biblical interpretation. Such information brings its own problems of interpretation. An archaeological find is not usually self-interpreting, but forms part of a picture of the past reconstructed from quite diverse sources. It is, important not to explain *ignotum per ignotius*; that is, an unknown by something yet more obscure. Background information is important, but it can be used to propose completely opposite meanings of a single text; thus background studies can develop a quasi-scriptural status in their interpretative authority. It is, therefore, important to recognize simultaneously the importance and the dangers of background information in interpretation. For instance, in Daniel 6:6, 11, 15 (Aramaic 6:7, 12, 16) there is an unusual Aramaic word for the way the people assembled before the king. A standard dictionary basing itself on occurrences of seemingly related forms in Aramaic other than biblical Aramaic concludes that the word means 'shew tumultuousness, come thronging'.[72] But, however erudite the linguistic observation, it does not seem to fit the context. Oriental kings would not tolerate disorderly thronging in their presence, and the word must be understood in a way that suits all three of the contexts in which it is used. Context comes first. It is important to remember that with few exceptions ancient texts, including those in the Bible, were written

---

71. Information, especially from later traditions, is helpfully used to mark out points on the route of the exodus in G. I. Davies, *The Way of the Wilderness: A Geographical Study of the Wilderness Itineraries in the Old Testament* (Society for Old Testament Study Monograph Series 5; Cambridge: Cambridge University Press, 1979).

72. F. Brown, S. R. Driver and C. A. Briggs, *A Hebrew and English Lexicon of the Old Testament, with an Appendix Containing the Biblical Aramaic* (Oxford: Clarendon, 1907), p. 1112.

in order to be understood. Difficulties naturally arise, but if a background explanation cannot be squared with the text of a passage, it is to be rejected. A student should view acquiring a knowledge of background information about the OT as a long-term process that gradually produces beneficial results rather than as a quick way to decide on one interpretation rather than another.

### Chronological development

An issue that combines theology and history is the question of historical development. Except for the few who deny any history in the OT, it is widely acknowledged that there is historical development within the OT. Central to Christian interpretation is the idea of the relative order of elements in the OT.[73] There is not only development through time, but there is also progression in revelation. But one encounters quickly the difficulty of knowing what the relative order of parts of the OT is. This is particularly the case when the traditional view of the order of composition of OT books is compared with that in standard textbooks of OT criticism. Whereas the OT gives a picture of the Law of Moses as established at the beginning of Israelite history, and of the prophets calling the Israelites back to obedience to the Law, it is a useful generalization to say that modern scholarship has generally posited the reverse order: among the earliest to write were prophets such as Hosea and Amos in the eighth century BC, and only after them, round the time of the exile in the sixth century and slightly later did the written Law, the Pentateuch, take its shape.[74] However, this critical model of the history of Israelite literature still lacks external confirmation, even though it seeks to explain data which have not yet received adequate attention from scholarship broadly supporting the view that the Law preceded the prophets.

---

73. Witness Paul's arguments in Romans 4:10 and Galatians 3:17 based on relative chronology in the OT.
74. This scheme was developed by Eduard Reuss (1804–91), who by 1834 had concluded that 'the prophets . . . [are] older than the law, and the Psalms more recent than both'. Reuss, *Geschichte des Alten Testaments* (2nd edn.; Braunschweig: C. A. Schwetschke, 1890), p. vii.

One of the false notions frequently used to date texts relative to each other is how primitive they seem to be. The assumption is that cultures evolved at such a rate and with such consistency that over a period of centuries it is quite clear which elements are earlier than the others. For instance, Hermann Gunkel, commenting on the relative dating of psalms, stated:

> Indeed, in the earliest history of man all religion existed only in the form of the worship service, while a cultless piety developed only later. This conjecture is supported also by Babylonian parallels, namely, the Babylonian psalm poetry. This Babylonian poetry, which, as a whole, precedes the Israelite, belongs to the context of the worship service. There is the further illustration, from the history of Protestant hymnody, that the 'chorale' is older than the 'spiritual song'.[75]

Gunkel's argument is basically that in whatever culture we look at religious songs, the ones based round cult or public ceremony will be the earliest form to appear, and that religious expressions by individuals outside the cult will only appear later. In fact, this search for the primitive pervades Gunkel's classification of psalms. But Gunkel is not alone among formative figures in OT criticism to have such an approach. Wellhausen in his *Prolegomena* embraces just such an overarching story. The history of Israelite literature is traced from the golden era of classical prophets whose statements awe us with vivid and stark expression, through to the writings of a much more scribal class with an institutionalized religion. Similarly, in his view, the early strands of the Pentateuch (J) were ones containing a primitive, anthropomorphic picture of God, whereas the later sections (P) had developed a much more philosophical and abstract conception of God. Wellhausen made no secret of the fact that he took a dim view of the final stage, seeing it as the institutionalization of legalistic Jewish religion.[76]

What is important to note here is that so much of the recon-

---

75. Hermann Gunkel, *The Psalms: A Form-Critical Introduction* (tr. Thomas M. Horner; Philadelphia: Fortress, 1967), p. 5.

76. Wellhausen, *Prolegomena*, pp. 361–362.

struction of both political and literary history was predicated on a certain evolutionary principle rather than on any firm external controls marking primitivity and later development. To some extent one could say that the general shape of the story that would be told was fixed prior to examination of the text. The result was that the biblical text was able to be fitted into the Wellhausenian scheme very well, but this provided no guarantee that the Wellhausenian scheme was the correct one.

There is no intrinsic reason for a Christian approach to deny cultural progression or the gradual accumulation of human knowledge. The student must, therefore, consider developmental schemes critically to consider which elements result from a presupposition of cultural evolution, and which are actually justified by the data themselves.

In relation to this there is also the issue of progressive revelation. The phrase 'progressive revelation' is used to describe how more and more revelation is unfolded through the time line of the Bible's narrative. Thus, for instance, the character of Israel's messianic hope became clearer through the OT narrative; indeed, the very concept of Messiah was not there through the whole period described. Progressive revelation in some ways provides a counterpart to a presupposition of cultural evolution and the same data may sometimes be explained by either model. However, at times there is a clash between the concept of development through time espoused in biblical texts and the concept of development applied to the text by modern scholars. A right approach should not deny development, but should seek to view it under a model consistent with the nature of Scripture.

### Towards the New Testament

In most academic discussion of the OT the NT is viewed as beyond the purview of the subject. This is understandable as the OT was presumably able to be interpreted to some degree before the NT came along. However, there is often a sense that the NT is somehow foreign to the OT, and therefore should be avoided in interpretative discussion of the OT. However, this scarcely does justice to the OT, which, at least in prophetic writings, is so often looking ahead to something other than itself. Why insist that an ostensibly prophetic text is considered without regard to any claimants to fulfilment? Similarly, the OT contains within itself considerable elements of typology (i.e. linked, recurring patterns in history). The return of the Judaean captives from Babylon is described in terms marking it as in some ways a repeat of the exodus from Egypt (e.g. Isaiah 43:16–21), and the return of treasure to Jerusalem after the exile seems to parallel the earlier plundering of Egypt as the Israelites left it (Ezra 1:7–11; Exodus 12:35–36). Thus the OT itself invites observation of recurring situations. In the light of this there is no a priori reason why NT typological applications of the OT should be rejected as valid interpretations.

This brings us on to a crunch issue for Christian students. According to the NT (e.g. Luke 24:27) Jesus claimed that the OT was essentially about himself. This claim cannot be understood merely as a claim that there are several key OT passages which prefigure Christ, but rather must be understood as maintaining that there is something fundamental throughout the whole OT which points us in the direction of Christ. To appreciate this it is necessary to move beyond mere ideas of an OT statement predicting something in the NT, and to discern something in the OT that could be about Christ, even in the passages that are not in the form of prophetic predictions, since such passages make up the overwhelming bulk of the OT. This will inevitably lead to considering the possibility that themes or accounts of events themselves reflect something related to Christ. This may be in a portrayal of justice, in an account of deliverance, or even in a story giving an example of the opposite of what Christ is. Links made between the OT and Christ, however, must not be without discipline. Students need to define criteria controlling this exercise, but can at least carry out the exercise of seeing reflections of Christ in OT material in the knowledge that OT writers themselves saw reflections of their own period in the history of the times that preceded them.[77]

---

77. A useful book for beginning to think about Christian application of the OT is Graeme Goldsworthy's *Gospel and Kingdom: A Christian Interpretation of the Old Testament* (Exeter: Paternoster, 1981).

## Conclusion

To summarize the strands of the preceding discussion, studying the OT is vital for serious Christian theology. It is also a minefield. This is so partly because of the complexity of the subject itself, the period of time covered by the OT, and the interdisciplinary approach this requires. But the likeness between OT studies and a minefield is also caused by ideological factors. In studying the OT and literature about the OT one is entering an area where result is dependent on the approach taken, and there are elements in approaches taken within the academy that a student with a faith commitment will want to avoid. Even in seemingly objective disciplines, such as archaeology, wider paradigmatic commitments are frequently brought to bear on investigation. This rarely takes place at the surface level, but may have an influence on the broader picture within which a scholar seeks to make sense of isolated data. The challenge for the student is not to feel discouraged by the vastness of the subject, but to take pleasure in developing competent knowledge of various parts of it gradually. The very size of the subject in relation to the size of our own intellect should arouse the humility exhorted by the prophet:

> He has told you, man, what is good:
> and what does the Lord require of you
> but to do justice, and to love mercy,
> and to walk humbly with your God? (Micah 6:8, my tr.)

## Resources

### *Bibliography*
Below is a brief general OT bibliography, which may be used to supplement rather than replace topic-based reading lists. Further regular articles and book reviews appear in the Religious and Theological Studies Fellowship's (RTSF's) journal *Themelios*.

Arnold, Bill T. and Bryan E. Beyer, *Encountering the Old Testament: A Christian Survey* (Grand Rapids: Baker, 1999), 512 pages. For those who like pictures, potted summaries of debates, and do not have much time, this is not a bad starting point. Further reading is listed and should be sought.

Bray, Gerald, *Biblical Interpretation: Past and Present* (Leicester: Apollos, 1996), 608 pages. A wide-ranging survey of how people have understood the Bible throughout the history of the church. Excellent for historical perspective on modern debates.

Bruce, F. F., *The Canon of Scripture* (Downers Grove: IVP, 1988), 349 pages. A treatment of why particular books are in the Bible, and why some are not.

Dillard, Raymond B., and Tremper Longman III, *An Introduction to the Old Testament* (Leicester: Apollos, 1995), 473 pages. A must. A clear book-by-book introduction to the OT from an evangelical perspective.

Dorsey, David A., *The Literary Structure of the Old Testament: A Commentary on Genesis–Malachi* (Grand Rapids: Baker, 1999), 330 pages. With this you can quickly turn up any OT book and find out how someone has seen literary structures in it. You may not be convinced by all examples, but it can save a lot of time, and engender considerable enjoyment in reading the text.

Ellis, E. Earle, 'The Old Testament Canon in the Early Church', in M. J. Mulder (ed.), *Mikra: Text, Translation, Reading and Interpretation of the Hebrew Bible in Ancient Judaism and Early Christianity* (Assen: Van Gorcum/ Philadelphia: Fortress, 1988), pp. 653–690. Contains a robust challenge to the view that at the time of the NT a plurality of OT canons were in use. Christians at the earliest stage sought to identify which OT books were Scripture on the basis of Palestinian authorities.

Garrett, Duane A., *Rethinking Genesis: The Sources and Authorship of the First Book of the Pentateuch* (Grand Rapids: Baker, 1991), 273 pages. Seeks to establish an early date for Genesis on a variety of grounds.

Halpern, Baruch, *The First Historians: The Hebrew Bible and History* (University Park, PA: Pennsylvania State University, 1996), 321 pages. A response to those scholars who deny that there can be any real knowledge of history in the Bible.

Handy, Lowell K. (ed.), *The Age of Solomon: Scholarship at the Turn of the Millennium* (Leiden: E. J. Brill, 1997), pp. 1–56, 106–153. This volume contains papers with responses between A. R. Millard, supporting the basic historicity of the biblical narratives about Solomon, and J. Maxwell Miller, who is more sceptical. There are also important papers by K. A. Kitchen.

Hasel, Gerhard F., *Old Testament Theology: Basic Issues in the Current Debate* (4th edn.; Grand Rapids: Eerdmans, 1991), 272 pages. A move towards a positive theology of the Bible.

Hasel, Gerhard F., *Understanding the Book of Amos: Basic Issues in Current Interpretations* (Grand Rapids: Baker, 1991), 171 pages. A brief but penetrating analysis of trends in Amos scholarship and pointing towards a profitable path for research.

Hoffmeier, James K., *Israel in Egypt: The Evidence for the Authenticity of the Exodus Tradition* (Oxford: Oxford University Press, 1997), 263 pages. Develops a positive evaluation of the evidence for the correctness of a number of biblical traditions about Egypt and the exodus.

Jobes, Karen H., and Moisés Silva, *Invitation to the Septuagint* (Carlisle: Paternoster, 2000), 351 pages. A first-rate introduction to the Greek OT – particularly useful for those trying to develop insight into how the OT is quoted in the NT.

Kitchen, K. A., *On the Reliability of the Old Testament* (Winona Lake, In: Eisenbrauns, 2003), 672 pages. Set to be a classic. It draws together a vast amount of information related to the reliability of the Old Testament.

Long, V. Philips, Iain W. Provan and Tremper Longman, *A Biblical History of Israel* (Louisville, KY: Westminster John Knox, 2003).

Longman, Tremper, III, *Old Testament Commentary Survey* (3rd edn.; Leicester: IVP, 2003), 144 pages. An ideal companion to help you purchase and read the better commentaries. The second edition (1995) also supplied guidance on other works besides commentaries.

McConville, J. Gordon, *Teach Yourself the Old Testament* (London: Hodder & Stoughton, 1996), 168 pages. A good starting point to get orientated in OT discussion.

Millard, A. R., and D. J. Wiseman (eds.), *Essays on the Patriarchal Narratives* (Leicester: IVP, 1980), 223 pages. Some of these essays contain interesting arguments for the historicity of the patriarchs.

Motyer, J. A., *The Prophecy of Isaiah* (Leicester: IVP, 1993), 544 pages. Maintains that the whole book of Isaiah is a composition by Isaiah and that there are overarching themes and structures for the whole book.

Payne, J. Barton (ed.), *New Perspectives on the Old Testament* (Waco, TX: Word, 1970), 405 pages. A useful, if somewhat dated, collection of essays on a wide range of OT subjects, but with key essays on Deuteronomy, Esther and Daniel.

Whybray, R. N., *The Making of the Pentateuch: A Methodological Study* (Journal for

the Study of the Old Testament Supplement Series 53; Sheffield: JSOT
Press, 1987), 263 pages. Questions the need for more than one author to
have written the Pentateuch, positing that a single author might have
composed the whole during the exile or later.

Yamauchi, Edwin M., *Persia and the Bible* (Grand Rapids: Baker, 1990), 578
pages. A useful resource for discussion of Ezra, Nehemiah, Esther,
Daniel, and anything Persian in the Bible.

Alongside these isolated books it will be worthwhile for students to
consult various commentary series. Often the most insightful treatment of a passage is not by a commentator espousing an approach
treating the text as Scripture. However, it is as well to consult widely,
including works by people who treat the Bible explicitly as God's
Word. A few series of commentaries that aim to acknowledge the
Bible's authority deserve specific mention. The Tyndale OT
Commentaries (Leicester: IVP) are generally brief. The New
American Commentary series (Nashville: Broadman & Holman) is
more extensive, and is less devotional than the NIV Application
Commentary (Grand Rapids: Zondervan). Probably the most aca-
demic of the conservative evangelical commentary series is the New
International Commentary on the OT (Grand Rapids: Eerdmans).
All such series aim to reach a wide audience and some are thus quite
lightweight in their treatment. Market forces within evangelicalism
militate against the production of highly technical commentaries.
Mainstream evangelical publishers prefer relatively larger print runs
of books with their accompanying economies of scale and cheaper
prices for customers. Most academic publishers are content with
smaller print runs and higher prices for customers. This means that
for detailed or technical treatment of an issue students may only
have available discussions from a secular academic perspective that
they do not share. This is where the ability to detach information
from paradigm is particularly important.

The Society for Old Testament Study is the main academic
organization for OT study in the UK. Membership is for accom-
plished scholars, but everyone can benefit from the *Book List*,
which is produced every year, and which lists, topically arranged, a
large range of books on the OT that have appeared in the previous year or so, with concise comment. This can help a student get

abreast of what is being written, and by consulting back issues (i.e. for a couple of years after a particular book was published) you might even get a concise summary of a book you've been set to read!

### The Web

Web resources change constantly, and the majority of sites dealing with the OT are not really academic. The value of the Web is to get orientation in debates on an issue and to be able to find references and written material. The following Web pages are therefore only to be seen as starting points in investigation.

#### Archaeology

The Biblical Archaeological Society (http://www.bib-arch.org), which publishes among other things the bimonthly journal the *Biblical Archaeology Review*, is the main forum for archaeological discussion without excessive technicality. *BAR* tries to stir up debate and almost all the big names in biblical archaeology will contribute here at one time or another. A site defending the full historicity of the biblical narrative is http://christiananswers.net/archaeology/home.html.

#### Bibliography

Though not really an academic site, http://www.bible.org/docs/ot/otbooks.htm is not a bad place to search for bibliography on individual books of the OT. The RTSF site (http://www.uccf.org.uk/coursework/rtsf/resources.php) contains some basic bibliography and lists of RTSF booklets. For those not scared off by German, http://www.isatex.de provides bibliographical links and URLs for a large range of online OT journals. Though access to the whole journal is usually restricted, a summary of an article is usually online.

#### Dead Sea Scrolls

A good introduction to the history of Dead Sea Scroll scholarship, with lots of links to other Dead Sea Scroll resources is http://www.rci.rutgers.edu/~religion/iho/dss.html. Another widely respected site is http://orion.mscc.huji.ac.il.

### General

Many resources can be reached via http://www.tyndale.cam.ac.uk. Go via the 'Online Resources' tab to search for books or organizations on the Web. The Society for Biblical Literature (http://www.sbl-site.org) is a huge organization, run on a secular basis, which organizes large conferences covering every aspect of biblical studies. The Evangelical Theological Society (http://www.etsjets.org) covers a range of subjects including the OT, and provides a forum for discussion.

### Language

If you learn Hebrew for a year or more you might consider joining the B-Hebrew newsgroup (http://www.ibiblio.org/bhebrew) and posting questions you have there. The group can also cope with more advanced questions.

## 2. BEGINNING TO STUDY THE NEW TESTAMENT

### Alistair I. Wilson

*Alistair I. Wilson, a minister of the Free Church of Scotland, teaches New Testament at the Highland Theological College in Dingwall in the Scottish Highlands. He studied theology at the University of Edinburgh and the Free Church College, Edinburgh, and his PhD from the University of Aberdeen is on 'Matthew's Portrait of Jesus the Judge'.*

### Approaching New Testament study

This guide is written for students entering their first or second year of degree level study in a British institution of higher education. I hope that it will be helpful to students at other levels, in other kinds of institutions, in other nations and, indeed, to some who are not involved in formal education or who have left their formal student days behind, but readers should understand that I have a particular readership in mind as I write.[1]

It is important to indicate clearly what I am not going to do, as well as what I hope to do. This chapter is *not* an 'Introduction to the New Testament'. Not only would this task demand much more

---

1. I am grateful to my teaching colleagues at Highland Theological College for reading various drafts of this chapter and for numerous helpful suggestions that have improved it substantially. All remaining deficiencies are my own responsibility.

space than I have available, but also there are numerous helpful volumes available that you may consult for such discussions (for selected examples, see the section 'Resources' at the end of the chapter). My intention is rather to write an introduction to the *practice of studying* the New Testament (NT), with particular reference to study of the NT in an academic institution. What I have written comes from reflection on several years' experience of teaching undergraduate students and my hope is that this chapter will help you to find academic study of the NT an enjoyable, enriching and even spiritually strengthening experience (as well, perhaps, as warning you of a few pitfalls!).

Studying the NT in an academic institution is, in some respects, a very different task from studying the NT in other settings such as a church service or a home Bible study. You will have to learn information and evaluate opinions that are (or, at least, are widely perceived to be) of little consequence to most readers of the Bible. Yet, fundamentally, your task as a student of the NT is the same as that of every reader of the NT: to grasp (and, of course, live out) the meaning of the text as accurately and as fully as possible. In addition, if you are so privileged as to have the opportunity to study the NT intensively for several years, you will surely wish to develop skills that enable you to pass on what you have learned to others as effectively as possible.

If you have not yet begun your course and have some time before the course begins, there are several things that you can usefully do to prepare for your studies. However, if you have already begun your course, then it is never too late to begin to do these things!

### Read the New Testament
Read as much of the NT as possible, in as large portions as possible. The NT documents must be your primary sources. Some beginning students may not be familiar with the text of the NT at all, or may know only a few favourite passages. Too many people make judgments and pronouncements about the NT on the basis of what others say about it rather than their own reading of the text. As a student of the NT, you will want to ensure that your

views about the NT are firmly founded in the biblical text. Other students will have grown up with the NT in their family and in their church. Strangely, this great blessing can also prove to be a problem for the beginning student. One of the greatest problems facing someone who has grown up reading the NT is the sense of familiarity with the material. This familiarity may well be more perceived than real, but it can prevent the student from grappling with the biblical text as fully as he or she might. Aim to read the biblical documents as coherent compositions rather than as collections of inspiring anecdotes and sayings. Try to read shorter documents in a single sitting, if possible. Look for the plot in a narrative or the major argument in a letter. Ask questions of the text as you read, such as:

- Why did the author include this comment?
- How does this verse or passage relate to those that precede and follow it?
- Have I read something like this before in another part of the Bible?

### Practise your written English

Ensure that you are able to communicate your views clearly. It matters little that you have the most profound grasp of NT theology if you are unable to communicate what you know in a form that can be grasped by others. You should aim to write in as simple and unambiguous prose as possible. While you may well have to read some extremely complex and pretentious prose in the course of your academic studies, you will find that most tutors (who will have to read numerous essays on the same subject in a short period of time) will not be impressed by such style. You might practise by writing out one-page summaries of books, chapters and articles you have read, or of subjects you have been studying. Ask someone who will be both truthful and helpful to read what you have written and to point out any faults so that you can correct them ('Faithful are the wounds of a friend', Proverbs 27:6 [AV] !). This discipline will also provide you with a helpful resource for examination revision. Be sure to use your computer software's facilities for checking your spelling and grammar, but beware of placing all your trust in these features in case 'ewe right' nonsense![2]

When writing an essay on a particular topic, you should take great care to follow whatever specific instructions the college or tutor provides. There are, however, several commonly recognized features of a good piece of work that may be highlighted here:

1. *The work must be presented clearly.* Provide an *introduction*, which defines your task and indicates how you intend to carry it out. Then write the *body* of the essay, perhaps dividing it into manageable sections using subheadings. Finally, provide a *conclusion*, which briefly summarizes your conclusions without introducing any new ideas or material.

2. *The essay must draw on primary sources.* That is to say, the student must allow the subject of the essay to speak for himself/ herself/itself. If the essay is on John's Gospel, ensure that you engage with the biblical text directly, not simply quoting the commentaries. If the essay is on the Dead Sea Scrolls, find a copy of a translation of the scrolls and read them first hand. If the essay is on the writings of Rudolf Bultmann, then it is essential that Bultmann's own writings are consulted, not simply the summaries of his critics or supporters.

3. *An argument must be presented on the basis of evaluation of evidence and fair discussion of the various views that have previously been expressed.* That is, when you are writing on a contested issue concerning which there are two main views, A and B, you should fairly present view A, then fairly present view B, then evaluate both according to the evidence, then present your own view, using carefully expressed arguments. To this end you should regard

---

2. The Open University provide a useful online 'Toolkit' on 'The Effective Use of English', with particular reference to academic writing at the following address:

http://www3.open.ac.uk/learners-guide/learning-skills/english/index. htm. Other similar resources may be found through use of a good Internet search engine.

the task of gathering a representative bibliography as a vital part of the process of writing.

Time spent on good presentation, careful gathering of evidence, and thoughtful, fair argumentation will prove to be of immense value to your studies.

### Get a general orientation to New Testament studies

One of the biggest challenges for a new student of NT studies is the task of fitting a great deal of new information about significant scholars and their ideas into some overall framework. If time allows, you will be helped greatly by reading about the history of NT studies. Two books are particularly useful in this respect. First, *Interpretation of the New Testament 1861–1986* (Oxford: Oxford University Press, 1988) by S. Neill and T. Wright provides a sparkling overview of the modern history of NT studies and will provide you with orientation to a whole host of important figures and debates. Second, G. Bray has written *Biblical Interpretation: Past and Present* (Leicester: Apollos, 1996), in which he not only provides short narrative accounts of the manner in which the Bible (both OT and NT) has been interpreted through the ages from the early church to the present day but also provides a huge number of brief biographical sketches of significant figures, ancient and modern. A particularly valuable and distinctive aspect of Bray's book is that he includes information about many living scholars who are currently contributing to the world of NT studies, broadly classified according to their geographical and theological backgrounds, whose books students will frequently encounter on their reading lists. It will prove extremely useful to you as a new (or possibly not-so-new) student to have this book to hand when engaging with contemporary scholarship.

### Be prepared to listen and think

It is important that you approach your studies with an open attitude. The task of the student of the NT is, ultimately, to discover the truth, and there is no reason for such a student to hold back from investigating any and every issue. Evangelical students coming to academic study of the NT frequently encounter several obstacles to gaining the most from their studies. First, they will often be quite familiar with the biblical texts and will probably have heard many sermons on those texts. There is, therefore, a strong inclination to believe that they already know a great deal about the NT and that the purpose of their academic studies is simply to confirm that fact and to add the seal of approval of an academic degree. Second, evangelical students may well believe that modern biblical scholarship is simply an obstacle to trusting the plain meaning of the text and that their task is, therefore, to resist the influence of scholarship as much as possible. Such beliefs can have an extremely detrimental effect on a student's course if they are not recognized and dealt with at an early stage.

In the first place, they will probably present themselves in an arrogant manner. The student who holds fast to such convictions may well appear disrespectful of the views of others, whether they are tutors, fellow-students or authors. In the second place, such convictions may well lead to the student being deprived of further opportunities to deepen his or her understanding of the Bible. Of course, a student who has been well taught in home and church over a number of years will indeed come to academic study with an enviable head start. There is, however, always opportunity for further growth in knowledge and understanding through more intense engagement with the biblical text and through interaction with other people (whether in person or through reading literature). Likewise, many of the theories of modern biblical scholarship should be treated with some caution and be carefully evaluated, but it is impossible to evaluate an argument carefully to which one has not listened. As a wise student you will not shun biblical scholarship, but you will test it. That which is *valuable* may be accepted (even if this requires you to change some long-held opinions). That which is *refuted by the evidence* must be rejected. That which is *ambiguous* may be considered with interest without a final judgment until such time as the uncertainty is resolved. Thus, if you are looking forward to the beginning of a course of NT studies, you may prepare by making a deliberate decision to listen carefully and respectfully to whatever views are expressed by tutors, fellow-students and authors.

You may determine to learn from all such engagement, even when learning means respectfully and carefully rejecting the views of others.

## Studying the New Testament as a Christian

It is, of course, possible to study the NT without any Christian faith commitment. Students in most British universities will discover that some of their NT tutors profess a Christian faith (although evangelical students may well find that certain tutors hold beliefs quite different from their own), while others may study the NT from the perspective of Jewish faith, other non-Christian religious faith or no religious faith at all. Such scholars of the NT may well discover important insights into the meaning of the language of the NT or the historical background to the text or the contemporary significance of the text, and the attentive student may learn a great deal from them. Nonetheless, it is my conviction that the fundamental character of the NT as the breathed-out (2 Timothy 3:16) utterance of the only God and Father of the Lord Jesus Christ demands that true interpretation of the NT can be achieved only by those who have been brought into a restored relationship with the Father and are equipped by the Holy Spirit of God (1 Corinthians 2:6–16; Romans 8:5–9). The following remarks assume that you are studying the NT as an evangelical Christian.

Fundamental convictions, such as that which I have just identified with respect to the divine origin of the NT, are sometimes known as 'presuppositions'.[3]

Some tutors or fellow-students may try to persuade you that presuppositions are particular to evangelical students and are bound to hinder truly 'objective' study of the NT. This is simply not the case. The German evangelical scholar G. Maier has

---

3. An important discussion of presuppositions may be found in D. G. McCartney and C. Clayton, *Let the Reader Understand* (2nd edn.; Phillipsburg: P&R, 2002), pp. 5–81.

discussed the way in which people interpret the Bible in his book *Biblical Hermeneutics*,[4] and, in line with others before him, has demonstrated that 'there is no presuppositionless exegesis or biblical research'.[5]

That is to say, it is impossible to read the biblical texts without presuppositions. Every author, tutor and student holds some. Thus there is nothing wrong with holding firmly to certain presuppositions. In fact, you do hold certain presuppositions and so the real question is whether or not they are valid.[6]

D. McCartney and C. Clayton identify 'rationalism', or the supremacy of human reason, as the basic presupposition of many modern people, tracing this view to the philosopher R. Descartes (1596–1650). They go on to write:

-------------------

4. Wheaton: Crossway, 1994.

5. Ibid., pp. 42–43. Cf. R. Bultmann, 'Is Exegesis without Presuppositions Possible?' in S. Ogden (tr. and ed.), *New Testament and Mythology* (London: SCM, 1985), pp. 145–153. Bultmann declares, 'no exegesis is without presuppositions, because the exegete is not a *tabula rasa* but approaches the text with specific questions'. See also E. V. McKnight, 'Presuppositions in New Testament Study', in J. B. Green (ed.), *Hearing the New Testament* (Grand Rapids: Eerdmans/Carlisle: Paternoster, 1995), pp. 278–300, who discusses the presuppositions held by various interpreters, and K. J. Vanhoozer, 'The Reader in New Testament Interpretation', in Green, *Hearing the New Testament*, pp. 301–328, who considers the philosophy of reading.

6. See the essay by A. Schlatter, 'Die Bedeutung der Method für die theologische Arbeit', *Theologischer Literaturbericht* 31 (1908), pp. 5–8. An English translation is found in R. W. Yarbrough 'Adolf Schlatter's "The Significance of Method for Theological Work": Translation and Commentary', *Southern Baptist Journal of Theology* 1.2 (1997), pp. 64–76, in which Schlatter writes (p. 67), 'the historian in his historical work can never deny himself in such a way, can never annihilate his convictions – and also should not – in such a way that they do not determine his historical observations and judgements. Attempts to make of oneself a lifeless mirror, which only picks up and passes on life that is foreign to itself, are fruitless and both logically and ethically wrong.'

When it comes to the Bible . . . the modern non-Christian's basic presupposition will result in an approach different from that of the Christian. For non-Christians, statements claiming to have come from God cannot be allowed to escape testing by a human reasoning process that has begun by *assuming that it has no need of God*. They assume that reason would operate the same way whether or not the true God exists. Thus, many modern students of the Bible evaluate whether biblical statements are true on the basis of criteria that are external to the Bible itself, and this cuts them off from having their own thinking critiqued by God's Word . . . But Christians are persuaded by the Holy Spirit that the Bible is God's true voice. Christians, under the Holy Spirit's tutelage, use reason to decide *what* God is saying in his Word, and their reason, starting from the correct presuppositions, can recognize the wisdom and truthfulness of what is said, but they do not use reason to decide *whether* what he says is true on the basis of some external criteria. What criteria could be more ultimate than God's speech? Are our thoughts higher than God's thoughts?'[7]

In order to illustrate this point, it may be useful to look briefly at the way in which several notable contributors to NT studies have indicated the presuppositions that underpin their views about the NT text. For example, Rudolf Bultmann, in his famous essay 'New Testament and Mythology' (1941) writes:

We cannot use electric lights and radios and, in the event of illness, avail ourselves of modern medical and clinical means and at the same time believe in the spirit and wonder world of the New Testament. And if we suppose that we can do so ourselves, we must be clear that we can represent this as the attitude of Christian faith only by making the Christian proclamation unintelligible and impossible for our contemporaries.[8]

_____

7. D. G. McCartney and C. Clayton, *Let the Reader Understand* (2nd edn.; Phillipsburg: P&R, 2002), pp. 8–9.

8. R. Bultman, 'New Testament and Mythology', in *New Testament and Mythology and Other Basic Writings* (London: SCM, 1984), pp. 4–5.

Bultmann is unambiguous in his assertion that modern advances in science have ruled out the possibility of realities such as those indicated by the NT text. Thus modern science, understood to be the expression of human reasoning at its height, acts as the ultimate arbiter of what is true. Note carefully that Bultmann is not debating the meaning of the biblical text; he understands perfectly well what the text says. He simply uses an external criterion to decide what he will accept.

More recently, Barnabas Lindars writes concerning John's Gospel:

> the multi-dimensional character of the Gospel obviously precludes the idea that it is a straight historical record of what actually happened and what Jesus actually said in his ministry. It is a mistake to suppose that there was any direct reporting of Jesus in his earthly life. The Synoptic Gospels are based on a variety of traditions, some oral and some written, which embodied the memories of people who knew Jesus, and evolved over a long period. Similarly John is dependent on the work of predecessors, and it should not be assumed that the underlying materials were substantially different from those used by the Synoptic writers.[9]

Immediately you see the word 'obviously', alarm bells should ring in your mind and a whole host of questions should be asked. What is a 'straight historical record'? How do we know that there was no 'direct reporting of Jesus in his earthly life'? Do all scholars agree about what Lindars asserts so confidently? It is not necessary to decide whether any of Lindars' comments are *correct* at this point. All you need to notice is that Lindars writes with some presuppositions, which show through in his writing.

Finally, in describing his approach to the NT, Bart Ehrman addresses his readers as follows:

> My approach will be strictly historical, trying to understand the writings of the early Christians from the standpoint of the professional historian

---

9. B. Lindars, R. B. Edwards, J. M. Court, *The Johannine Literature* (Sheffield: Sheffield Academic Press, 2000), p. 36.

who uses whatever evidence happens to survive in order to reconstruct what happened in the past.[10]

This may sound entirely appropriate. Yet there is, it seems to me, reason to be concerned about the claim that the approach of Ehrman's work will be 'strictly historical'. What does that say about the way in which he will evaluate the biblical texts? When the biblical text includes accounts of the 'powerful acts' of Jesus – for example, in Luke's Gospel (written by an ancient historian, Luke 1:1–4) – by what criteria will these accounts be evaluated?

Given the above, let me suggest several ways in which you may approach academic study of the NT in a distinctively *Christian* manner.

### Study the New Testament as part of the God-breathed Christian Bible

The NT documents are truly examples of ancient literature, but they are not simply ancient literature. Historic Reformation theology has expressed the Christian view thus:

> The authority of the Holy Scripture, for which it ought to be believed, and obeyed, dependeth not upon the testimony of any man, or Church; but wholly upon God (who is truth itself) the author thereof: and therefore it is to be received, because it is the Word of God.
> (Westminster Confession of Faith, 1.2)

This conviction will lead to at least two responses. First, you will read the NT in the context of the whole biblical canon, both OT and NT. In fact, it is impossible to understand the NT documents correctly without recognizing the foundational significance of the OT, not only as NT authors cite texts from the OT in building their arguments but in the pervasive presence of concepts such as creation, covenant, sacrifice, Messiah, age to come and so on.

The Christian church has only one Bible, which is composed of

---

10. B. D. Ehrman, *The New Testament: A Historical Introduction to the Early Christian Writings* (Oxford: Oxford University Press, 2000), p. 14.

two 'testaments'. This fact has not always been properly reflected in academic biblical studies, but in recent years authors such as Brevard S. Childs,[11] Walter Moberly[12] and Graeme Goldsworthy[13] have pioneered a revival of 'biblical theology' as an academic discipline as they have sought to read both the OT and the NT as essential constituent parts of a single Christian Bible.[14] There is a grave danger that intensive study of the NT can lead, in theory or in practice, to neglect of the OT. If you recognize that God is the ultimate author of both the OT and the NT, then you will want to ensure that you regard (and actually treat) the OT as an indispensable portion of the Christian canon.

Second, you will treat the Bible as of ultimate importance as a revelation from God. The most obvious place to start in grasping this is 2 Timothy 3:16. Paul's starting point is that 'all Scripture' is 'God-breathed' (NIV).[15] That is to say, the text has its origin in God himself. The context of this passage makes it clear that Paul's primary referent when using the term 'Scripture' is the OT. Yet for the Christian the text has a wider application to that which has become recognized as Scripture, the NT.

It is important to recognize that many biblical texts make some

---

11. See especially B. S. Childs, *Biblical Theology of the Old and New Testaments* (London: SCM, 1993).

12. See especially R. W. L. Moberley, *The Bible, Theology and Faith* (Cambridge: Cambridge University Press, 2000).

13. See especially G. Goldsworthy, *According to Plan* (Leicester: IVP, 1991).

14. For useful overviews of the current state of the discipline see B. S. Rosner and T. D. Alexander, *New Dictionary of Biblical Theology* (Leicester: IVP, 2000), and S. J. Hafemann (ed.), *Biblical Theology: Retrospect and Prospect* (Leicester: Apollos, 2002). Other important contributors to this renaissance in biblical theology are C. Seitz (see, e.g., *Word Without End* [Grand Rapids: Eerdmans, 1998]), and F. Watson (see, e.g., *Text and Truth* [Edinburgh: T. & T. Clark, 1997]).

15. Cf. ESV 'Breathed out by God'. These translations are much more satisfactory renderings of the Greek term *theopneustos* than the traditional 'inspired', which does not reflect the *theo-* component of the word and has all kinds of misleading connotations in modern English.

kind of explicit claim to express God's own voice (e.g. Deuteronomy 4:2; Jeremiah 1:2; 1 Thessalonians 2:13).[16] Thus to adopt this view of the divine origin and character of the NT text is not to impose an alien theological category upon the text, but is to allow the text to be read on its own terms.

The implication of this position is that you will recognize that the NT text is entirely true.[17] That is to say, whatever God intends the language of the NT to convey may be accepted entirely. Thus statements relating to historical events, metaphorical descriptions, and theological reflections may all be regarded as true, when due account is taken of the intention of the particular words. This is not to say that you will necessarily be able to *demonstrate* to the satisfaction of others that the NT is true in its statements. Some historical problems will not be solved unless further evidence comes to light, and many theological statements are incapable of 'proof'. In such cases confidence in the God-breathed character of the NT will lead to trust, founded on the testimony of the Holy Spirit.

### Study as an act of Christian discipleship
The Greek word normally translated 'disciple' is *mathētēs*, which is related to the verb 'to learn'. Perhaps you are taking a course in NT studies as part of a general theological training, in order to prepare for some kind of Christian service. Frequently, a student in this position will have some sense of 'calling' to be involved in overseas mission work, youth ministry, preaching, counselling, student

---

16. See the substantial discussion in W. Grudem, 'Scripture's Self-Attestation and the Problem of Formulating a Doctrine of Scripture', in D. A. Carson and J. D. Woodbridge (eds.), *Scripture and Truth* (Leicester: IVP, 1983).

17. One foundational text for this position is the account of Jesus' words 'Your word is truth' in John 17:17 (cf. Psalm 119:60). On Jesus' view of the Bible, see J. W. Wenham, *Christ and the Bible* (Leicester: IVP, 1972). The phrase 'entirely true' (or possibly 'entirely reliable') is intended as a positive synonym for the commonly used, but more negatively expressed, term 'inerrancy' – a term I am happy to accept so long as it is appropriately defined to reflect the diverse uses of scriptural language.

evangelism and so on, and theological training is required by the Christian organization with which he or she wishes to work. The theological training, however, may be regarded as a means to an end – and a distracting means at that. 'What benefit for evangelizing the world', one might say, 'is there in learning about the views of some sceptical scholar?' If you consider your theological studies to be a distraction from true discipleship, you will find that you are not motivated in your work. You may well be rather cynical about what you are asked to read and consider and you will probably fill your time with many activities in 'real life Christianity'. Rather than taking this dismissive view, treat your studies as an opportunity to prepare for the ministry God has for you and, in fact, as an act of service in itself (Ephesians 6:7). Time well spent during a course of theological studies will shape your character, your ability to think and evaluate and your Christian faith. Value this time and use it well.

### Study as an act of Christian worship

Jesus declares that 'You shall love the Lord your God with all your heart, and with all your soul, and with all your strength, and with all your mind; and your neighbour as yourself' (Luke 10:27 NRSV). The careful use of your mind is not detached from worship but is part of a holistic approach to worship in which we offer all that we are to God (Romans 12:1). In fact, 'the renewing of your mind' is called for in the very same context (Romans 12:2). John 14:21 also links love of Jesus with faithfulness to his commands, which are found in Scripture.[18] Not only are we called to live in obedience to these commands but, as a prior necessity, we are required to ensure that we have understood them also.

### Study as an act of Christian witness

Peter exhorts his readers (1 Peter 3:15–16 ESV):

> in your hearts regard Christ the Lord as holy, always being prepared to
> make a defence to anyone who asks you for a reason for the hope that is

---

18. McCartney and Clayton, *Reader*, p. 244.

in you; yet do it with gentleness and respect, having a good conscience, so that, when you are slandered, those who revile your good behaviour in Christ may be put to shame.

Serious study of the NT will lead you into a greater familiarity with the biblical text and therefore a greater appreciation of who God is, what he has done for his people and how that impacts you as an individual. If you are diligent, you will also gain a fuller appreciation of the various views that have been expressed regarding the NT, both positive and negative, and the underlying convictions that account for these views. As an educational process, serious study of the NT should enable you to construct and present arguments coherently. This knowledge and training should enable you to be more effective as an apologist. At the same time it is crucially important that you note the context of the call to be ready to give a reason. The answer must be given 'with gentleness and respect' so that the very character of the answer may be as effective a testimony to the truth of the Gospel of Jesus Christ as the content of the answer.

### Study in the context of the Christian community
A course in academic NT studies will undoubtedly raise issues that challenge the Christian student. You will be required to read books by authors who do not share your views. You will be confronted by features in the biblical text that raise big and important questions. It is essential that you deal with these issues in the context of supportive Christian fellowship, that you have people around you who are willing to talk things through, praying for you and with you.

Some students will study in theological colleges that, like my own institution, are self-consciously 'worshipping communities'. Such an environment is a great help to getting theological studies into proper perspective. Other students, however, will be working in institutions with a very different ethos. In such a situation the need to study as part of a Christian community is not lessened but intensified. The Christian student should seek out other Christian students for support and fellowship. In such situations local groups of the Religious and Theological Studies Fellowship can be of great benefit, providing a context for mutual encouragement.

As a student of the NT you should also seek to develop an approach to interpreting the NT that integrates academic studies with use of the NT in the life of the church. A determination to treat the Bible in one way in church but another way entirely in academic studies might seem to offer a way forward when wrestling with difficult issues, but it is inevitably going to lead to tensions. If scholarship has produced valid insights into the biblical text, then these insights are as important to all Bible readers as they are to the theological student. The challenge is to weigh the supposed insights in order to evaluate their true worth to the church and then to convey those valid insights to the wider church in a way that can be understood and appreciated.

## What is the New Testament?

The NT may be accurately described as literature, as history and as theology.[19] I will now consider each of these aspects of Scripture in turn.

### Literature

The NT documents are examples of human communication. They are more than this, but they are no less. This means that it is of crucial importance to understand how communication works if we are to understand the NT correctly.

In the broadest terms it is possible to recognize a number of literary types or 'genres' among the NT documents. These are normally identified as 'gospel', 'history', 'letter' and 'apocalyptic'. In many ways this is a useful analysis. It recognizes that some documents are like each other and unlike others. Yet this simple analysis may lull the student into a false sense of sophistication in that these four categories may not do full justice to the individual

---

19. A helpful discussion of these three angles on the NT can be found in P. J. Achtemeier, J. B. Green and M. M. Thompson, *Introducing the New Testament: Its Literature and Theology* (Grand Rapids: Eerdmans, 2001), pp. 1–13.

characters of the documents that may be placed within any one of these categories. For example, we might legitimately claim that both Romans and Philemon are letters. It only takes a moment's reflection, however, to recognize that there are significant differences between these two literary works, not simply in terms of their length, but in terms of their style and purpose. Of course, these two diverse documents come from the same author. If we now consider the difference between Philippians and Hebrews, we see even more pronounced differences.

It is also possible to compare the biblical documents with other ancient genres of literature to which we have access. We know that Philippians is a letter, for example, not because Paul explicitly states, 'I am writing a letter', but because what he writes conforms broadly to the typical pattern of an ancient Hellenistic letter.[20]

On a smaller scale, recognition of the NT as a collection of literary works will alert the student to the need to appreciate the various ways in which words are used. George B. Caird has written an exceptionally helpful book entitled *The Language and Imagery of the Bible*[21] in which he considers literary features such as hyperbole (overstatement), litotes (understatement; see Acts 21:39), irony (see 1 Corinthians 4:8; 2 Corinthians 12:13), simile and metaphor and so on. It is as important that you develop your skills in reading a text as a student of the NT as it would be if you were studying English literature. Attempt to develop literary sensitivity in much the same way as you might attune your ear to musical compositions, so that you are able to hear the nuances of the language of the NT.

The importance of correctly recognizing literary 'genres' (whether those of complete documents or of small portions of a document) lies in the fact that our decision on genre has a profound impact on the 'rules' by which we read literature. Most readers know what to expect when the words 'once upon a time'

---

20. For very interesting information about ancient letters see the classic book by A. Deissmann, *Light from the Ancient East* (Peabody: Hendrickson, 1995).
21. London: Duckworth, 1980.

introduce a narrative and they read the following account of
talking animals or magical beans without any measure of shock or
concern, because they enter willingly into the agreement which the
genre of literature establishes between the reader and the text –
that all disbelief will be suspended throughout this fictional tale.
Political satire and other forms of comedy depend on the fact that
material associated with one form of discourse may be couched in
the language forms of another genre and thus be made to sound
amusing. The reader knows that this material is not normally communicated in this way, but enjoys the humorous association. To
make a mistake regarding a literary genre, however, can have very
significant consequences. One famous example of this is the panic
associated with Orson Welles's 1938 radio broadcast of H. G.
Wells's science-fiction novel *The War of the Worlds*. When a (fictional) radio news announcer declared that Martians had invaded a
(real) small town in the US, some listeners treated that announcement as they had learned to treat declarations by radio news
announcers (i.e., as fact) and considerable panic ensued. This is a
classic example of a genre mistake.[22]

Though less dramatic, the impact of genre mistakes when
reading the NT is no less significant for correct interpretation of
the biblical texts. When Jesus says, 'And if your eye causes you to
stumble, pluck it out' (Mark 9:47 RSV), what kind of response is he
demanding? When Paul writes to the Corinthians: 'you have begun
to reign, without us' (1 Corinthians 4:8; my tr.), is he making a
statement of fact? When John records his vision of the holy city
Jerusalem coming down from heaven (John 21), does he indicate
that this city is cubic (21:16)? In each case you will only be able to
appreciate the meaning of this language if you correctly recognize
its literary genre. Likewise, if the authors of the Gospels write
accounts that include literary features normally associated with
historical narrative, then it is important to read these texts according to the normal conventions for reading such a literary genre. We

---

22. Fascinating information on this event can be found at 'The War of the
    Worlds Broadcast: An Historical Perspective', http://www.war-ofthe-
    worlds.co.uk/.

have no right to read a text as if it were symbolic if all its literary signals suggest that it is historical.

Reading the NT as literature demands hard work, but it can protect you from the common inclination among Christians to make random selections from the NT documents, remove them from their contexts and treat them as personal messages from God – a process with huge potential for misinterpretation. Reading the NT documents as literary works in their own right can also heighten your appreciation of the creativity and profundity of these ancient texts.

### History

To say that the NT is 'history' is an accurate statement, but it must be qualified. In fact, only one of the documents within the NT canon has traditionally been regarded as formally a work of history: the Acts of the Apostles. More recently, scholarship has recognized the essential unity of the Gospel of Luke and Acts as two parts of a single work and so an increasing number of scholars are tending to identify 'Luke-Acts' as a kind of historical work. This use of the word 'history' indicates a particular kind of literary work that recounts events in a particular manner and with a particular purpose. However, it should be clear to any reader of the NT that each of the documents in the canon is in some sense 'history', to the extent that it provides accounts of incidents that took place previously (e.g. Galatians 2:1–11) or makes reference to persons and events within the life of the early Christian community or more widely within the ancient Graeco-Roman world (e.g. Luke 1:5; 2:1–2; 3:1–2), even when that particular document does not formally belong to the literary category of 'historical narrative'.

This is to say that 'history' can be understood in at least two ways. First, it can be understood to refer to the totality of human experience. Every event that takes place in every place at every moment to every person might be described as human history. The NT claims that God works out his purposes in and through the realities of human experience. Second, 'history' may be understood to refer to the accounts of past human events. These cannot provide an exhaustive chronicle of all that took place within a period of time (not that such a work would be particularly interesting or useful even if it could be done), and so they are necessarily selective. The author selects material to include or exclude on the basis of what serves his purpose best. Selectivity does not disqualify a work from being history, nor does a particular purpose on the part of the author. Indeed, these are required of every historian.

Of fundamental importance to your appreciation of the purpose of the NT texts is the fact that throughout the Bible God is presented as the God of creation who acts within the history of his people. Perhaps the primary example of this is the exodus, but the principle runs right through to the astonishing statement that 'the Word became flesh and lived [pitched his tent] among us' (John 1:14 NRSV). Again and again the NT authors refuse to allow their readers to banish their statements about Jesus to the realm of private opinion and personal perception.

### *Theology*

To say that the NT is 'theology' is to claim that the primary purpose of the various documents that compose the NT is to speak of God. Understood in a rich sense the 'theology' of the NT is its testimony to the character of God himself, particularly as seen in the Lord Jesus Christ; the nature of his dealings with the world, and with his chosen people in particular; and his purposes for his people. When these diverse texts are understood to be the very Word of God, we are confronted by texts in which God speaks primarily of himself.

Thankfully, recent academic NT studies have given far greater prominence to this fundamental aspect of the NT than was the case several decades ago, perhaps substantially due to the impact of 'redaction criticism' (see below). A sensitive reading of the NT will seek to consider the theological voice of the texts on several levels.

First, each individual document may be treated in its own right to determine its distinctive theological emphases. Thus we should not be surprised to discover that the dominant theological themes in 1 Corinthians are rather different from those in Revelation, and we will appreciate the NT most fully when we allow each document to have its own theological voice heard. Clearly, this point is related to an appreciation of the NT documents as literary works in their own right. If one's primary method for seeking theological insight from the NT is to draw isolated texts from diverse documents without reference to their wider contexts, then neither the literary coherence nor the theological contribution will be recognized. While this might seem to be a simple task, there are occasions where tensions may apparently exist even within a single document. Helpful in this regard is the recent series of volumes from Cambridge University Press entitled 'New Testament Theology', in which there are several outstanding studies of the theology of individual NT documents.

Second, one may consider the theology of a particular author. In the history of NT interpretation most attention has, unsurprisingly, been paid to Paul and John. A variation on this theme is the number of studies that have been devoted to 'the theology of Jesus', although, of course, this can only be derived from the four canonical Gospels, all of which were authored by other people. This is a very important task for the student of the NT because it moves further beyond the task of identifying a variety of isolated statements to the task of considering how they might cohere. Some despair of finding any coherence,[23] but many modern interpreters are more optimistic. One of the problems faced by those who wish to carry out this task is the fact that there is less certainty today among many interpreters as to which documents may be ascribed to a particular author. Thus should the material in Ephesians, Colossians and the Pastoral Epistles be included in an account of Paul's theology? The answer given to that question will undoubtedly shape the final description of Paul's theology. Likewise, should the Gospel according to John be considered along with one, two or all three of the Letters of John?

Third, one may consider 'the theology of the NT'. If the task of writing a theology of Paul raises problems, then they are minor compared to the task facing the writer of a NT theology, because in this case some attempt must be made to find coherence between Paul and James and between Peter and Luke. Several methods have been employed over the years and most have

---

23. E.g. H. Räisänen, *Paul and the Law* (Philadelphia: Fortress, 1983).

received criticism. Perhaps one of the most nuanced attempts is that of G. B. Caird, in his posthumously published book.[24] Other notable attempts include those by G. E. Ladd[25] and D. Guthrie.[26]

There are clearly different perspectives from which it is possible to treat the theology of the NT. One is to analyse the thought of the NT authors carefully, to describe what they thought and to stop there. Description of the theology of the NT is, in this case, a purely historical exercise. Throughout the Christian church, however, the theology of the NT has been recognized as more than the description of what ancient men thought: as the very Word of God. Thus, in order to empathize fully with the perspective of the NT authors themselves, you will want to submit your thinking to the theological message you are studying. Careful analysis of the individual theologies and collective theology of the NT is a vital task, but unless you have taken the step of listening for God's voice, you have not heard what these writers were called to convey.

## Interpreting the New Testament

### Do you need Greek?

The NT documents as we have them were all written in *koinē* (common) Greek. This is not simply an accident of history but is the result of God's providence, and so the task of equipping oneself to read these documents in their original language is a matter of some importance. Some years ago (and still today in certain institutions), a candidate for ministry would have no choice but to study NT Greek. Depending on your reasons for studying the NT, you may find that you are given no choice as to whether or not to undertake Greek studies. If you have some reasonably successful experience of learning a foreign language, you should certainly attempt to learn Greek, as there are numerous advantages:

---

24. *New Testament Theology* (Completed and edited by L. D. Hurst; Oxford: Oxford University Press, 1994).
25. *A Theology of the New Testament* (rev. edn.; London: Lutterworth, 1993).
26. *New Testament Theology* (Leicester: IVP, 1981).

1. You can read the biblical text directly without being absolutely dependent on the work of other translators, thus allowing you to notice stylistic features disguised in English translation.
2. You can use standard Greek lexica (a dictionary of NT Greek is called a 'lexicon'; plural 'lexica').
3. You can use commentaries based on the Greek text, which are often among the finest treatments of the text.

If you do take up study of Greek, please remember that this will require commitment and hard work. Be prepared to give your best to your studies of the 'nuts and bolts' of the language so that you can eventually appreciate its finer points. Remember also that a little knowledge can be a dangerous thing, so be careful not to make dogmatic statements about what a text 'really means' until you have completed a substantial amount of language study, thought the issue through, read some dependable books on the subject and perhaps discussed the text with another competent person; knowledge of Greek will prove most effective when used with wisdom.

If, however, your experience tells you that you are not good at learning languages, it may be wise for you to forego learning Greek formally as part of your studies, since poor results may adversely affect your overall course. The student who makes this choice has two main options, which are not mutually exclusive. The first is that the student continues to learn Greek but does so informally, working through a textbook in whatever spare time can be found. The second is that the student becomes competent in using the main tools that provide access to the work of Greek scholars. A useful tool in this respect is W. D. Mounce, *Greek for the Rest of Us* (Grand Rapids: Zondervan, 2003).

If, on the other hand, you are naturally gifted in learning languages, then take every opportunity to learn whatever languages you can. Learn the Greek of the NT. Then you can develop your vocabulary further so that you can work with the Septuagint (the Greek translation of the OT, usually signified by LXX). Knowledge of Hebrew will allow you not only to read the OT but also to compare the quotations of the OT found in the NT with the Hebrew text and, more generally, to understand the Hebraic language and concepts that permeate the NT. Other languages, such as Syriac or Coptic, may prove useful to those who go on to advanced studies. If you have or can acquire competence in French or German, you will find these modern languages very useful also, as there is a great deal of important secondary literature written in these languages. If you are considering pursuing your studies to postgraduate level, then some skills in French and German will be valuable at least, and probably essential.

### The Old Testament

It is impossible to understand the NT fully without knowledge of the OT. This is so for at least three reasons. First, the OT and NT form a theological unity. Thus, many of the fundamental concepts of the OT Scriptures are largely presupposed by the NT authors and so brief references to a theme in the NT must be given substance by reference to the OT. A notable example is the NT understanding of God. Second, the NT either quotes or paraphrases portions of the OT frequently, sometimes drawing on the known Hebrew text, sometimes on the Septuagint, and sometimes on a text otherwise unknown (possibly specially amended by the NT author to draw out a particular point). As examples, you might consider the way the OT is used in Matthew's infancy narrative, Paul's letter to the Romans or the letter to the Hebrews. Third, frequent allusions to OT language in the NT will only be picked up and correctly interpreted by a reader who is already attuned to the language of the OT. Notable in this respect is Revelation, which is full of echoes of the OT in virtually every verse but which contains no specific quotations of the OT. The way to gain knowledge of the OT is much the same as for the NT. There is no substitute for reading the text. Many students may find, however, that they are daunted by the sheer scale of the OT canon and by the unfamiliarity of the material it contains. If you are not taking a formal class on the OT, you may find it useful to read some of the recent and helpful commentaries in the New American Commentary series or the NIV Application Commentary series. These series both provide the complete biblical text divided into portions (thus helping you to avoid the danger of reading *about* the text *rather than* reading the text) along

with helpful comments on the original meaning, Christian significance and application of the text. Several other commentary
series would likewise provide useful background reading for NT
studies.

## Early Judaism

Although not part of the Christian canon, many documents from
'Second Temple Judaism'[27] are important sources of information
that can aid the interpreter of the NT. It is very important, however,
that you recognize from the outset that you may not simply identify
the thought and literature of so-called Second Temple Judaism with
the thought and literature of the OT. While there are clearly major
points of similarity, there are also some notable developments from
the OT in many of the writings of early Judaism and you should be
careful to treat both bodies of materials carefully and on their own
terms. It is also essential to recognize that there are significant
differences between the theological and political perspectives of
individual documents, and so you should be careful not to presume
that all Second Temple literature speaks with one voice. From a
Christian perspective, the literature of early Judaism is a remarkable
resource for understanding the ancient world and, indeed, a provi-
dential gift preserved throughout the years, but it is not part of the
Christian canon (i.e. it is not the Church's Scripture) and must be
given its appropriate status in the task of biblical interpretation.
Several categories of literature are available to the modern student
of the NT. As students often only hear about these bodies of literature without actually reading them, and as engagement with primary
sources is fundamental to good scholarship, I have provided a brief
excerpt from a representative of each kind of literature in a further
attempt to encourage you to engage with primary sources. Such
brief citations clearly do not provide an alternative to more sus-
tained reading of the various texts available in English translation,
but they do, at least, point you in the right direction and will perhaps

---

27. This term is used to refer to the period between the completion of the
'Second Temple' in c. 516 (see Ezra 3 – 6) and either the construction
(begun first century BC) or the fall (70 AD) of Herod's temple.

stimulate further reading.[28] The main categories of Jewish literature
are as follows.

## Apocrypha

This term is used to refer to a collection of Jewish documents that
includes historical works, wisdom literature and fiction. The term
and the literature it refers to can draw strong reactions from evangelical students. If you regard the use of the Apocrypha as
inappropriate, you should beware of *over*reacting to *religious* use by
rejecting a valuable source of *historical* and *literary* information that
can illuminate study of the NT. An example may illustrate my
point. In order to understand the political and religious circum-
stances in which Jesus proclaimed the kingdom of God, it is
necessary to appreciate the tensions surrounding the so-called
Maccabean Revolt. One of our most important witnesses to these
events is the document known as 1 Maccabees, which is part of
the Apocrypha. While numerous textbooks may provide the
outline of events, the student will gain a great deal from first-hand
exposure to the primary text. I reproduce a short selection below
that relates to the brutal regime of the Seleucid ruler Antiochus IV
('Epiphanes'):

> Now on the fifteenth day of Chislev, in the one hundred and forty-fifth
> year, they erected a desolating sacrilege upon the altar of burnt offering.
> They also built altars in the surrounding cities of Judah, and burned
> incense at the doors of the houses and in the streets. The books of the
> law which they found they tore to pieces and burned with fire. Where
> the book of the covenant was found in the possession of any one, or if
> any one adhered to the law, the decree of the kingdom condemned him
> to death. They kept using violence against Israel, against those found
> month after month in the cities . . . But many in Israel stood firm and
> were resolved in their hearts not to eat unclean food. They chose to die
> rather than to be defiled by food or to profane the holy covenant; and

---

28. An excellent source of many more selections from ancient documents
    with brief editorial comments is W. A. Elwell and R. W. Yarbrough,
    *Readings from the First Century World* (Grand Rapids: Baker, 1998).

they did die. And very great wrath came upon Israel. (1 Maccabees 1:54–58, 62–64 RSV).

Not only can you recognize the term 'desolating sacrifice', which is similar to language found both in the OT (Daniel 9:26–27; 11:31; 12:11) and the NT (Mark 13:14 and parallels), but you will also sense the strong religious and political currents present in Jesus' day. For more details about this ancient literature see D. A. deSilva, *Introducing the Apocrypha* (Grand Rapids: Baker, 2002).

*Pseudepigrapha*
A substantial number of Jewish documents dating from 200 BC to AD 100 were written under the names of famous figures from Jewish history. Among these 'falsely (*pseud*) titled (*epigrapha*)' works, *1 Enoch* is particularly notable. One famous, although debated, passage relates to the Son of Man:

> And they had great joy, and they blessed and praised and exalted because the name of that Son of Man had been revealed to them. And he sat on the throne of his glory, and the whole judgment was given to the Son of Man, and he will cause the sinners to pass away and be destroyed from the face of the earth. (*1 Enoch* 69:26–27)

It is not difficult to see similarities between this passage and Matthew 25:31–46, although the question of possible literary relationship is complicated by some uncertainty as to whether this section of *1 Enoch* dates from before or after the writing of Matthew's Gospel.

*Dead Sea Scrolls*
The accidental discovery of some ancient scrolls in a cave on the north-western shore of the Dead Sea in 1947, and the subsequent discovery of ten further caves and numerous other documents and fragments, has revolutionized academic study of the NT. In fact, it has even had a significant impact on the life of the ordinary Bible reader, as can be seen by the numerous references to readings supported by the Dead Sea Scrolls (DSS) in a modern translation like the NIV. Many interesting passages in the DSS can

be cited; you should browse through an English translation of the DSS if at all possible to get a proper flavour of these texts. Particularly interesting are 1QpHab (the commentary, or 'pesher' on Habakkuk) and 1QM (the War Scroll, which describes the climactic battle between the 'sons of light', represented by the community members, and the 'sons of darkness'). The passage I have chosen is a frequently quoted passage that presents one perspective on the piety of the Qumran community. It comes from 1QS 11.2–15 (i.e. a document found in cave 1 at Qumran, entitled 'Serekh' [Hebrew for 'rule' – the document is normally known as the 'Community Rule'], column (*not* chapter) 11, lines (*not* verses) 2 to 15:

> As for me, my justification lies with God. In His hand are the perfection of my walk and the virtue of my heart. By His righteousness is my transgression blotted out . . . As for me, to evil humanity and the counsel of perverse flesh do I belong. My transgressions, evils, sins and corrupt heart belong to the counsel of wormy rot and those who walk in darkness . . . As for me, if I stumble, God's loving-kindness forever shall save me. If through sin of the flesh I fall, my justification will be by the righteousness of God which endures for all time . . . By His righteous truth He has justified me; and through His exceeding goodness shall He atone for all my sins. By His righteousness shall He cleanse me of human defilement and the sin of humankind – to the end that I praise God for His righteousness, the Most High for his glory.[29]

Clearly, this text is of considerable relevance to the question of whether all Jews in Paul's day were 'legalistic', and so deserves consideration in any discussion of Paul's theology of justification. Such texts require careful treatment, however. You must ask what the author meant by his words; have you understood him on his own terms? Also, remember that the fact that one Jew thought like this does not demonstrate that others shared his views.

---

29. M. Wise, M. Abegg and E. Cook, *The Dead Sea Scrolls: A New Translation* (London: HarperCollins, 1996), pp. 142–143.

## Josephus

The life story of Josephus reads like an exceptionally imaginative work of fiction: a prodigious young Jewish man, having personally tried the main Jewish philosophies of his day, becomes involved in the Zealot movement against Rome in the Jewish War (AD 66–70). Captured by the Romans when he remains the sole survivor of a suicide pact, he predicts that the Roman general Vespasian will become emperor. When this prophecy becomes a reality, Josephus is rewarded by being brought to Rome, where, under the patronage of the Flavian family, he writes voluminous works about his life, the entire history of the Jewish people (including a retelling of the OT narrative) and the Jewish War. Strange as his story is, the writings of Josephus are of immense importance to a full understanding of the religion, culture and politics in the time of Jesus and the early Christian community. The following passage from Josephus is particularly famous, not simply because it refers to Jesus but because it does so in a way that is rather surprising for a man who, apparently, remained a Jew and never converted to Christianity. It is known as the 'Testimonium Flavianum' and is found in *Antiquities* 18.3.3.

> At this time there appeared Jesus, a wise man, *if indeed one should call him a man*. For he was a doer of startling deeds, a teacher of people who receive the truth with pleasure. And he gained a following both among many Jews and among many of Greek origin. *He was the Messiah.* And when Pilate, because of an accusation made by the leading men among us, condemned him to the cross, those who had loved him previously did not cease to do so. *For he appeared to them on the third day, living again, just as the divine prophets had spoken of these and countless other wondrous things about him.* And up until this very day the tribe of Christians, named after him, has not died out.[30]

What reasons can you suggest for the view of many scholars that the italicized portions of the text were not written by Josephus but were

---

30. This text has been taken from J. P. Meier, *A Marginal Jew*, vol. 1 (New York: Doubleday, 1991), p. 60. Meier has an excellent discussion of this text from Josephus that is both cautious and clear.

added by a Christian at a later date?[31] Do you think they are correct
in their argument? Bear in mind that the only texts we have had of
this passage in Josephus, until recently, all contain the full text.
However, an Arabic version has been discovered, which appears to
reflect the scholars' reconstruction of the original reading.[32]

### Rabbinic literature

This is possibly the most problematic category for the student of
the NT. The rabbinic literature dates to the early third century AD
(c. AD 200), when the various traditions were put into written form
in the Mishnah by Rabbi Judah Ha-Nasi ('the Prince'). The
Mishnah forms the heart of a mass of literature that explains and
interprets this material, including the Tosephta, and the two
Talmuds (Jerusalem and Babylonian). Much of this material is
highly inaccessible to the new reader, but one of the most interesting and frequently quoted portions of rabbinic literature is the
'tractate' of the Mishnah (indicated by a small 'm') known as 'Pirqe
Aboth' (pronounced, and sometimes written, 'Avoth'), translated
as 'the sayings (or ethics) of the Fathers'. In describing the way in
which the 'oral Torah' was transmitted from Moses to the time just
prior to the writer's own day, *m*Aboth 1:1 reads as follows:

> Moses received the Torah at Sinai and handed it on to Joshua, Joshua to
> elders, and elders to prophets. And prophets handed it on to the men of
> the great assembly. They said three things: Be prudent in judgment.
> Raise up many disciples. Make a fence for the Torah.[33]

This text not only provides insight into the authority vested in the
oral traditions but it also illuminates the way in which traditions

---

31. Note that the historian Eusebius cites the long version of Josephus's text
    in Book 1 (c. 300 AD) of his *Church History* (1.11). See the discussion in
    P. L. Maier, *Eusebius: The Church History* (Grand Rapids: Kregel, 1999),
    pp. 377–379.
32. See Elwell and Yarbrough, *First Century World*, pp. 123–124.
33. J. Neusner, *The Classics of Judaism* (Louisville: Westminster/John Knox
    Press, 1995), pp. 72–73.

were transmitted. Paul echoes the same kind of language when he speaks of the transmission of traditions about the Lord's Supper and the resurrection (1 Corinthians 11:23; 15:3). With cautious use, the sayings found in the Mishnah provide good examples of the general way in which religious Jews (particularly Pharisees) would have thought and acted in the NT period.

It is not necessary for you to know these materials in great detail, especially in the early stages of your studies. However, if you are willing to investigate some of these documents, you will gain a first-hand appreciation of Jewish thought in the first century. For example, the account of the brutal religious oppression of Antiochus IV and the resultant revolt by Mattathias and his sons (the Maccabean Revolt) will be far more vividly impressed on your mind if you read the ancient narrative in 1 Maccabees 1 – 2 than if you simply get the details from an introductory textbook. Likewise, the 'Dead Sea Scrolls' will become more than simply a phrase, if you take the time to read through one or two of the most famous documents (perhaps the Community Rule, 1QS; the War Scroll, 1QM; or the Habakkuk Pesher, 1QpHab) than if you have only heard that this great body of literature has something vaguely useful to contribute to study of the NT.

Beyond the important Jewish materials mentioned above, two other bodies of literature will prove to be important to you as a student of the NT.

### Graeco-Roman sources

Many pieces of literature have survived from the period of ancient history when Greek culture and Roman politics dominated the world stage. Included among them are works of ancient history, biography, myth and more. While only a few make direct reference to events recounted in the NT, these literary works are important sources of information on the wider context of the NT, particularly with respect to politics and religion.[34] Among the many works by Greek and Roman writers available to us, one of the most

---

34. For important texts, discussion and bibliography, see H.-J. Klauck, *The Religious Context of Early Christianity* (London: T. & T. Clark, 2000).

famous is Suetonius' *Lives of the Caesars*. In his account of the laws
and edicts of 'the Deified Claudius', we read:

> The Jews he expelled from Rome, since they were constantly in
> rebellion, at the instigation of Chrestus.[35]

This reference is widely thought to be a misunderstanding of the
fact that there were tensions between the mainly Jewish Christians
(who followed 'Christos') and the non-Christian Jews, a distinction
unrecognized by the Roman emperor. This edict explains why
Priscilla and Aquila were in Corinth when Paul was there (Acts
18:2), although the NT does not provide any background information on the event.

### Early Christian writings

Although these documents clearly post-date the documents of the
NT canon, some shed light on the way early interpreters preserved
and used the text of the NT. Notable among such sources are the
writings of the so-called Apostolic Fathers.[36] One particularly
important document in this collection is known as 1 Clement. This
letter, sent from Christians in Rome to fellow-Christians in
Corinth, is perhaps the earliest Christian document known, apart
from the NT documents (dating from AD 95 or 96):

> Let us therefore be humble, brothers, laying aside all arrogance and
> conceit and foolishness and anger, and let us do what is written. For the
> Holy Spirit says, 'Let not the wise man boast about his wisdom, nor the
> strong about his strength, nor the rich about his wealth; but let him who
> boasts boast in the Lord, that he may seek him out, and do justice and
> righteousness' [Jeremiah 9:23–24; 1 Corinthians 1:31]. Most of all, let us
> remember the words of the Lord Jesus, which he spoke as he taught
> gentleness and patience. For he said this: 'Show mercy, that you may

---

35. Suetonius, *Lives of the Caesars* (tr. Catharine Edwards; Oxford World's
    Classics; Oxford: Oxford University Press, 2000), p. 184.
36. A useful English edition is J. B. Lightfoot, J. R. Harmer and M. W. Holmes,
    *The Apostolic Fathers* (Leicester: Apollos, 1989).

receive mercy; forgive that you may be forgiven. As you do, so shall it be done to you. As you give, so shall it be given to you. As you judge, so shall you be judged. As you show kindness, so shall kindness be shown to you. With the measure you use, it will be measured to you. (1 Clement 13:1–2)[37]

This citation is interesting in that it clearly preserves material found in the NT (1 Corinthians 1:31; Matthew 5:7; 6:14; 7:1–2), but, in the case of Jesus' words, in a rather different form. This might reflect independent tradition or might simply be a loose rendering of the canonical material.

### 'Criticism'

Many evangelical students will be concerned that they must deal with 'biblical criticism' in their NT courses, because they understand 'criticism' to mean a destructive, rationalistic attitude towards the biblical text. Unfortunately, many practitioners of biblical criticism have exemplified exactly that kind of attitude. This sad fact does not, however, mean that biblical criticism is necessarily rationalistic. In fact, the word 'criticism' is derived from the Greek word group that indicates 'judgment'. In this sense, every conscientious student of the NT should be a 'critical' scholar. For this reason, I am deeply uncomfortable with the tendency to describe non-evangelical and sceptical biblical scholarship as 'critical scholarship'. This seems to me to be unfortunate on two counts. First, it allows a perfectly good word to be hijacked and distorted, so that 'critical' effectively becomes a synonym for 'sceptical'. Second, it suggests that evangelical scholarship is '*un*critical', which is another way of saying that it is gullible. It is your responsibility as an evangelical student to ensure that your tutors never encounter a more 'critical' student when it comes to fairly gathering, analysing and assessing the available evidence.

There are several well-known 'critical methods' you will inevitably encounter. There are also several more recent trends in NT studies of which you should be aware. You must recognize that

---

37. Lightfoot, Harmer and Holmes, *Apostolic Fathers*, p. 35.

there is no obligation upon you to adopt the views encountered. What is most important, however, is that you should accurately understand the views of the major proponents of the various critical methods and be able to summarize them fairly before evaluating them in accordance with how well they account for the available evidence. In fact, careful analysis of the way in which a scholar with rationalistic presuppositions uses a method may lead you to the conclusion that the scholar has proposed a method which may be valuable to you, if only the method is employed using a different set of presuppositions. On the other hand, a particular method might be seriously flawed and subject to criticism regardless of the world view from which the scholar who employs it is working. Thus you should beware of claiming that a method is 'good' or 'bad' until it has been scrutinized with respect to underlying philosophy and effectiveness in drawing out the meaning of the text.

We will now briefly consider key aspects of the following 'critical methods': textual criticism, source criticism, form criticism, redaction criticism, structuralism, post-structuralism and deconstruction, canonical approach, narrative criticism / reader-response criticism, ideological approaches, social-science approaches and rhetorical criticism.[38] There are many useful discussions of the various critical methods and I do not wish to reproduce that work here. Instead, I have attempted to gather a selection of quotations from key representatives of the various methods that indicate their intentions in their own words.

*Textual criticism*
Textual criticism is the term applied to the task of determining the true text of the NT, which can then be the subject of historical and theological analysis. This task used to be known as 'lower criticism' as opposed to 'higher criticism', which dealt with the historical/theological issues. It involves assessing the

---

38. A particularly clear and helpful introduction to these approaches may be found in D. Wenham and S. Walton, *Exploring the New Testament*. Vol. 1: *Introducing the Gospels and Acts* (London: SPCK, 2001), chs. 4 and 5.

numerous manuscripts (abbreviated MSS [pl.] or MS [sing.]), which have been preserved to the modern day (often described as 'extant' or 'available'), as to their accuracy in representing the original text of the NT. This requires competence in Greek. Few people have had such an impact on the careful use of NT textual criticism in the twentieth century as Professor Bruce Metzger, who taught at Princeton Theological Seminary. In the preface to his classic book on the subject, he outlines the need for the method:

> The necessity of applying textual criticism to the books of the New Testament arises from two circumstances: (a) none of the original documents is extant, and (b) the existing copies differ from one another. The textual critic seeks to ascertain from the divergent copies which form of the text should be regarded as most nearly conforming to the original. In some cases the evidence will be found to be so evenly divided that it is extremely difficult to decide between two variant readings. In other instances, however, the critic can arrive at a decision based on more or less compelling reasons for preferring one reading and rejecting another.[39]

Detailed engagement with the intricacies of textual criticism will only be possible for those who pursue Greek studies to an advanced level, but it is important for you to recognize from the start of your studies that before anything can be said about the NT text, you have to decide what the NT text is! For a useful survey of the main views on the best way to do textual criticism see particularly D. A. Black (ed.), *Rethinking New Testament Textual Criticism* (Grand Rapids: Baker, 2002). The United Bible Societies have published an indispensable book that explains the rationale for each decision taken by the editorial committee of the UBS Greek NT.[40]

---

39. B. M. Metzger, *The Text of the New Testament* (Oxford: Oxford University Press, 1968), p. v.

40. B. M. Metzger (ed.), *A Textual Commentary on the Greek New Testament* (New York: United Bible Societies, 1971).

## Source criticism

This is investigation of whether the authors of the canonical Gospels have drawn on other sources for some of their material. Luke's preface to his Gospel (Luke 1:1–4) certainly suggests that Luke used various sources in drawing up his narrative. These sources might be other canonical works or they might be documents or traditions otherwise unavailable to us. In attempting to explain the various similarities and differences between the three Synoptic Gospels the most widespread belief among NT scholars is that Mark was written first, and that Matthew and Luke used Mark and another hypothetical source named 'Q' (standing for the German word for source, *Quelle*). A standard work is *The Four Gospels: A Study of Origins* by B. H Streeter.[41] Streeter explains the phenomena he seeks to explain as follows:

> The authentic text of Mark contains 661 verses. Matthew reproduced the substance of over 600 of these. Mark's style is diffuse, Matthew's succinct; so that in adapting Mark's language Matthew compresses so much that the 600 odd verses taken from Mark supply rather less than half the material contained in the 1068 verses in the longer Gospel. Yet, in spite of this abbreviation, it is found that Matthew employs 51% of the actual words used by Mark . . . If we leave out of account all passages where there is reason to suspect that Luke has used a non-Marcan source, it appears on an approximate estimate that about 350 verses (i.e. just over one half of Mark) have been reproduced by Luke. When following Mark, Luke alters the wording of his original a trifle more than Matthew does; on the other hand he retains many details which Matthew omits, and he does not compress the language quite so much. The result is that on average Luke retains 53% of the actual words of Mark, that is, a very slightly higher proportion than Matthew.
>
> From these various figures it appears that, while Matthew omits less than 10% of the subject matter of Mark, Luke omits more than 45%, but for much of this he substitutes similar matter from another source. Each of them omits numerous points of detail and several complete

---

41. London: Macmillan, 1924.

sections of Mark which the other reproduces; but sometimes they both concur in making the same omission.[42]

Although these figures may appear rather confusing, the main point is simple: it appears that the various Gospels have some interrelationship. The so-called Synoptic Problem is, 'What is the nature of this relationship, if in fact it exists?' Whatever solution you eventually adopt, there is no escaping the evidence of the texts and your responsibility is to account for that evidence as best you can. For a recent account of the main proposed solutions, see D. A. Black (ed.), *Rethinking the Synoptic Problem* (Grand Rapids: Baker, 2002).[43]

*Form criticism*

The classic work on *Formgeschichte* (a German term more properly translated 'form history') was done by three German scholars: K. L. Schmidt,[44] M. Dibelius[45] and R. Bultmann. Bultmann's classic work is *History of the Synoptic Tradition*, in which he states that the purpose of form criticism is (quoting M. Dibelius), 'to rediscover the origin and the history of the particular units and thereby to throw some light on the history of the tradition before it took literary form'.[46] Bultmann goes on to explain:

> The proper understanding of form-criticism rests upon the judgement that the literature in which the life of a given community, even the

---

42. Streeter, *Four Gospels*, pp. 159–160.

43. For a clear survey of the issues and a view which boldly goes against the majority, see M. Goodacre, *The Synoptic Problem: A Way Through the Maze* (London: Continuum/Sheffield Academic Press, 2001).

44. His major work is *Der Rahmen der Geschichte Jesu* (Berlin: Trowitzsch, 1919).

45. Most notably, *Die Formgeschichte des Evangeliums* (Tübingen: Mohr [Siebeck, 1919]).

46. R. Bultmann, *The History of the Synoptic Tradition* (Oxford: Basil Blackwell, 1963), p. 4, citing M. Dibelius's article (no title supplied) in *Theologische Rundschau* N. F. 1 (1929), p. 187.

primitive Christian community, has taken shape, springs out of quite definite conditions and wants of life from which grows up a quite definite style and quite specific forms and categories. Thus every literary category has its 'life situation' (*Sitz im Leben*: Gunkel), whether it be worship in its different forms, or work, or hunting, or war.[47]

It is important to note that not all those who saw value in the method shared Bultmann's views on the historical value of the traditions about Jesus. Notably, Vincent Taylor, in his important book *The Formation of the Gospel Tradition*, writes:

> It is on this question of eyewitnesses that Form-Criticism presents a very vulnerable front. If the Form-Critics are right, the disciples must have been translated to heaven immediately after the resurrection. As Bultmann sees it, the primitive community exists *in vacuo* [Latin: 'in isolation / a vacuum'], cut off from its founders by the walls of an inexplicable ignorance. Like Robinson Crusoe it must do the best it can. Unable to turn to any one for information, it must invent situations for the words of Jesus, and put into His lips sayings which personal memory cannot check. All this is absurd.[48]

Taylor clearly comes to the text with an entirely different reconstruction of the events from Bultmann. A key question, therefore, to ask of the reconstructions of form criticism (along with many other forms of critical method) is, 'On what evidence do you build your reconstruction?' While such reconstructions may be of limited value, the practice of identifying material of different kinds of 'form' (e.g. 'parable', 'pronouncement story') is very useful for ensuring appropriate interpretation and should not be dismissed lightly.

*Redaction criticism*
This method grew out of form criticism and sought to recognize the truly theological nature of the Gospels. It is particularly asso-

---

47. Bultmann, *Synoptic Tradition*, p. 4.
48. (2nd edn.; London: Macmillan, 1935), p. 41.

ciated with three German scholars: W. Marxsen (working on Mark), H. Conzelmann (working on Luke) and G. Bornkamm (working on Matthew). The realization that the authors of the Gospels were communicating a theological message was a major advance, but the redaction critics tended to be very ready to attribute variations in the various accounts to theological motives without regard to historical accuracy. In his famous essay on the Matthean version of the stilling of the storm, Bornkamm first indicates that Mark presents this event as a straightforward miracle story and then argues that Matthew has made several significant changes in order to emphasize the theme of discipleship. He then writes:

> If this observation is correct it means: Matthew is not only a hander-on of the narrative, but also its oldest exegete, and in fact the first to interpret the journey of the disciples with Jesus in the storm and the stilling of the storm with reference to discipleship, and that means with reference to the little ship of the Church.[49]

The redaction critics correctly saw that the authors of the Gospels were more than 'cut and paste' editors but were theologians in their own right. However, they attributed to these evangelists a willingness substantially to modify their traditions to serve their theological ends. When considering the contribution of redaction criticism it is important to ask whether the emphasis of a theme by one author necessitates a willingness to misrepresent the facts of the situation, recognizing that selectivity is not the same thing as creation of events from nothing.

*Structuralism*
This approach to the biblical texts, which is the application of the 'structural linguistics' of Ferdinand de Saussure (1857–1913), is rather difficult to grasp. It argues that words have no meaning

---

49. G. Bornkamm, 'The Stilling of the Storm in Matthew', in G. Bornkamm, G. Barth and H. J. Held, *Tradition and Interpretation in Matthew* (London: SCM, 1963), p. 55.

apart from their difference from other words. According to this philosophy, the interpreter must seek the 'deep structure' of the text. Structuralism traces its root to the analysis of Russian folk tales by V. Propp in the 1920s by which he discovered that a common structure could be traced in many stories. This is often associated with the work of A. J. Greimas and his method known as 'actantial analysis'. This method allows the reader to represent a story using a diagram with six key figures or 'actants', as follows:

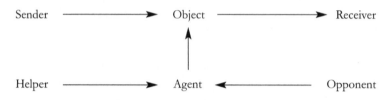

The sender initiates an act, which involves conveying an object to a receiver. He commissions an agent to perform it. The agent is challenged by an opponent, but is helped by a helper. Some recent interpreters have found Greimas's diagram a useful tool in highlighting the major elements of a narrative, without necessarily accepting structuralism as a whole. For example, N. T. Wright employs Greimas's diagram while explicitly rejecting some aspects of structuralism that he describes as 'decidedly anti-historical'.[50] Wright uses several diagrams of the kind suggested by Greimas to represent the various scenes of the parable of the wicked tenants (Mark 12:1–12). The first is as follows:

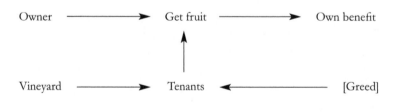

---

50. N. T. Wright, *The New Testament and the People of God* (London: SPCK, 1992), p. 70.

Wright explains:

> The story begins with the owner planting a vineyard, in order (as it
> appears) to get fruit for himself, using tenants as his agents, despite (as it
> appears) their greed.[51]

To the extent that this method helps to identify the key moments
in a narrative it has value. To the extent that it reduces the impact
of other significant details in a narrative, it must be modified or
challenged.

### Post-structuralism and deconstruction

These approaches have in common a rejection of definitive
'meaning' in the biblical text. Post-structuralism emphasizes the
potential for multiple meanings in a text. Deconstruction seeks to
identify excluded readings and give them priority, which, of course,
must happen again and again as different readers seek to 'liberate'
previously 'marginalized' readings. Perhaps the most notable recent
proponent of this kind of approach is Stephen D. Moore. Here is a
short section of an essay on the way in which Jesus the historical
figure is presented in literature:

> Writ(h)ing in pain on his cross, Jesus can at last be read: 'Truly this man
> was God's son' (Mk 15:39). He is in the process of becoming a book.
> Nailed, grafted onto the tree, Jesus' body is becoming one with the
> wood. His flesh, torn and beaten to a pulp, joined by violence to the
> wood, is slowly being changed into processed woodpulp, into paper, as
> the centurion looks on. As tree and budding book, Jesus is putting
> forth leaves, the leaves of a gospel book, whose opening sentence the
> centurion has just read: [*archē tou euangeliou Iēsou Christou huiou theou*: 'the
> beginning of the good news of Jesus Christ, Son of God'].[52]

---

51. Wright, *New Testament*, p. 74.
52. S. D. Moore, 'Ugly Thoughts: On the Face and Physique of the Historical
    Jesus', in J. C. Exum and S. D. Moore (eds.), *Biblical Studies, Cultural Studies:
    The Third Sheffield Colloquium* (Sheffield: Sheffield Academic Press, 1998),
    p. 377.

Indeed, Moore's prose is witty and arresting, but it is hard to avoid the sense that Moore is simply playing with the biblical text as it communicates something of absolute importance.

## Canonical approach

This approach to the NT is associated with the name of Brevard S. Childs. Childs's work was initially directed towards the OT,[53] which was his area of expertise, but he has since applied his insights to the NT and to the Bible as a whole. His 'approach'[54] developed out of a concern that, in the context of much academic study of the Bible, the biblical text was not being treated on its own terms. He writes:

> The critic presumes to stand above the text, outside the circle of
> tradition, and from this detached vantage point adjudicate the truth and
> error of the New Testament's time-conditionality. In contrast, the
> canonical interpreter stands within the received tradition, and, fully
> conscious of his own time-conditionality as well as that of the
> Scriptures, strives critically to discern from its kerygmatic witness a way
> to God which overcomes the historical moorings of both text and
> reader.[55]

Robert Wall explains:

> In brief, the 'canonical approach' of Childs posits hermeneutical value in
> the Bible's final literary form . . . which supplies the normative written
> witness to Jesus Christ.[56]

---

53. His classic work is *Introduction to the Old Testament as Scripture* (London: SCM, 1979).

54. He does not appreciate the description 'canonical criticism', despite the widespread use of this phrase. See his *Old Testament as Scripture*, pp. 82–83.

55. B. S. Childs, *The New Testament as Canon* (London: SCM, 1984), pp. 51–52.

56. R. W. Wall, 'Reading the New Testament in Canonical Context', in Green, *Hearing the New Testament*, p. 371.

However, Childs does not reject standard critical positions on the biblical text. Instead, he brackets them out of consideration as the canonical form of the text is considered. He continues:

> The principal concern of the canonical approach can be briefly summarized. Its aim is not to provide a short-cut to exegesis, nor is it to offer an interpretation of each passage within the New Testament. Rather, it seeks to sketch a different vision of the biblical text which profoundly affects one's concept of the enterprise, but which also makes room for the continuing activity of exegesis as a discipline of the church.[57]

Many benefits have come out of Childs's work, but you should also question whether it is possible to treat the final form of the biblical text as authoritative while all the time accepting many of the conclusions of mainstream 'critical' scholarship.

### Narrative criticism / reader-response criticism

Arising out of a new interest in the final form of the biblical text, combined with insights from students of literature, 'narrative criticism' pays particular attention to the signals within the NT text that indicate how the text was intended to be read. One of the foremost scholars of narrative criticism is M. A. Powell, who has recently written a fascinating book that works out the principles of this kind of approach in dealing with specific texts from Matthew's Gospel. In a brief historical survey of the discipline, he writes:

> Narrative criticism was defined as a text-oriented approach to Scripture as opposed to the author-oriented mode of traditional historical study. Meaning could be determined by paying attention to the form, structure, and rhetorical dynamics of the work itself, without reference to background information regarding what the author may or may not have intended.[58]

---

57. Childs, *New Testament as Canon*, p. 53.

58. M. A. Powell, *Chasing the Eastern Star* (Louisville: Westminster/John Knox Press, 2001), p. 67.

Now Powell suggests that 'narrative criticism' should be under-stood in relation to a broader category of 'reader-response criticism',

> as a subset or variety of reader-response criticism. The latter is a broad field that encompasses several different systems of interpretation. There is simply *descriptive reader-response*, which seeks to catalog the variety of interpretations given for a given text and to understand what factors influence this diversity . . . An important subset of descriptive reader-response criticism is *Wirkungsgeschichte*, the German approach that attempts to catalog the variety of interpretations that have been offered for any given text throughout history . . . Reader response also encompasses many overtly *ideological approaches* that seek to read texts from the perspective of readers who are informed in particular ways. For instance, *womanist* readings attempt to read literature from the perspective of African-American women . . . And then there is *narrative criticism*, a basic discipline that is practiced by almost all reader-response critics yet sometimes despised by them when it is not combined with other approaches . . . Narrative criticism is unique among reader-response approaches in that it does not concern itself with the actual responses of real people. Instead, narrative criticism seeks to determine a range of expected responses that might be attributed to a text's implied readers. The concept of *implied readers* . . . refers essentially to an imaginary set of people who may be assumed to read a given text in the way they are expected to read it, bringing to their reading experience the knowledge, competence, beliefs, and values that appear to be presupposed for the text in question.[59]

Appreciation of literary features of the text is without doubt a good thing, but emphasis on the role of the reader (which, in some measure, is quite valid) can quickly lead to rampant subject-ivism that does not hear anything outside the reader's own ideas and values. You will benefit from thinking through these issues carefully, so that you neither reject valid insights nor are led into unhelpful interpretation.

---

59. Powell, *Eastern Star*, pp. 63–64.

## Ideological approaches

Closely related to reader-response criticism, 'ideological' approaches to the NT are not simply those that come to the text with certain presuppositions. We have already seen that there can be no other kind of reading of the NT. Rather, they are approaches to the text that give priority to the concerns of a particular issue, whether that is gender or sexuality or race or economic position. Sandra Schneiders, an advocate of feminist biblical interpretation comments:

> Feminist biblical interpretation is a species of liberationist hermeneutics, which also includes class interpretation such as that which functions within Latin American theology and racial interpretations such as African American or black hermeneutics. What these types of interpretation have in common is their starting point in the experience of the oppressed, their presupposition that there is no such thing as a neutral scholarship that pursues and attains purely objective knowledge, and their goal of social transformation.[60]

The fact that most modern NT interpretation has come from Western, white, economically prosperous males inevitably means that at least some of that biblical interpretation has been biased towards the interests of that community. It is no bad thing to hear the readings of people from other perspectives. However, you should beware of the suggestion that one's gender or economic status itself validates or invalidates a particular reading of the text.

## Social-science approaches

Stephen Barton explains that disciplines from the 'social sciences' have become important in study of the NT:

> Conventionally, these include sociology, social (or cultural) anthropology, and psychology . . . The main presupposition that underpins the use of the social sciences in NT interpretation is that the text of the NT is a

---

60. S. M. Schneiders, 'Feminist Hermeneutics', in Green, *Hearing the New Testament*, p. 349.

product, not just of historical conditioning, but of social and cultural conditioning as well. To the extent that cultural factors and social forces played a part in the lives of the individuals and groups that produced the NT or to which the NT refers, sociological analysis is legitimate and necessary.[61]

There are clearly many benefits for interpretation of the NT texts in appreciating the social setting of the early Christian communities. 1 Corinthians stands out as a document that can be understood more fully when you appreciate something of the social setting of the Corinthian church. At the same time, you will want to ask whether any given interpretation places more weight on a reconstruction of the social setting of a hypothetical community than on the NT text itself.

*Rhetorical criticism*
Ben Witherington III, a notable evangelical advocate of the application of research into ancient rhetoric to the NT documents, writes:

> Rhetorical criticism can be thought of as part of literary criticism, but it has a decidedly historical interest. It tells us a great deal about how the different NT authors structured their writings. Rhetoric is by definition the art of persuasion, and particular literary devices and forms were used in antiquity to persuade a hearer or reader to some position regarding the issue that the speaker or writer was addressing. Attention to the rhetorical dimension of Paul's letters has revealed how certain forms of argument or exhortation function in his letters, and thus how those forms ought to be interpreted.[62]

Most commentators are sceptical of any suggestion that Paul had formally studied the classic handbooks of rhetoric by authors such

---

61. S. C. Barton, 'Historical Criticism and Social-Scientific Perspectives', in Green, *Hearing the New Testament*, pp. 67–68.
62. B. Witherington III, *Conflict and Community in Corinth* (Grand Rapids: Eerdmans, 1995), p. xii.

as Quintillian, but it seems likely that even in Jerusalem where Paul was trained under Gamaliel, the pervasiveness of Greek culture ('Hellenization') would have allowed ample opportunity to become acquainted with rhetorical forms. When considering the proposals of advocates of rhetorical criticism, you should ask whether the text in question fits naturally into the rhetorical structure or whether it is being forced for the sake of conforming to an expected model.

No student will be expected to adopt these various methods, either whole or even in part. However, no student can legitimately reject these various methods unless he or she understands what is being rejected.[63]

### An example

Having briefly outlined the various approaches that might be employed when analysing the NT, it may be useful now to illustrate some of these methods by means of a worked example. A similar approach is taken by C. L. Blomberg in his very helpful book *Jesus and the Gospels* (Leicester: Apollos, 1997), pp. 108–110. I will attempt to indicate how a select few of the above methods might be applied to the particular NT texts and I hope to suggest several questions students might ask with respect to the method in question.

As the text for consideration I have chosen Mark 5:21–43 (NASB), because the passage is found in all three Synoptic Gospels and so it is possible to illustrate issues of source, form and redaction criticism; and because it is a narrative and so it is possible to evaluate the text using narrative tools.

---

63. See the important discussion of evangelicals and biblical criticism in M. A. Noll, *Between Faith and Criticism* (Leicester: Apollos, 1991). One of the most useful books on critical methods is D. A. Black and D. S. Dockery (eds.), *Interpreting the New Testament: Essays on Methods and Issues* (Nashville: Broadman & Holman, 2001). This volume is written in a more accessible style than some introductory textbooks and covers a wide range of topics from a conservative stance. See also the important essays in Green, *Hearing the New Testament*.

| Matthew 9:18–26 | Mark 5:21–43 | Luke 8:40–56 |
|---|---|---|
| | | [40] And as Jesus returned, the people welcomed Him, for they had all been waiting for Him. |
| [18] While He was saying these things to them, | [21] When Jesus had crossed over again in the boat to the other side, a large crowd gathered around Him; and so He stayed by the seashore. | |
| a *synagogue* official came and bowed down before Him, and said, 'My daughter has just died; but come and lay Your hand on her, and she will live.' [19] Jesus got up and *began* to follow him, and *so did* His disciples. | [22] One of the synagogue officials named Jairus came up, and on seeing Him, fell at His feet [23] and implored Him earnestly, saying, 'My little daughter is at the point of death; *please* come and lay Your hands on her, so that she will get well and live.' [24] And He went off with him; and a large crowd was following Him and pressing in on Him. | [41] And there came a man named Jairus, and he was an official of the synagogue; and he fell at Jesus' feet, and *began* to implore Him to come to his house; [42] for he had an only daughter, about twelve years old, and she was dying. But as He went, the crowds were pressing against Him. |
| [20] And a woman who had been suffering from a hemorrhage for twelve years, came up behind Him and touched the fringe of His cloak; [21] for she was saying to herself, 'If I only touch His garment, I will get well.' [22] But Jesus turning and seeing her said, 'Daughter, take courage; your faith has made you well.' At once the woman was made well. | [25] A woman who had had a hemorrhage for twelve years, [26] and had endured much at the hands of many physicians, and had spent all that she had and was not helped at all, but rather had grown worse – [27] after hearing about Jesus, she came up in the crowd behind *Him* and touched His cloak. [28] For she thought, 'If I just touch His garments, I will get well.' [29] Immediately the flow of her blood was dried up; and she felt in her body that she was healed of her affliction. [30] Immediately Jesus, perceiving in Himself that the power *proceeding* from Him had gone forth, turned around in the crowd and said, 'Who touched My garments?' [31] And His disciples said to Him, 'You see the crowd pressing in on You, and You say, "Who touched Me?"' [32] And He looked around to see the | [43] And a woman who had a hemorrhage for twelve years, and could not be healed by anyone, [44] came up behind Him and touched the fringe of His cloak, and immediately her hemorrhage stopped. [45] And Jesus said, 'Who is the one who touched Me?' And while they were all denying it, Peter said, 'Master, the people are crowding and pressing in on You.' [46] But Jesus said, 'Someone did touch Me, for I was aware that power had gone out of Me.' [47] When the woman saw that she had not escaped notice, she came trembling and fell down before Him, and declared in the presence of all the people the reason why she had touched Him, and how she had been immediately healed. [48] And He said to her, 'Daughter, your faith has made you well; go in peace.' |

woman who had done this. 33 But the woman fearing and trembling, aware of what had happened to her, came and fell down before Him and told Him the whole truth. 34 And He said to her, 'Daughter, your faith has made you well; go in peace and be healed of your affliction.'

35 While He was still speaking, they came from the *house of* the synagogue official, saying, 'Your daughter has died; why trouble the Teacher anymore?' 36 But Jesus, overhearing what was being spoken, said to the synagogue official, 'Do not be afraid *any longer*, only believe.' 37 And He allowed no one to accompany Him, except Peter and James and John the brother of James. 38 They came to the house of the synagogue official; and He saw a commotion, and *people* loudly weeping and wailing. 39 And entering in, He said to them, 'Why make a commotion and weep? The child has not died, but is asleep.' 40 They *began* laughing at Him. But putting them all out, He took along the child's father and mother and His own companions, and entered *the room* where the child was. 41 Taking the child by the hand, He said to her, 'Talitha kum!' (which translated means, 'Little girl, I say to you, get up!'). 42 Immediately the girl got up and *began* to walk, for she was twelve years old. And immediately they were completely astounded. 43 And He gave them strict orders that no one should know about this, and He said that *something* should be given her to eat.

23 When Jesus came into the official's house, and saw the flute-players and the crowd in noisy disorder, 24 He said, 'Leave; for the girl has not died, but is asleep.' And they *began* laughing at Him. 25 But when the crowd had been sent out, He entered and took her by the hand, and the girl got up. 26 This news spread throughout all that land.

49 While He was still speaking, someone came from *the house of* the synagogue official, saying, 'Your daughter has died; do not trouble the Teacher anymore.' 50 But when Jesus heard *this*, He answered him, 'Do not be afraid *any longer*, only believe, and she will be made well.' 51 When He came to the house, He did not allow anyone to enter with Him, except Peter and John and James, and the girl's father and mother. 52 Now they were all weeping and lamenting for her; but He said, 'Stop weeping, for she has not died, but is asleep.' 53 And they *began* laughing at Him, knowing that she had died. 54 He, however, took her by the hand and called, saying, 'Child, arise!' 55 And her spirit returned, and she got up immediately; and He gave orders for *something* to be given her to eat. 56 Her parents were amazed; but He instructed them to tell no one what had happened.

## Textual criticism

The use of textual criticism would highlight, among other relatively minor issues, the fact that the inclusion of the words 'named Jairus' in Mark 5:22 is disputed, as is the specific identification of Peter in Luke 8:45. The student must ask several questions, which most beginning students will be hard-pressed to answer other than by drawing on discussions in commentaries, and particularly in B. M. Metzger's *Textual Commentary*. These questions should include, 'Which manuscripts (MSS) – that is, "external evidence" – support the different readings? How significant are these witnesses? Which arguments from style and context – "internal evidence" – support the different readings? Which is the "harder" reading? Which reading best explains the existence of the others?'

## Source criticism

I have already identified, in the parallel columns, that there are three accounts of this incident: one in each of the Synoptic Gospels. It will also be clear that there are substantial points of both similarity and difference. If we focus on just one tiny detail, it is interesting to note that, while at certain points all three accounts use their own distinctive phrases, both Matthew 9:20b and Luke 8:44 use exactly the same Greek phrase *proselthousa opisthen hēpsato tou kraspedou tou himatiou autou* (having come up behind [him], touched the fringe of his garment). In both accounts this phrase is identical in vocabulary, word forms and word order – quite remarkable in a flexible language like Greek. Yet Mark's account reads *elthousa en tō ochlō opisthen hēpsato tou himatiou autou* (having come in the crowd behind [him], touched his garment). Notice that this does not include the same *pros* prefix on the first verb, it adds the phrase *en tō ochlō* (in the crowd) and it omits *tou kraspedou* (the fringe). Why might Matthew and Luke differ from what is the fullest account in precisely the same way at precisely the same point? Could it be that they were drawing from a common source?

## Form criticism

This interwoven narrative clearly presents two incidents in what might be described as 'miracle stories' or, more specifically, 'healing stories'. In fact, they come towards the conclusion of a group of such miracle stories that begins in 4:36. Might there have been a particular use for materials of this sort in the life of the early church (a *Sitz im Leben*)? Might they have been used as an apologetic tool to answer the question 'Who is this?' (Mark 4:41)? Of course, we have no external evidence to support an answer. Would such a use demand that the church had created the accounts? I would suggest not. The fact that these two narratives are 'bracketed' together not only in Mark (who favours this method of presentation) but in Matthew and Luke also suggests that they were understood to 'belong together' although this feature may simply reflect the necessary progression of the story.

### Redaction criticism

Several questions might arise when the three accounts of these events are compared. Why is Matthew's account (found in the longer Gospel) so much more condensed than Mark's? Why is Mark the only author to include the Aramaic phrase *talitha kum*? Why does Mark have to explain what the Aramaic phrase means?

### Narrative criticism

The story progresses with great power and pathos. Does the 'sandwich' effect reflect Mark's distinctive use of this literary tool, or is it simply a necessary aspect of the two-part story? Might the implied readers be those who themselves were oppressed and marginalized and here find Jesus identifying with their kind?

### Social-science approaches

According to B. Witherington:

> The social significance of the story should not be overlooked, for we see Jesus aiding both a male of high status (Jairus) and a woman who was an outcast and marginalized because of her physical condition.[64]

---

64. B. Witherington III, *Mark: A Socio-Rhetorical Commentary* (Grand Rapids: Eerdmans, 2001), p. 185.

## Ideological approaches

Elizabeth Struthers Malbon comments on Mark's narrative:

> The haemorrhaging woman emerges from the great crowd . . . that
> followed Jesus, giving evidence of the presence of women in the crowd,
> a presence generally 'obscured by the androcentric nature of the
> language which uses masculine forms for common gender.' Yet by her
> emerging, the haemorrhaging woman distinguishes herself from the
> other women and men of the crowd; she is bold, for her faith is strong
> . . . The healing of the haemorrhaging woman is unique in the Markan
> Gospel . . . in taking place solely at the woman's initiative (5:28–29) . . .
> As Schierling points out, the haemorrhaging woman has suffered as
> Jesus: 'Only here and in relation to Jesus is the word "suffering" [*paschō*,
> 5:26; 8:31; 9:12] ever mentioned . . . Mark recognizes the suffering of this
> woman in society as similar to that which Jesus experienced before his
> death.'[65]

## Structuralism

We might present one aspect of the account of the healing of the
woman using 'actantial analysis' as follows:

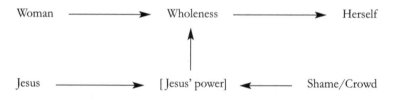

The woman initiates contact with Jesus with the intention of
achieving wholeness (perhaps only physically) for herself. She
appears to believe that Jesus has power to achieve this end,
although this is not explicitly stated. The full realization of wholeness is threatened by her reticence to make herself known to Jesus
for some unstated reason – presumably because of her fear of
how Jesus or the crowd will regard her. However, Jesus ensures

---

65. E. M. Struthers, *In the Company of Jesus* (Louisville: Westminster/John
Knox Press, 2000), pp. 50–51.

that the woman experiences true wholeness by identifying her and reassuring her of the reality that has taken place.

### Post-structuralism and deconstruction

It is hard for someone who believes that meaning lies in the text to begin to illustrate an approach which rejects that idea. However, as a faltering attempt, one might draw attention to the fact that Jesus crossed over to the 'other side' of the lake (Mark 5:21) and suggest that he deals graciously with a man who, as a representative of official Judaism, is on the 'other side' (opposition) from Jesus, with a woman who must stand on the 'other side' (alienation) of the street, and with a girl who was on the 'other side' (separation) of death. Or, perhaps, alternatively one might note that the Aramaic word *kum* sounds like the English word 'come!' and emphasize that this narrative is part of Mark's call to discipleship.

## Resources

### Bibliography

When studying and writing on the NT, you should aim to use as wide a range of literature as possible. When writing a formal academic paper, you must construct a bibliography at the end of the paper that lists all the resources used in the writing of the paper in alphabetical order according to the author's surname. The bibliography should not be restricted to those resources actually cited in footnotes, but you should attempt to demonstrate your use of all resources by means of footnotes.

A good bibliography will not appear by accident! It will be the product of careful and thoughtful research. If you have to construct the bibliography for an essay, it is likely that the tutor will have begun the task for you by supplying a short list (an 'indicative bibliography') of relevant books and articles. If this is the case, then you should respect that list and aim to locate and use most of the items included on it. The tutor has constructed the list by including those works he or she considers to be the most accessible or most significant contributions on the topic in question. Having once been a novice theological student, I know how

tempting it is for an evangelical student to dismiss the list of
books on the indicative bibliography and to gather together a rich
range of evangelical studies in their place. Although the possibility
of gathering an impressive group of academically respectable
evangelical studies is possible now in a way that it has not been
previously, and although I well understand the temptation, I would
urge you to resist it firmly! Such an approach will almost certainly
be penalized, not only in institutions not evangelical by confession
but also in those that are. Let me explain why I would penalize a
student who had not drawn on a wide range of literature.

First, it suggests incomplete research. It is important that you
read a variety of views to get an accurate perspective on a subject.
You should read the work of the various authors first hand in order
to appreciate the full impact of their points. Second, it may indicate
a rather defensive attitude, which is not prepared to listen to the
views of others when they stand in opposition to a personal view.
Third, it may indicate a tendency to look for easy answers in ready
locations and to be unwilling to exert the effort to locate some
further materials. Fourth, not to follow specific instructions and
recommendations with respect to reading materials betrays a lack of
judgment, since these are provided for the benefit of the student.

All quotations from sources must be indicated by quotation
marks around the relevant citation and a footnote indicating bibliographical information and the specific page reference. Even
substantial dependence on a paragraph or section of another work
written up in your own words should be acknowledged by a footnote. Failure to acknowledge citation of the work of another author
is plagiarism and is an academic offence of the highest order.
Students should treat this aspect of their work with the utmost care.

It is very important that you form good habits with respect to
the formatting of footnotes and bibliographies. See the *SBL
Handbook of Style*, ed. Patrick H. Alexander et al. (Peabody:
Hendrickson, 1999).

It may be useful to consider an example of how the various
resources available to you contribute to a piece of research. Let us
imagine that a class has been set the following assignment: *Write an
exegesis [explanation] of Galatians 1:1–10.* You are being asked to write
a careful explanation of the meaning of the text (*not* a sermon!).

What should you include in the bibliography? There are a number of categories of sources which you may use.

*Biblical text*

Some students will study the passage based on an English translation, while others will base their studies on the Greek text.[66] Versions of the biblical text are *not* normally included in the bibliography, but it is worth indicating which version of the English or Greek text is being used in a footnote when you first use it. If a number of translations are quoted for comparison, indicate which is being used by means of an abbreviation in brackets after the quotation. I am well aware that some students will come to the study of the NT with deeply held convictions about the text of the NT. (These usually relate to the superiority of the so-called 'Textus Receptus' [TR], which underlies the Authorized Version [AV] and the New King James Version [NKJV] translations of the NT.) Nonetheless, I would urge you to read the passage under scrutiny in several modern translations to gain a sense of which features of the passage are most significant and perhaps most subject to debate. I would also urge you to read the biblical text carefully and to make some initial observations *before* reading the other resources. This practice will allow you to develop your own skills of analysis rather than simply relying on those of the commentators. If you wish to study a passage from the Gospels, a 'Synopsis', which places parallel accounts side by side in columns, is an exceptionally useful tool.[67]

*New Testament introduction*

A general orientation to the wider literary, historical and religious context of the passage may be found in one of several sound single-volume introductory volumes. These books often approach the task in quite different ways and so it is probably useful to consult more than one. Particularly commendable are P. J. Achtemeier,

---

66. The Bible Society may be able to provide theological students with standard critical editions of the Greek NT at substantial discount. See http://www.biblesociety.org.

67. The standard 'Aland' editions are also available from the Bible Society.

J. B. Green and M. M. Thompson, *Introducing the New Testament: Its Literature and Theology* (Grand Rapids: Eerdmans, 2001); R. E. Brown, *An Introduction to the New Testament* (New York: Doubleday, 1997); D. A. Carson, D. J. Moo and L. Morris, *An Introduction to the New Testament* (Leicester: Apollos, 1992);[68] D. Wenham and S. Walton, *Exploring the New Testament*. Vol. 1: *A Guide to the Gospels and Acts* (London: SPCK, 2001); I. H. Marshall, S. Travis and I. Paul, *Exploring the New Testament*. Vol. 2: *A Guide to the Epistles and Revelation* (London: SPCK, 2002). Such volumes might provide much useful discussion of whether Paul was writing to Christians in 'North Galatia' or 'South Galatia', for example.

### Bible atlas
Paul writes his letter to Christians in Asia Minor. A Bible atlas may provide helpful information about the specific locations mentioned in the passage.

### Bible dictionaries
A Bible dictionary will provide a concise discussion of a particular topic. For example, the reader may find an article on the word 'apostle'. Some dictionaries, such as the *Anchor Bible Dictionary*[69] and the series of NT dictionaries from IVP[70] have extended articles, which are extremely valuable for academic study. Dictionary articles should normally be used to get an overview of a topic, which is then followed up using more detailed studies. The more recent and substantial dictionaries will often provide a bibliography of up-to-date resources that the student may use for further research.

---

68. A new and substantially revised edition of this important book is in preparation.

69. D. N. Freedman (ed.), *The Anchor Bible Dictionary*, 6 vols. (New York: Doubleday, 1993).

70. J. B. Green et al., *Dictionary of Jesus and the Gospels* (Leicester: IVP, 1992); G. F. Hawthorne et al., *Dictionary of Paul and his Letters* (Leicester: IVP, 1993); R. P. Martin and P. H. Davids (eds.), *Dictionary of the Later New Testament and its Developments* (Leicester: IVP, 1998); C. A. Evans and S. E. Porter, *Dictionary of New Testament Background* (Leicester: IVP, 2000).

## Theological dictionaries/wordbooks

For detailed investigation of an important theological term such as 'apostle' or 'gospel', the student should turn to one or more of the multivolume dictionaries such as the *Theological Dictionary of the New Testament* (*TDNT*),[71] the *Exegetical Dictionary of the New Testament* (*EDNT*),[72] the *New International Dictionary of the New Testament Theology* (*NIDNTT*)[73] and so on. Such resources offer vast amounts of information about words and/or concepts. Do beware, however, of the so-called etymological fallacy, the idea that in order to find out what a word means in one location, one should study what it meant in much older texts and in very different contexts. Also beware of the idea that a concept is only present if certain key words are used. Concepts can, in fact, be expressed using a great diversity of phrases. Used carefully, however, these dictionaries are very useful resources.

## Commentaries

Commentaries are useful because they gather a lot of different kinds of information about a particular verse or passage in the Bible into a single location. Some are very brief and selective and may strongly press one view. Others may be huge and exhaustive and it may be difficult to discern what the author's own opinion is. It is important to use a number of commentaries representing a variety of theological positions and always to use every commentary critically. I have indicated which series are entirely evangelical in their stance (E). Of course, the term 'evangelical' will be understood in different ways by different people and a variety of perspectives will be found in many of these series. Many of the series I have not marked as entirely evangelical, nonetheless contain individual volumes written by evangelicals.

---

71. G. Kittel and G. Friedrich (eds.), 10 vols. (Grand Rapids: Eerdmans, 1964–76).
72. H. Balz and G. Schneider (eds.), 3 vols. (Grand Rapids: Eerdmans, 1990–93).
73. C. Brown (ed.), 4 vols. (Exeter: Paternoster, 1975–78).

*Anchor Bible (AB)*. Technical. Recent volumes have been of particularly high quality.

*Baker Exegetical Commentary on the New Testament (BECNT)* – (E). Some excellent volumes have appeared in this new series.

*Bible Speaks Today (BST)* – (E). Written for a popular readership and fairly brief, but based on solid scholarship.

*Black's (or Harper) New Testament Commentary (BNTC/ HNTC)*. Many useful volumes by top scholars. Serious but readable.

*Cambridge Greek Testament Commentary (CGTC)*. Older series. Not too technical, but based on the Greek text.

*Expositor's Bible Commentary (EBC)* – (E). Some excellent volumes, often bound in a single volume with more average works.

*Eerdmans Critical Commentaries (ECC)*. Very technical.

*International Critical Commentary (ICC)*. An old series, revived recently with several superb but technical studies.

*Interpretation (Int)*. Several excellent volumes (notably Hays on 1 Corinthians) with a view to application.

*New American Commentary (NAC)* – (E). Conservative and scholarly. Several excellent contributions.

*New Century Bible (NCB)*. Concise, useful exegesis. Some classic volumes.

*New International Biblical Commentary (NIBC)*. Recent series. Divided into accessible exposition followed by more detailed notes.

*New International Commentary on the New Testament (NICNT)* – (E). An outstanding series, particularly some of the more recent volumes.

*New International Greek Testament Commentary (NIGTC)* – (E). Essential reading for the reader with Greek. Some recent volumes are huge!

*New Testament Commentary (NTC)* – (E). Readable exegesis by competent scholars.

*NIV Application Commentary (NIVAC)* – (E). Brief but solid exegesis with contemporary application.

*Pillar New Testament Commentary (PNTC)* – (E). Substantial exegetical works with theological sensitivity.

*Tyndale New Testament Commentary (TNTC)* – (E). Concise exegesis. Some notable contributions.

*Word Biblical Commentary (WBC)*. Detailed technical studies reflecting a very diverse range of critical perspectives.

You might, for example, use a number of commentaries in order to help you to see how Galatians 1:1–10 fits into the structure of the letter as a whole, what unusual features are found here and what purpose Paul intends to accomplish by his words.

### Monographs

This is simply a way of describing book-length studies on a particular topic. It often requires a little more work to locate relevant studies, but a look through the footnotes relating to the text in substantial modern commentaries should enable the student to find one or two important books. Many monographs are published as part of academic series, often related to academic societies or journals. With respect to our test case of Galatians 1:1–10, is there perhaps a book on the theme of 'gospel' in Paul that you might use? Or perhaps you might find a study of apostleship, or of Paul's opponents.

### Journal articles

Students may be hesitant to delve into journals because some are highly technical and rather forbidding. However, it is well worth searching out a few articles from journals for several reasons. First, articles are often more up to date than books because the time between completion of writing and publication is usually shorter. Second, journal articles are often more narrowly focused than other kinds of writing, and one may find more detail on one's topic. Third, the student is able to demonstrate the professional skill of knowing where to look for information.

Here are just a few of the many significant journals of which the student should be aware:

*Themelios.* An evangelical theological journal aimed particularly at undergraduate students. Includes a substantial number of book reviews.

*Bulletin for Biblical Research (BBR).* A broadly evangelical journal covering both OT and NT studies and containing mainly technical articles. A few substantial book reviews are included.

*Journal for the Study of the New Testament (JSNT).* An important refereed journal of NT studies, which includes articles for a diverse

range of perspectives at a demanding level, including a significant number by evangelical scholars. A few brief book notes are
usually included.

*New Testament Studies (NTS)*. Major journal for technical NT studies.
Articles may be published in English, French or German.
Generally, not for the beginner but a resource to keep in mind.

*Tyndale Bulletin (TynBul)*. An important academic journal produced
by Tyndale House, Cambridge, covering the whole range of
theological topics but with a particular emphasis on biblical
studies articles.

Back issues of many evangelical journals (including *Westminster
Theological Journal* and *Trinity Journal*) are now available on CD-
ROM from Galaxie Software (www.galaxie.com).

If representatives from a variety of theological positions of all
the classes of resources above are gathered and used carefully,
your bibliography will be powerful.

*Buying books and journals*

Every student of the NT should begin to build up a library of
resources that will enable him or her to interpret the NT in future
life and ministry. While a theological library should provide many
resources during the period of an academic course, the wise
student will recognize that the course will soon come to an end
and that a personal library should be developed in the meantime, if
at all possible.

Many books and magazines will compete for finite resources, so
you will do well to think carefully before spending money on books.
It is well worth browsing Internet-based booksellers and second-
hand book catalogues for discounted books rather than always
paying full price for new copies. Aim to purchase books stra-
tegically. Draw up a list of those books you regard to be most
important to purchase, and don't be easily distracted from that list
into less important buys that eat into limited financial resources.
Remember, the fundamental rule is, 'Try before you buy.' This is
best done by using a book in a library or borrowing a copy from
someone before spending your own money on a copy. However,
when this is not possible, take careful note of the advice of others

who have 'tried' the book for you and have written reviews in journals and magazines. One particularly helpful source of recent reviews (and a useful bibliography of NT books and commentaries) is the online *Denver Journal*, which can be found at the website of Denver Seminary.

Students who seek up-to-date bibliographical information are strongly advised to purchase two volumes:

D. A. Carson, *New Testament Commentary Survey* (5th edn.; Leicester: IVP, 2001)

G. D. Fee, *New Testament Exegesis* (3rd edn.; Westminster/John Knox Press, 2002)

### The Internet

The Internet or World Wide Web (www) has opened up easy access to a huge volume of information. Unfortunately, since there is no regulation of what is placed on the Internet, you must be extremely careful about what you use in your studies. Some sites will present material with no academic credibility and use of such material in an essay will only harm your grade. Sites related to an academic institution will usually have some measure of credibility, but even this cannot be taken for granted. As a rule of thumb, you will be wise never to include information found only on a single Internet site. If, however, the same view is presented in reputable publications, then by all means make reference to the website as well. Perhaps the greatest benefit the Internet offers to you as a student of the NT is the access it provides to ancient primary sources that would otherwise be available only in specialist libraries.

There is now an accepted method of citation of web addresses. See *The SBL Handbook of Style* ed. Patrick H. Alexander et al. (Peabody: Hendrickson, 1999).

### Gateways

These sites do not attempt to present the information you require. Instead, they provide a convenient reference point where you may find links to numerous other sites.

Of particular importance with respect to the NT is www.ntgateway.com.

Two sites of particular importance to biblical studies in general are www.tyndale.ca.ac.uk and http://www.torreys.org/bible/

Numerous sites provide access to non-canonical texts such as the 'Pseudepigrapha' (OT and NT) and images and selected translations of the Dead Sea Scrolls. These can all be found at one of the sites listed above.

It is vital that you provide proper references for any material you use from an Internet site, since use of unacknowledged material is an act of plagiarism.


## Conclusion

Serious study of the NT should be rewarding and even enjoyable (although don't believe anyone who tells you it will be easy). There are endless opportunities to learn fascinating new things about language, history and cultures distant from our own in numerous ways. If you approach your studies with anticipation and enthusiasm, you will experience a rich and stimulating intellectual journey. In the midst of wrestling with all kinds of 'criticisms' and ancient documents, however, take time to remember that your primary responsibility is to read and interpret the texts of the NT carefully in order not simply to hear accurately the voices of a past age (although that is important in itself) but to hear the voice of the living God, to live the life that the texts bring and to share these life-giving words with others. May the Father give us his Spirit, who will lead us into all truth concerning Father, Son and Holy Spirit as found in the NT, and indeed the whole Bible.

© Alistair I. Wilson, 2003.

## 3. ENCOUNTERING BIBLICAL INTERPRETATION

**Antony Billington**

*Antony Billington has taught Hermeneutics at London Bible College since 1991. For five years he was also Director of Distance Learning at the college, before beginning part-time PhD research in the theological significance of biblical narrative.*

This chapter is to the discipline of biblical interpretation what *The Rough Guide to Egypt* is to Egypt.[1] It aims to provide a brief overview of a huge area, rich in history, diverse in shape, and richly rewarding for those who have the opportunity to visit it. A map may not be the territory, but it's a crucial thing to have when exploring an unknown landscape. This chapter, like the others in the volume, offers a plan and a guide, to provide an indication of the shape of the landscape, so that those who want to do so can explore more fully at a slower pace afterwards. The footnotes aim to provide what amounts to a selective but representative collection of resources which show that there's no

---

1. The substance of the material in this chapter has developed over the last twelve years, teaching groups in churches, Christian organizations, conferences, and yearly cohorts of undergraduate students at London Bible College. I am grateful for the interaction on all such occasions, which has served to shape these ongoing reflections.

shortage of material for any who want to investigate this topic in
further detail.[2]


## Orientation: getting our bearings

'What?!' At least, that's how most normal people respond when
they ask what subject I teach, and I reply, 'Hermeneutics.' So, we'll
need to begin by answering the question *What is hermeneutics?* If the
conversation hasn't drawn to a close with the mere mention of the
word, a second question regularly comes on the heels of the first –
*Why is it important?* After this, the rare, still-interested person might
wonder what such a discipline involves, which leads to a third
question – *Where is its focus of interest?* These three questions and
the answers to them form the framework for this section of orientation.

### What is biblical hermeneutics?
The term 'hermeneutics' is sometimes said to find its origin in the
name *Hermes*, who was the messenger for the gods, transmitting and
interpreting their messages. At its most basic level, then, 'hermeneutics' has to do with *interpretation*; and so 'biblical hermeneutics' refers
specifically to the interpretation of the *Bible*. That brief explanation
does for many; but (as anyone who has hung around with theologians long enough will know) the answer to the question is
inevitably more involved than a shorthand definition suggests, and
can be explored from different angles.

---

2. I have resisted the urge to include references to websites, even though
   there is plenty of fine material available on the Internet and even though
   its importance as a resource is increasing exponentially. However, the
   printed and bound page on a library shelf is still more stable than a web-
   page address. Still, those who take the time, conduct careful searches, and
   are prepared to wade through the rough with the smooth, will find many
   valuable resources online.

## a. Prescriptive and descriptive approaches

Hermeneutics can be defined as a study of the *principles* of interpretation. This emphasizes what we might think of as the *prescriptive* aspect of hermeneutics: it *prescribes* that we do certain things in order to understand a text. In fact, this has been the classic approach to hermeneutics – to develop rules for interpreting the text.[3] It seeks to deal both with the issue of what the text *meant* in the past in its original setting (sometimes we give the designation 'exegesis' to this task) *and* the question of what the text *means* now to the contemporary reader (we sometimes call this 'application').[4] In line with this, Grant Osborne, uses 'hermeneutics' as the overall term, and 'exegesis' and 'contextualization' ('the cross-cultural communication of a text's significance for today') as the two aspects of that larger task.[5] As such, while the term

3. Walter C. Kaiser, Jr and Moisés Silva, *An Introduction to Biblical Hermeneutics: The Search for Meaning* (Grand Rapids: Zondervan, 1994), p. 15; William W. Klein, Craig L. Blomberg and Robert L. Hubbard, Jr, *Introduction to Biblical Interpretation* (Dallas: Word, 1993), p. 4; Robert H. Stein, *Playing by the Rules: A Basic Guide to Interpreting the Bible* (Grand Rapids: Baker, 1994), p. 17; W. Randolph Tate, *Biblical Interpretation: An Integrated Approach* (2nd edn.; Peabody: Hendrickson, 1997), p. ix.

4. Note, e.g., the subtitles of the following books: Ron Julian, J. A. Crabtree and David Crabtree, *The Language of God: A Commonsense Approach to Understanding and Applying the Bible* (Colorado Springs: NavPress, 2001); J. Scott Duvall and J. Daniel Hays, *Grasping God's Word: A Hands-on Approach to Reading, Interpreting, and Applying the Bible* (Grand Rapids: Zondervan, 2001); Dan McCartney and Charles Clayton, *Let the Reader Understand: A Guide to Interpreting and Applying the Bible* (2nd edn.; Phillipsburg: Presbyterian & Reformed, 2002).

5. Grant R. Osborne, *The Hermeneutical Spiral: A Comprehensive Guide to Biblical Interpretation* (Downers Grove: IVP, 1991), p. 5. Gordon D. Fee and Douglas Stuart, *How to Read the Bible for all its Worth* (2nd edn.; Bletchley: Scripture Union, 1993), p. 25, think of hermeneutics more narrowly as the *application* of the message of the Bible in the contemporary world – what the text means to us now. They do recognize, however, that the term has traditionally covered both the tasks of exegesis *and* application.

'hermeneutics' only really came into vogue in the seventeenth century, the discipline itself – of interpreting and appropriating biblical texts – dates right back to pre-Christian times, through the apostolic age, the patristic period, the medieval church, the Reformation and beyond, down to today.[6]

We need to acknowledge, however, that the relationship between 'exegesis' and 'application' is somewhat problematic. We have regularly worked on the assumption that the tasks can be neatly parcelled out: we do our exegetical work in a detached manner, and then (and only then) do we apply the text in a separate operation. In fact, however, most of the time it's inevitably more messy than that: the tasks are blurred and the boundaries fuzzy; we do our exegesis out of a framework of various convictions and biases; we discover that Scripture addresses us even before we've begun the application stage! Application is neither separate from, nor coterminous with, exegesis; there is a 'permeable barrier' between the two.[7]

Not all are happy with this 'prescriptive' answer, however. They emphasize what we might call the *descriptive* angle of hermeneutics, where we don't *prescribe* rules for understanding, but *describe* how understanding is possible. Hermeneutics is here concerned with the theory of understanding itself. Putting it somewhat simplistically, if the first definition refers to the *practice* of interpretation, this second definition refers to the *theory* that comes to realization in the practice of interpretation. It's the definition preferred by Anthony Thiselton:

---

6. Many of the standard textbooks devote a chapter to the history of biblical interpretation: e.g. Klein, Blomberg and Hubbard, *Biblical Interpretation*, pp. 21–51. For a fuller treatment, see Gerald Bray, *Biblical Interpretation: Past and Present* (Leicester: Apollos, 1996).

7. Daniel M. Doriani, *Putting the Truth to Work: The Theory and Practice of Biblical Application* (Phillipsburg: Presbyterian & Reformed, 2001), pp. 18–27.

It remains helpful to distinguish hermeneutics as critical and theoretical reflection on these processes [of understanding] from the actual work of interpreting and understanding as a first-order activity.[8]

Indeed, it's important to note that the study of biblical interpretation necessarily takes place in a context of philosophical understanding.[9] We need not be suspicious of this, or defensive about it. Thiselton's major works on hermeneutics have taken philosophy seriously, with the firm conviction that philosophical hermeneutics enables the biblical texts to speak more clearly.[10] In

---

8. Anthony C. Thiselton, 'Biblical Studies and Theoretical Hermeneutics', in John Barton (ed.), *The Cambridge Companion to Biblical Interpretation* (Cambridge Companions to Religion; Cambridge: Cambridge University Press, 1998), pp. 95–113; here p. 95.

9. In addition to Thiselton's essay (previous note), see the following helpful summaries: Craig Bartholomew, *Reading Ecclesiastes: Old Testament Exegesis and Hermeneutical Theory* (Analecta Biblica 139; Rome: Pontifical Biblical Institute, 1998), pp. 5–29; David E. Klemm, 'Hermeneutics', in John H. Hayes (ed.), *Dictionary of Biblical Interpretation* (Nashville: Abingdon, 1999), vol. 1, pp. 497–502; Dan R. Stiver, *The Philosophy of Religious Language: Sign, Symbol and Story* (Oxford: Blackwell, 1996), pp. 87–111.

10. His two major textbooks are *The Two Horizons: New Testament Hermeneutics and Philosophical Description with Special Reference to Heidegger, Bultmann, Gadamer and Wittgenstein* (Exeter: Paternoster, 1980); and *New Horizons in Hermeneutics: The Theory and Practice of Transforming Biblical Reading* (London: HarperCollins, 1992). He has helpfully summarized some of the contours of his work in several places, notably: 'The Use of Philosophical Categories in New Testament Hermeneutics', *Churchman* 87.2 (1973), pp. 87–100; and 'Address and Understanding: Some Goals and Models of Biblical Interpretation as Principles of Vocational Training', *Anvil* 3.2 (1986), pp. 101–118. An excellent example of how the philsophical issues can help deal with a contentious issue (homosexuality, in this case) in biblical interpretation is his 'Can Hermeneutics Ease the Deadlock? Some Biblical Exegesis and Hermeneutical Models', in Timothy Bradshaw (ed.), *The Way Forward? Christian Voices on Homosexuality and the Church* (London: Hodder & Stoughton, 1997), pp. 145–196.

the lead essay of the first volume of a series devoted to Scripture and hermeneutics, Craig Bartholomew shows the necessity of wrestling with philosophical issues in biblical interpretation from a Christian perspective.[11]

One such area requiring engagement is postmodernism.[12] Underlying the diverse forms of postmodernism, as the designation suggests, is a move beyond modernism, particularly when it comes to the debated area of how we know things. Reason was the guiding principle of the period of the Enlightenment, or modernity, with its view of objective knowledge, its quest for certainty in building on secure foundations, and its confidence in science to supply truth about the world to the autonomous knower. Postmodern thinkers have called into question the possibility of the power of human reason to provide a universal point of view. No world view can claim the status of 'grand story' in a world of fragmentation, diversity and ambiguity. There are no foundational truths by which realities can be known; knowledge is rooted in one's situation and presuppositions; thinking takes place within particular frameworks – which leads to the view that something might be 'true' within the framework, but not absolutely true. The intellectual climate of postmodernism has given birth to diverse approaches to biblical interpretation, some of which we'll consider in the sections that follow.

In summary, depending on how it's defined, hermeneutics can be either prescriptive – *what* we should do in order to understand a

---

11. Craig Bartholomew, 'Uncharted Waters: Philosophy, Theology and the Crisis in Biblical Interpretation', in Craig Bartholomew, Colin Greene and Karl Möller (eds.), *Renewing Biblical Interpretation* (The Scripture and Hermeneutics Series Vol. 1; Carlisle: Paternoster, 2000), pp. 1–39. In keeping with philosophical concerns, the second volume in the series is devoted to language: Craig Bartholomew, Colin Greene and Karl Möller (eds.), *After Pentecost: Language and Biblical Interpretation* (The Scripture and Hermeneutics Series Vol. 2; Carlisle: Paternoster, 2001).

12. For a recent survey from a Christian perspective, see Millard J. Erickson, *Truth or Consequences: The Promise and Perils of Postmodernism* (Downers Grove: IVP, 2001).

text, or descriptive – *how* understanding is possible. Carl E. Braaten manages to capture both senses as he writes:

> Traditionally, hermeneutics dealt with the rules to be observed in Biblical exegesis [our 'prescriptive' angle]. Today it enjoys a wider reference. Hermeneutics is a fundamental inquiry into the conditions which must obtain in the understanding of history and historical documents [our 'descriptive' angle]. Thus, it embraces both the methodological rules to be applied in exegesis as well as the epistemological presuppositions of historical understanding.[13]

Purists might insist that we reserve the term 'hermeneutics' for the descriptive task, and use 'biblical interpretation' for the prescriptive task. It's important to be aware of the difference in opinion even if, in the final analysis, we find it difficult to maintain a clear distinction between the two aspects. In fact, much of what we consider in this chapter is necessarily more inclusive than either one definition on its own suggests.

### b. General and special hermeneutics

A distinction can also be made between *general* hermeneutics and *special* hermeneutics. What is meant by *general* hermeneutics is reflection on principles of interpretation more *generally*. What is involved in reading *any* text? Even the most ardent fundamentalist who would otherwise refuse to contaminate Scripture by getting involved in the 'shady' business of hermeneutics has to use general principles to read Scripture – getting the book the right way up and moving from left to right across the page (if reading English) for starters! Even the ability to read is itself a crucial and overlooked part of this 'general' understanding brought to Scripture. The moment I open and read my copy of the NIV (or RSV, or NRSV, or GNB), I am already dependent on literally thousands of hours others have spent poring over ancient texts, and using 'normal' methods of research and translation, in order to bring me the

---

13. Carl E. Braaten, *History and Hermeneutics* (New Directions in Theology Today Vol. 2; London: Lutterworth, 1968), p. 131.

version of the Bible from which I happen to be reading.

However – and here's the other side of the coin – we are not reading any *general* text; we are reading the *biblical* text. In which case, we may need to appeal not just to general principles for understanding, but ask whether there are some *special* principles to apply. With regard to the Bible, there are a number of factors we could consider. Scripture is a *canon*, a collection of authoritative documents, which requires that each part be read in the light of the whole. There is the notion of *tradition* to consider – those who have gone before us who have themselves been formed and informed by Scripture. Then there is the current believing *community* or *church* to which we belong, which also shapes our understanding in certain ways. There is also our *experience* of God's grace and rebuke in our lives. Not to mention the *Holy Spirit*, or the fact that we are handling the *Word of God*, through which, we believe, *God* himself addresses us. All these 'special' features need to be considered in our reading of Scripture.[14]

Of course, for much of the last two thousand years, this is exactly what most Christians have said. It's only during the last three hundred years or so, aided and abetted by Enlightenment thinking, that scholars have been told to set aside their presuppositions and read the Bible 'like any other book' (although whether anyone could ever really do that, of course, is open to debate). In recent years, however, an increasing number of scholars have called for a special, *theological* hermeneutics, where reflection on biblical interpretation is informed by *theological* considerations, and asks what the aims of a specific *Christian* use of it might be.[15] One of the most prominent voices, Francis Watson, writes:

---

14. Many of these features are addressed in Joel B. Green and Max Turner (eds.), *Between Two Horizons: Spanning New Testament Studies and Systematic Theology* (Grand Rapids: Eerdmans, 2000).

15. Cf. Stephen E. Fowl, 'Introduction', in Stephen E. Fowl (ed.), *The Theological Interpretation of Scripture: Classic and Contemporary Readings* (Blackwell Readings in Modern Theology; Oxford: Blackwell, 1997), pp. xii–xxx: 'In brief, I take the theological interpretation of Scripture to be that practice whereby theological concerns and interests inform and are informed by a reading of Scripture' (p. xii).

The text in question is the biblical text; for the goal is a theological hermeneutic within which an exegesis oriented primarily towards theological issues can come into being. This is therefore not an exercise in general hermeneutics.[16]

Theological hermeneutics enables us to maintain a commitment to the authority of Scripture without that commitment being tied too tightly to the agenda of Enlightenment reasoning; and it places Scripture in the church as the primary context for interpretation and formation, seeking to do justice to the role of worship, tradition and the Spirit. It also means that biblical texts can be interpreted in the light of their subject matter, Jesus, which in turn leads to exciting proposals about breaking down the traditional boundaries (also largely established during the Enlightenment) between Old Testament and New Testament studies, and between biblical studies and systematic theology.[17]

Debate continues, however, as to how much weight should be given to tradition, to the community, to the Spirit in interpretation. Moreover, it may be a mistake to set the general and the special in complete opposition to each other. We may consider it vital to seek a distinctly theological hermeneutics, but the theological questions can themselves be pursued within the context of general hermeneutical reflection. Kevin Vanhoozer's work has been important here.[18] Vanhoozer argues that *all* hermeneutics is theological, that

16. Francis Watson, *Text, Church, and World: Biblical Interpretation in Theological Perspective* (Edinburgh: T. &T. Clark, 1994), p. 1. Watson has continued his project in *Text and Truth: Redefining Biblical Theology* (Edinburgh: T. & T. Clark, 1997). For a briefer way into his concerns, see 'The Scope of Hermeneutics', in Colin E. Gunton (ed.), *The Cambridge Companion to Christian Doctrine* (Cambridge Companions to Religion; Cambridge: Cambridge University Press, 1997), pp. 65–80.

17. Green and Turner, *Between Two Horizons*; Watson, *Text and Truth*.

18. Kevin J. Vanhoozer, *Is There a Meaning in this Text? The Bible, the Reader, and the Morality of Literary Knowledge* (Leicester: Apollos, 1998). For an overview, see 'Language, Literature, Hermeneutics and Biblical Theology: What's Theological About a Theological Dictionary?' in Willem A.

our ability to understand *any text* – not just the biblical text – is
ultimately dependent on God. His exploration of 'meaning' begins
with the triune God, with the creation of human beings in his
image, and with language as his gift for communion in covenant
relationship. As he says in one of his essays:

> *All hermeneutics, not simply the special hermeneutics of Scripture, is 'theological'* . . .
> I stake my claim that the Bible should be read like any other book, and
> that every other book should be read like the Bible, from within a
> Christian worldview.[19]

Vanhoozer leans on the Jewish philosopher George Steiner, who
argues that *any* work of art, *any* work of literature, *any* claim 'of the
capacity of human speech to communicate meaning and feeling is,
in the final analysis, underwritten by the assumption of God's
presence'.[20] So, my ability to read the newspaper, to reply to emails,
to enjoy jokes, to engage with the material that informs this essay,
to communicate *anything at all*, is ultimately dependent on the one
who has created me with that capacity, who is himself the supreme
speaker.

If this is the case, our wrestling with the meaning of words,
with literary context, with historical background – with everything
that involves looking at biblical texts as communicative acts – is
not dishonouring to God. On the contrary, it is precisely as we do
those things that we honour the manner in which God has chosen

---

VanGemeren (ed.), *New International Dictionary of Old Testament Theology and Exegesis* (Carlisle: Paternoster, 1996), vol. 1, pp. 15–50.

19. Kevin J. Vanhoozer, 'The Spirit of Understanding: Special Revelation and
    General Hermeneutics', in Roger Lundin (ed.), *Disciplining Hermeneutics:
    Interpretation in Christian Perspective* (Leicester: Apollos, 1997), pp. 131–165,
    here pp. 160, 132; his italics; cf. Vanhoozer, *Meaning*, pp. 378–381, 407, 414.
    A number of Vanhoozer's essays, including the one cited here, are now
    conveniently gathered together in Kevin J. Vanhoozer, *First Theology: God,
    Scripture and Hermeneutics* (Leicester: Apollos, 2002).
20. George Steiner, *Real Presences: Is There Anything In What We Say?* (London:
    Faber & Faber, 1989), p. 3.

to speak to us, and the means by which we are to seek to under-stand his Word properly. In short, special hermeneutics goes hand in hand with the general – precisely for theological reasons.

### Why is it important?

The importance of hermeneutics is illustrated every time we read Scripture and seek to appropriate it for today. This is especially foregrounded in difficult passages where stakes are high, such as texts on the relationship between men and women in the church and home, or on sexuality. But even if we take a fairly innocuous passage – John 2 for example – we have to face some questions. Do we simply say that the story of Jesus turning water into wine at a wedding (2:1–11) teaches us that marriage is a good thing? Or, more specifically, that when *Jesus* is invited into a marriage, good things happen? (Many a wedding sermon has been built around exactly this notion!) What do we learn from the second part of the chapter, where Jesus clears the temple (2:12–25)? Do we *literalize* it, and conclude that we should go into the nearest cathedral and overturn the postcard stands and the bookmark racks? Or do we *internalize* it, and say that when Jesus comes into our hearts, which are his 'temples', he cleans all the muck out? Or, do we cut a middle, moralizing path and conclude simply that there's a right and a wrong place for righteous anger?

The issue is not whether we can do without hermeneutics, but that we *have* to have hermeneutics: will it be good or bad, faithful or unfaithul? Whenever we ask questions about moving from the 'there and then' of the biblical text to the 'here and now' of the contemporary world, we are necessarily doing hermeneutics. This means that it is not a rarefied academic discipline to be left behind in a course on theology or a book on biblical studies, but that it's part and parcel of faithful discipleship and church life.

### Where is its focus of interest?

This question is most helpfully tackled by looking at several three-fold cords. The danger in each case is to focus on one aspect of the trio to the exclusion of the other two; the plea in each case is to do justice to the three factors together in an integrated manner.

## a. Author – text – reader

Interpretation requires us to keep several items in view: a text, an author and a reader. Interpreting the Bible can be seen as a conversation between the *text* and its *author*, on the one side, and the *reader* on the other. As with any dialogue, it needs to be understood *as a whole*; ignoring the role of any of the elements risks misunderstanding. Responsible hemeneutics, then, will focus on a cluster of issues surrounding the author, the text and the reader, and it will do so in a way that does justice to *all three* factors together. Meaning depends on what the author intended, what the words and sentences in the text say, and what the reader understands as he or she reads, reflects and responds.

The literary relationship between author, text and reader dominates Vanhoozer's discussion in *Is There a Meaning in This Text?*[21] Vanhoozer documents how each of these factors has been 'undone', especially in postmodern philosophy and literary theory – which doubts that there is 'meaning' in a text, and focuses much more on how readers themselves provide 'meaning' as they read. Part I ('Undoing Interpretation') of the book thus sets up the discussion, to which Part II ('Redoing Interpretation') replies.[22] He challenges the largely current consensus that meaning is relative to the encounter of text and reader, and seeks to 'redo' interpretation. The *author*, he argues, is a communicative agent, and to describe meaning is to describe the author's intended action. *Texts* are complex literary acts, which embody intention, and need to be understood at the levels of words, genre and, ultimately, the entire canon of Scripture. In reading, *readers* are called not to play or create, but to encounter an 'other' that calls us to respond and 'follow' the text.

We will revisit these areas in turn in the sections that follow. Before we do so, however, it will be worth looking at related ways of thinking about the focus of biblical hermeneutics.

---

21. Cf. also Tremper Longman III, *Literary Approaches to Biblical Interpretation* (Foundations of Contemporary Biblical Interpretation Vol. 3; Leicester: Apollos, 1987), pp. 19–45, reprinted in Moisés Silva (ed.), *Foundations of Contemporary Interpretation* (Leicester: Apollos, 1996), pp. 106–123.
22. Vanhoozer, *Meaning*, pp. 37–195 and 197–452 respectively.

*b. Behind the text – in the text – in front of the text*
These are terms that have come into use to distinguish different ways of thinking about texts.[23] First of all, the text can be treated as a *window* through which we look at what lies 'behind' it – at the author who wrote it and the situation from which and for which it was composed. Second, our attention may shift to consider the things 'in the text' itself: its genre, its structure, its themes. The text is now not so much a window we look *through*, as a *picture* or a *stained-glass window* we look *at*, which we study as a work in its own right. Third, we may then think of ourselves as readers who are 'in front of' the text. Here the text is treated more like a *mirror*, and we focus on the various factors that go into the reading process, the interaction between me and the text.

Some approaches to biblical interpretation can be distinguished in terms of how they emphasize one aspect of the interpretive process by a focus on 'behind the text' issues (say) to the exclusion of all else, or an emphasis on the world 'in front of the text' to the detriment of the other 'worlds'. Once again, however, study of one area does not necessarily exclude the others, as Tate has tried to show, proposing that study of the three 'worlds' offers the possibility of an 'integrated' hermeneutics.[24]

*c. History – literature – theology*
This is another triad used in reflections on biblical interpretation.[25] Used together, the categories recognize that what we have in John's Gospel (say) is truth in three dimensions. John is *history*, and the accounts recorded in his Gospel are based on historical occurrences, but he does not merely record bare historical facts. As a

---

23. This schema provides the main structure of Sandra M. Schneiders, *The Revelatory Text: Interpreting the New Testament as Sacred Scripture* (San Francisco: HarperCollins, 1991); and Tate, *Biblical Interpretation*.

24. Tate, *Biblical Interpretation*, pp. xxiv–xxvi, 234–252.

25. Craig Bartholomew, 'Introduction', in Bartholomew, Greene and Möller, *Renewing Biblical Interpretation*, pp. xxiii–xxxi; William R. Telford, 'Modern Biblical Interpretation', in John Barton (ed.), *The Biblical World* (London: Routledge, 2002), vol. 2, pp. 427–449.

piece of narrative *literature*, John tells a *story*, and his Gospel contains *stories*, but it does not offer us mere stories unrooted in space-time history. John's Gospel is *theological*, but is not simply a collection of timeless propositions of theological truth. Nor is the theology to be boiled off the narrative such that the latter can be discarded when the 'truths' have been caught for analysis in the theological test tube. Rather, John's *story* of Jesus is integral to his *theology* of Jesus. Once again, we can run the risk of subsuming one or two aspects of this triad under the others. We will do well to follow the suggestions offered by Tom Wright, among others, whose work seeks to integrate historical reconstruction, literary criticism, and theology.[26]

Now that we have some bearings on the map of biblical interpretation, the next three sections explore more fully the particular territories of author, text and reader.

## Unlocking the intention of the author

One of the most important ongoing debates in hermeneutics is whether it is possible to say what constitutes *the* valid meaning of a text, or whether there are *multiple* valid meanings. If only one meaning is valid, what criteria do we use to discover that meaning? One way of answering the question is to emphasize the intention of the author. We miss the importance of this when we're less concerned with what the author meant by the text, and more concerned with *what the text means to me*, an interpretive indulgence perhaps especially associated with group Bible studies. One way of counteracting this danger is to make the author's intention our first port of call. It means that when John tells us why he wrote his Gospel (in 20:30–31), we should give his statement serious attention: he writes self-consciously as an author

---

26. N. T. Wright, *The New Testament and the People of God.* Vol. 1:
    *Christian Origins and the Question of God* (London: SPCK, 1992),
    pp. 3–144.

with an intended purpose, who has used the wealth of material available to him towards a specific end, so that readers might see Jesus and believe.

E. D. Hirsch, Jr, is probably the best known in the field of literary theory for emphasizing the importance of the author. For Hirsch, the meaning of a text is to be identified with the author's intended purpose: 'A text means what its author meant.'[27] If we don't focus on the author, says Hirsch, we run the risk of relativizing interpretation, of rejecting 'the only compelling normative principle that could lend validity to an interpretation'.[28] Hirsch is dealing with literary theory in general, but his work has been adopted by many evangelical biblical scholars. A strong defence of identifying the meaning of a text with the author's intention is associated with Walter Kaiser.[29] More recently, Grant Osborne also builds on Hirsch, which shows how much a core principle this is for evangelical interpreters.[30]

Even so, we need to recognize that the notion of authorial intention has been called into question by many, although rumours of the author's demise have been greatly exaggerated, and a significant number of literary theorists and philosophers have clung to

---

27. E. D. Hirsch, Jr, *Validity in Interpretation* (New Haven: Yale University Press, 1967), p. 1.
28. Ibid., p. 5.
29. Walter C. Kaiser, Jr, *Toward an Exegetical Theology: Biblical Exegesis for Preaching and Teaching* (Grand Rapids: Baker, 1981); Kaiser and Silva, *Biblical Hermeneutics*, pp. 27–45.
30. Osborne, *Hermeneutical Spiral*, pp. 6–7, 393–395. See also Scott A. Blue, 'The Hermeneutic of E. D. Hirsch, Jr and its Impact on Expository Preaching: Friend or Foe?' *Journal of the Evangelical Theological Society* 44.2 (2001), pp. 253–269; Duvall and Hays, *Grasping God's Word*, pp. 167–174; Julian, Crabtree and Crabtree, *Language of God*, pp. 35–63; Klein, Blomberg and Hubbard, *Biblical Interpretation*, pp. 117–151; McCartney and Clayton, *Let the Reader Understand*, pp. 291–301; Stein, *Playing by the Rules*, pp. 17–36; and 'The Benefits of an Author-Oriented Approach to Hermeneutics', *Journal of the Evangelical Theological Society* 44.3 (2001), pp. 451–466.

the notion of intention (albeit with some qualifications).[31] The issue is debated even among those biblical interpreters who basically agree on assigning primary significance to the author, and not least where particular issues with biblical texts require further elucidation (such as the dual authorship of Scripture).[32] It's my intention (note that!) to map out in brief scope some of the discussions surrounding the debate about authorial intention – the qualifications to it and some of the implications of it for biblical interpretation – in the paragraphs that now follow.

***The intention of the author as basic to everyday communication***
We ordinarily work by attributing intentions to people, whether in everyday interactions or in written documents, ranging from milk bills to last wills.[33] We recognize satire, sarcasm and irony. We complain (or fume) when something someone says offends us. We correct or qualify ourselves when we feel someone has misunderstood us. Even artists refute interpretations sometimes offered of their work, and are concerned to have their communicative intentions acknowledged. The convention of footnotes in a piece such as this, attributing views to certain scholars, is another indication of the value implicitly attached to authors. Of course, communi-

---

31. For the 'undoing' of the author and 'resurrecting the author' in contemporary critical theory, see Vanhoozer, *Meaning*, pp. 43–97 and 201–280.
32. It's become common to note some gaps in Hirsch's view even while being sympathetic to his basic stance: e.g. Peter Cotterell and Max Turner, *Linguistics and Biblical Interpretation* (London: SPCK, 1989), pp. 37–76; Millard J. Erickson, *Evangelical Interpretation: Perspectives on Hermeneutical Issues* (Grand Rapids: Baker, 1993), pp. 11–32; V. George Shillington, *Reading the Sacred Text: An Introduction to Biblical Studies* (Edinburgh: T. & T. Clark, 2002), pp. 45–61; Vanhoozer, *Meaning*, pp. 74–85, 259–263; Timothy Ward, *Word and Supplement: Speech Acts, Biblical Texts, and the Sufficiency of Scripture* (Oxford: Oxford University Press, 2002), pp. 161–168, 204–205.
33. See D. A. Carson, *The Gagging of God: Christianity Confronts Pluralism* (Leicester: Apollos, 1996), pp. 102–105, 'Practical experience with the way people actually communicate confirms that accurate communication is possible.'

cation is not foolproof. We can deliberately manipulate or resist what someone says; we can misunderstand what an author says; or an author may not be particularly competent. Texts can also be multilayered and ambiguous, as any reader of poetry knows. But then, an author can intend a text to be so. None of these cases detracts from the notion of authorial intention; on the contrary, they *assume* it.

### The intention of the author as laid down in the text

Holding to a view of authorial intention is not the same as holding to a view which says that we can get inside the author's head. We rely on the *text* for an understanding of the author's intention.

In the 1940s and 1950s the notion of 'intention' was called into question by the so-called New Critics. Perhaps most famous here is the 1946 essay on 'The Intentional Fallacy' by William Wimsatt and Monroe Beardsley.[34] Essentially, Wimsatt and Beardsley were reacting to the view that placed considerable importance on capturing the mind of the author, perhaps even drawing on what was known about the author's life in order to do so. New Criticism called on interpreters to restrict their analysis to meanings *in the text* rather than on speculations from the author's history and biography. The literary work, once complete, is independent of its author, and is to be studied in its own right. New Critics didn't deny that authors had intentions, but held that we must not confuse that intent with what is actually expressed in the text. This was an important point to note, in so far as critics had spent so much effort discussing the author's background and psychology that they had lost sight of the written text the author had written!

Indeed, in the case of the Bible, we have no access to the author's intentions other than through the text itself. We cannot interview John to ask him why he wrote something in his Gospel; but we can read his Gospel, and establish meaning on the basis of what he has written. Hence, all argument about authorial intention

---

34. William K. Wimsatt, Jr, and Monroe R. Beardsley, 'The Intentional Fallacy', in William K. Wimsatt, Jr, *The Verbal Icon: Studies in the Meaning of Poetry* (New York: Noonday, 1954), pp. 3–18.

needs to be rooted in a careful reading of the text. Along similar lines, Cotterell and Turner use the designation *discourse meaning* to guard themselves 'against the misunderstanding that a text means precisely and only what the author meant', and 'to stave off the view that we really can speak of "text meaning" as though the text were autonomous'.[35]

### *The intention of the author and the significance for the reader*
Despite his emphasis on the author, Hirsch does not ignore the reader. He recognizes that different readers will draw out different implications from a text, and so he makes a distinction between 'meaning' and 'significance', where *meaning* is related to the intention of the author, and *significance* has to do with the relationship between the meaning and the reader's own situation.[36] This has been influential on the way some biblical scholars have formulated the relationship between the interpretation and the application of biblical texts, even if they have tweaked the distinction here and there.

Most of the tweaking involves pointing out what we have noted already: the difficulty of separating meaning (what it meant) from significance (what it means).[37] Robert Stein argues for a 'pattern of meaning', which includes the author's intention as well as *implications* which fall within that pattern. The exhortation not to get drunk with wine (Ephesians 5:18), by implication, presumably, doesn't mean it's OK to get drunk on beer or whiskey.[38] Erickson holds that 'meaning' and 'significance' should be changed to 'signification' and 'significance', which removes the tendency to identify 'meaning' with meaning *then* and 'significance' with meaning *now*, and allows

---

35. Cotterell and Turner, *Linguistics*, p. 69.

36. Hirsch, *Validity*, p. 8.

37. E.g. McCartney and Clayton, *Let the Reader Understand*, pp. 291–293; Vern S. Poythress, *God-Centered Biblical Interpretation* (Phillipsburg: Presbyterian & Reformed, 1999), pp. 69–94. Though cf. Vanhoozer, *Meaning*, p. 260: 'With regard to interpretation, the meaning/significance distinction continues to be both meaningful and highly significant.'

38. Stein, *Playing by the Rules*, pp. 26–29, 39–43; 'Benefits', pp. 458–460.

that the author might have intended *both* meaning and significance. For Erickson, the signification and the later significance are both aspects of the text's meaning.[39]

In a later essay Hirsch himself noted that the distinction between meaning and significance 'requires further elaboration'.[40] There are cases, he notes, where an author intends his utterance to be open-ended; in particular, a future-oriented intention may have an indefinite number of future applications:

> When I apply Shakespeare's sonnet to my own lover rather than to his, I do not change his meaning-intention but rather instantiate and fulfil it. It is the nature of textual meaning to embrace many different future fulfillments without thereby being changes.[41]

So, he qualifies his earlier claim that 'future applications of meaning, each being different, must belong to the domain of significance'. Rather, 'different applications do not necessarily lie outside the boundaries of meaning'. Some applications might belong to a text's 'meaning' rather than its 'significance', then, and 'meaning can tolerate a small revision in mental content and remain the same – but not a big revision'.[42]

### The author's intention as the author's intended action

'I now pronounce you husband and wife,' or 'You're fired,' spoken by an appropriate person in an appropriate context, are not merely

---

39. Erickson, *Evangelical Interpretation*, pp. 11–32.

40. E. D. Hirsch, Jr, 'Meaning and Significance Reinterpreted', *Critical Inquiry* 11.2 (1984), pp. 202–225, here p. 204.

41. Ibid., p. 210.

42. Ibid., pp. 210, 212, 221. Hirsch has further qualified his position in 'Transhistorical Intentions and the Persistence of Allegory', *New Literary History* 25 (1994), pp. 549–567. Here he notes that allegory is able to find meanings 'that neither the original author nor the original audience would have directly construed', and that it is implicit 'in the interpretation of all writings that are intended to apply across time – the kinds of writings, that is, that are found in literature, law, and religion' (p. 552).

making statements about things but *doing* things. That these are
obvious examples of the *performative* nature of language shouldn't
detract from the fact that words also operate like this in everyday
speech. It's normally clear in a given situation whether 'The bowl's
empty' is a *request* ('Please fill the bowl'), a *rebuke* ('I told you there
wouldn't be enough rice for everyone'), or a *question* ('I asked you
to buy some fruit, didn't I?').

Along such lines, an increasing number of scholars in biblical
hermeneutics are drawing on the resources of what philosophers
of language call *speech act theory*, and its basic insight that words and
sentences *do* things. Vanhoozer, for instance, argues that authorial
intention is based on the notion of the author as a communicative
agent. To describe meaning is to describe the author's intended
action, and this is not to be confused with 'what the author
planned to write' or 'unintentionally brings about'.[43] Texts are
*speech acts* performed by authors, communicative actions of communicative agents, and one needs to understand what an author is
*doing* – whether telling a story, making a promise, giving a warning,
or issuing a rebuke. Hence, we are not asking about the author's
motivations, or the results brought about by reading the text; we
are asking, 'What intentional acts has the author performed
through the words of this text?'

Vanhoozer also uses speech act theory to offer an account of
the nature of Scripture as God's communicative act.[44] God is a
communicative agent, and Scripture is his communicative action,
the source of our knowledge of God, the place in which the Son is

---

43. Vanhoozer, *Meaning*, p. 259. Watson, *Text and Truth*, pp. 95–126, also draws
    on speech act theory in his argument that biblical texts have a single 'literal
    sense' which is 'the communicative intention of the author'. See Scott A.
    Blue, 'Meaning, Intention, and Application: Speech Act Theory in the
    Hermeneutics of Francis Watson and Kevin J. Vanhoozer', *Trinity Journal*
    23.2 (2002), pp. 161–184.

44. Vanhoozer, *First Theology*, pp. 127–203. See also Nicholas Wolterstorff,
    *Divine Discourse: Philosophical Reflections on the Claim that God Speaks*
    (Cambridge: Cambridge University Press, 1996); and Ward, *Word and
    Supplement*.

testified to, and the means of God's gift of the Spirit. Scripture is the book of the covenant, the covenant of discourse, which establishes God's relationship with his people, and through which we enjoy communion with him.[45]

### The intention of the author and the inspiration of Scripture

The doctrine of Scripture, as traditionally understood, holds that God is the author of Scripture, but not independently of human involvement. God used the biblical authors such that the result of what they wrote was written in their language, with their vocabulary, in their distinctive style, and reflecting their situations, but which was nothing less than the words of God. Hence, when evangelicals have formulated a doctrine of Scripture, they have done so by confessing some form of *complementary* authorship, stating that God was in some way sovereign over the otherwise very ordinary, very human, and very *intentional* act of authorship.

It should be clear that this view of Scripture means that what John says and means is at the same time what God says and means. *God's* intention is only really accessible *through* John's intention, which is only accessible through the *text*. If we ask what God means, we have to ask what John means, and if we ask what John means, we have to study the text! As Caird notes:

> We have no access to the mind of Jeremiah or Paul except through their recorded words. A fortiori, we have no access to the word of God except through the words and the minds of those who claim to speak in his name . . . if we try, without evidence, to penetrate to a meaning more

---

45. It should be noted that other scholars are less interested in exploring the notion of Scripture as a divine speech act, and more interested in using speech act theory to examine the communicative acts in particular biblical passages. See, e.g., Thiselton, *New Horizons*, pp. 272–312; and Richard S. Briggs, *Words in Action: Speech Act Theory and Biblical Interpretation* (Edinburgh: T. & T. Clark, 2001). For a survey, see Richard S. Briggs, 'The Uses of Speech-Act Theory in Biblical Interpretation', *Currents in Research: Biblical Studies* 9 (2001), pp. 229–276.

ultimate than the one the writers intended, that is our meaning, not theirs or God's.[46]

When we talk about God's word to his people *today*, we have to go back to his word spoken *once and for all* to his people through Ezekiel and John. This is just one of the reasons why we have to be careful of appeals to Spirit-inspired illumination that go against the text. The Spirit's role is not to author a *new* text, but to bring home the meaning of the text he has already authored.[47] We are not required to be dualists in our handling of the Bible, parcelling out our activity of interpretation as a detached, intellectual activity only after which we can expect the Spirit to do his work, either in applying the text or making us receptive to it. Those are doubtless aspects of his role, but he no less works *through* our faithful handling of the text, and not independently of it.[48]

In short, we understand what God says through what his prophets and apostles wrote in Scripture, and, in seeking to understand them, we seek to understand the texts they have written. Moreover, since the Bible is written in words to be understood by men and women, we can use the normal methods of understanding words and texts to read it. (More on this below.)

### The intention of the author and the canon of Scripture

Not satisfied by the argument of the previous section, someone might still push on whether (for instance) some Old Testament prophecies mean more than the prophets themselves envisaged (see 1 Peter 1:10–12). Do New Testament authors use the Old Testament in ways that go beyond the intention of the human author? Are there 'levels' of meaning in Scripture, such that

---

46. George Bradford Caird, *The Language and Imagery of the Bible* (London: Duckworth, 1980), p. 61; cf. Stein, 'Benefits', p. 464.

47. Duvall and Hays, *Grasping God's Word*, p. 197. In addition to their chapter on the role of the Spirit in interpretation (pp. 196–202), see Stein, *Playing by the Rules*, pp. 61–71; and Vanhoozer, *Meaning*, pp. 407–431.

48. Thiselton, *Two Horizons*, pp. 85–92.

God has a fuller or further intention beyond the human author's intention?[49]

We'll look at the debated area of the use of the Old Testament by New Testament writers more fully in the next main section. We may note, meanwhile, that even those who allow for a distinction between God's meaning and the human author's meaning, through an appeal to the wider canon or a 'fuller sense' (*sensus plenior*), still hold that the human author's meaning is to be seen as the *basis* for God's meaning. For Glenny, the divine fuller meaning is known by later revelation where Scripture explicitly interprets earlier passages:

> A later-revealed fuller divine meaning is not a new meaning of a text. It is a legitimate extension of the concept affirmed in the text in its original context, which is a part of the total divine meaning of that text.[50]

God means what he says through the human authors of Psalm 22 (or Isaiah 53 or Ezekiel 40 – 48), but also intends us to read those passages in the light of the canon as a whole. So, with respect to Scripture, the Christian reader must give account of two levels of authorship: the human author and the divine. But these must not be played off against each other. The divine author's meaning is to be perceived (1) through the human author, and (2) in the light of the canon as a whole.

---

49. Treatments of this topic in the general textbooks include Duvall and Hays, *Grasping God's Word*, pp. 175–195; Klein, Blomberg and Hubbard, *Biblical Interpretation*, pp. 119–132; McCartney and Clayton, *Let the Reader Understand*, pp. 159–174; Vanhoozer, *Meaning*, pp. 263–265. See also W. Edward Glenny, 'The Divine Meaning of Scripture: Explanations and Limitations', *Journal of the Evangelical Theological Society* 38.4 (1995), pp. 481–500; Douglas J. Moo, 'The Problem of *Sensus Plenior*', in D. A. Carson and John D. Woodbridge (eds.), *Hermeneutics, Authority and Canon* (Leicester: IVP, 1986), pp. 175–211; Vern Sheridan Poythress, 'Divine Meaning of Scripture', *Westminster Theological Journal* 48.2 (1986), pp. 241–279; Ward, *Word and Supplement*, pp. 253–263.

50. Glenny, 'Divine Meaning', p. 499.

### The intention of the author and historical criticism

The search for the intention of the author has tended to go hand in hand with the set of interpretive methods that have come to be called 'historical criticism'. The historical-critical method rose to prominence in the period of the Enlightenment, although interest in the historical meaning of the text goes back to the Reformation and before. Nevertheless, some forms of historical criticism were so wedded to Enlightenment thinking that they went hand in hand with a rejection of the miraculous, the transcendent, and the authority of Scripture.[51]

It's small wonder, then, that conservative scholars questioned, and continue to question, its value.[52] Even the term 'criticism' carries negative connotations. Criticize Scripture?! In fact, however, 'critical' must be understood in the sense of investigation and careful analysis, and stands in opposition not to faithful reading but to arbitrary, speculative interpretations. Most conservative scholars would thus question some of the underlying ideologies of the historical-critical method, but still recognize that God chose to speak in history, and so take seriously the need to subject the biblical text to careful scrutiny.[53]

In fact, it's now widely recognized that historical criticism was never the neutral enterprise its advocates thought it was. It's been challenged from many sides, and even declared 'bankrupt' by some, who point to its inability to deal with the real issues of people in their daily lives, and bring about transformation.[54]

---

51. The best historical survey is now Roy A. Harrisville and Walter Sundberg, *The Bible in Modern Culture: Baruch Spinoza to Brevard Childs* (2nd edn.; Grand Rapids: Eerdmans, 2002).

52. For a vigorous attack from a former advocate of historical criticism, see Eta Linnemann, *Biblical Criticism on Trial: How Scientific is "Scientific Theology"?* (tr. Robert W. Yarbrough; Grand Rapids: Kregel, 2001).

53. Grant R. Osborne, 'Historical Criticism and the Evangelical', *Journal of the Evangelical Theological Society* 42.2 (1999), pp. 193–210; Gordon J. Wenham, 'The Place of Biblical Criticism in Theological Study', *Themelios* 14.3 (1989), pp. 84–89.

54. Walter Wink, *The Bible in Human Transformation: Toward a New Paradigm for Biblical Study* (Philadelphia: Fortress, 1973).

Advocates of 'literary' and 'canonical' approaches to Scripture (see next section) frequently set out their perspective as an alternative paradigm to historical criticism. Even so, most of the critiques are arguably not directed to the method as such, which many still employ to some extent, but to its underlying historical positivism. Recent years have seen calls for a renewed historical criticism that is not histori*cist*, that is open to the transcendent and, within the context of a specifically Christian approach to Scripture, respects the 'otherness' of the text, allowing the text to challenge the interpreter's own world view.[55] Historical-critical study of the Bible remains a vital component of theological interpretation.[56]

Certain methods are associated with the historical paradigm of interpretation:[57] (1) *Textual criticism* seeks to determine what was the most likely reading among the variants in the many manuscripts of the text. (2) *Source criticism*, especially associated with studies of the Pentateuch and the Gospels, seeks to determine the sources used by a writer. (3) *Tradition criticism* elucidates the history

---

55. F. W. Dobbs-Allsopp, 'Rethinking Historical Criticism', *Biblical Interpretation* 7.3 (1999), pp. 235–271; Karl Möller, 'Renewing Historical Criticism', in Bartholomew, Greene and Möller, *Renewing Biblical Interpretation*, pp. 145–171. Contemporary literary and cultural theory has been marked by a 'historical turn' in some quarters – with the so-called new historicism. More a sensibility than a methodology, it questions the view that sees literature as an autonomous realm of discourse, and shows how the production and interpretation of texts are intermingled with contexts and ideologies. See Gina Hens-Piazza, *The New Historicism* (Guides to Biblical Scholarship; Minneapolis: Fortress, 2002).

56. Max Turner, 'Historical Criticism and Theological Interpretation of the New Testament', in Green and Turner, *Between Two Horizons*, pp. 44–70.

57. For overviews: Lorin L. Cranford, 'Modern New Testament Interpretation', in Bruce Corley, Steve W. Lemke and Grant I. Lovejoy (eds.), *Biblical Hermeneutics: A Comprehensive Introduction to Interpreting Scripture* (2nd edn.; Nashville: Broadman & Holman, 2002), pp. 147–162; McCartney and Clayton, *Let the Reader Understand*, pp. 303–312; Shillington, *Reading the Sacred Text*, pp. 224–242; Tate, *Biblical Interpretation*, pp. 3–12, 198–208.

of the traditions that make up texts. (4) *Form criticism* distinguishes various 'forms' in the text, classifies them into various groups, and seeks to correlate them with life settings in Israel or the early church. (5) *Redaction criticism* identifies how and why an author has edited traditions together. (6) *Composition criticism* moves beyond study of editorial changes to look at the overall shape of the final composition. (7) *Social-science criticism* draws on methods used in contemporary sociology and anthropology for considering the social dynamics of the communities out of which the texts arose.[58]

### The intention of the author and the task of exegesis

Most of the time, our understanding of what we read or hear is immediate and intuitive. Occasionally, we become aware of *trying* to understand, when the meaning of what somebody says, or what we read, is not immediately obvious; there are gaps to our under-standing, and the more obvious these gaps are, the more we become aware of the need for interpretation. With respect to the Bible, there are several possible gaps: there's a *linguistic* gap, since the Bible was written in languages different from our own; there's a *historical* gap between ourselves and the original writers; there's a *cultural* gap between the worlds of the Bible and our own. *Exegesis*, or *grammatical-historical exegesis* to give it the fuller designation

---

58. Many standard reference works carry sections and chapters on these 'criticisms'. On the Old Testament, see John Barton, *Reading the Old Testament: Method in Biblical Study* (2nd edn.; London: Darton, Longman & Todd, 1996); and Craig C. Broyles (ed.), *Interpreting the Old Testament: A Guide for Exegesis* (Grand Rapids: Baker, 2001). Still useful on the New Testament is I. Howard Marshall (ed.), *New Testament Interpretation: Essays on Principles and Methods* (rev. edn.; Exeter: Paternoster, 1979); but see now David Alan Black and David S. Dockery (eds.), *Interpreting the New Testament: Essays on Methods and Issues* (Nashville: Broadman & Holman, 2001); Joel B. Green (ed.), *Hearing the New Testament: Strategies for Interpretation* (Grand Rapids: Eerdmans, 1995); and Steven L. McKenzie and Stephen R. Haynes (eds.), *To Each Its Own Meaning: An Introduction to Biblical Criticisms and their Application* (2nd edn.; Louisville: Westminster/ John Knox, 1999).

preferred by some, recognizes these gaps and seeks to overcome them by discovering the meaning of the text in its original language and historical situation.

> On its most basic level, exegesis consists in expounding linguistic meaning in its appropriate historical context. The aim of the exegete is, in the first instance, philological and historical: the recovery of what words meant in their original context.[59]

Exegetes draw on the discipline of linguistics, which contributes to our understanding of how language works. Linguistics itself is divided into various branches, each of which emphasizes a different area, from study of the structure and meaning of individual words through to whole discourses in their social setting.[60] The significance of exegesis is indicated by the space devoted to it in the textbooks on hermeneutics.[61] We may note briefly just some of the levels at which it works.

---

59. Kevin J. Vanhoozer, 'Exegesis and Hermeneutics', in T. Desmond Alexander and Brian S. Rosner (eds.), *New Dictionary of Biblical Theology* (Leicester: IVP, 2000), pp. 52–64; here p. 56.

60. David Alan Black, *Linguistics for Students of New Testament Greek: A Survey of Basic Concepts and Applications* (2nd edn.; Grand Rapids: Baker, 2000). In addition to their book (*Linguistics*), Cotterell and Turner have each produced briefer introductions: Peter Cotterell, 'Linguistics, Meaning, Semantics, and Discourse Analysis', in VanGemeren, *New International Dictionary of Old Testament Theology and Exegesis*, vol. 1, pp. 134–160; Max Turner, 'Modern Linguistics and the New Testament', in Green, *Hearing the New Testament*, pp. 146–174.

61. Duvall and Hays, *Grasping God's Word*, pp. 28–82, 95–149; Julian, Crabtree and Crabtree, *Language of God*, pp. 65–159; Klein, Blomberg and Hubbard, *Biblical Interpretation*, pp. 155–255; McCartney and Clayton, *Let the Reader Understand*, pp. 119–158; Osborne, *Hermeneutical Spiral*, pp. 19–147; Tate, *Biblical Interpretation*, pp. 13–64. See also Gordon D. Fee, *New Testament Exegesis: A Handbook for Students and Pastors* (3rd edn.; Louisville: Westminster/John Knox, 2002).

### a. Words

In exegesis we get to grips with how words are used in the text. Should we conclude that Jesus is being rude when he addresses his mother as 'woman' (NIV) in John 2:4? Or should we render it as 'Dear Woman', or 'Mother', as some translations do? What about the word 'time', also in 2:4, sometimes translated as 'hour'? Or 'glory' in 2:11? Much of the work in this area has pointed out common mistaken linguistic assumptions (such as the appeal to root meaning, and the assumption that words always mean the same), and encouraged good practice in the handling of words.[62]

### b. Literary context

The exegete moves beyond the level of words to consider the *literary context* of the text, the words and sentences immediately preceding and immediately following the text under consideration, which extends to paragraphs and ultimately the whole book. With John 2:1–11, then, it's important to look back at the end of chapter 1. In 1:50–51, when Jesus promises Nathanael that he will see 'greater things', are we to understand the water-into-wine incident as one of the greater things Nathanael sees? In what ways is the cleansing of the temple, which follows (2:12–25), linked to the water-into-wine episode? Is it significant that John tells us that the water was that used by the Jews for ceremonial cleansing (2:6)? Jesus transforms the very water Judaism sets apart for cleansing! And in the very next incident, Jesus cleanses the *temple* – the very institution which mediated God's forgiveness to the people; and Jesus goes on to speak of *himself* as the temple, broken down and raised up (2:18–22). Furthermore, we might ask, how do these 'water' and 'temple' episodes fit in with other 'water' and 'temple' episodes in the rest of the Gospel? How does the rest of the Gospel help us understand what Jesus' 'time' (2:4) is? Where else in the Gospel does Jesus address his 'mother' (2:4)? John mentions that this was the first 'sign' (2:11); how does this sign fit with the other signs throughout the Gospel and contribute to John's overall purpose (20:30–31)?

---

62. D. A. Carson, *Exegetical Fallacies* (2nd edn.; Grand Rapids: Baker, 1996), especially pp. 27–64, is very helpful in this respect.

## c. Structure

That would bring us to ask whether or not there is any *structure* in the passage. Is it significant that 'Cana in Galilee' is mentioned in verses 1 and 11, which forms a literary bracket around the incident? Does the literary bracket between 2:1 and 4:54 mark those chapters out as a distinct unit in the narrative? Can we discern a structure when we set the individual passage in the flow of the Gospel as a whole? Though perhaps not so obvious in John 2, the study of structure is important in the study of other literary types, such as letters and poetry.

## d. Historical context

Exegesis also enquires about the *historical and cultural background* reflected in the text. Is it significant that the wedding takes place in Galilee? What form did weddings take in first-century Palestine? How important, socially speaking, was it for the bridegroom not to run out of wine? What was the significance of the ceremonial washing? And so on. John doesn't need to *explain* these things, because the import of them would be assumed by his original audience. Linguists have given the designation 'pragmatics' to the study of contextual meaning, of how more gets communicated than is said, because of what was presupposed between the original author and readers, but which cannot necessarily be assumed of readers today.[63] This requires exegetes to get to grips with aspects of the historical and cultural situation assumed by the text. Here, as elsewhere, we must be careful where there is lack of clear evidence about backgrounds; we need to use what knowledge we have available, but not pretend we have or know more than we do.

All of these are important aspects of exegesis, and the careful reader will try to get at the heart of the author's intention by considering *all* the different facets. This is one of the reasons why it's important to consult commentaries, which give information on the meaning of words, literary context, structure, and historical background, and inform us of the major opinions on the passage

---

63. Cotterell and Turner, *Linguistics*, pp. 90–105.

and help in our evaluation of them. Although we are dependent on the work of others, we can still read with great profit by keeping basic principles of exegesis in mind. If the territory seems huge (and it is), we need to be excited not daunted with the possibilities opened up to us in exploration.

## Unlocking the meaning of the text

We move here from the 'world behind the text' to the 'world in the text', the favoured sphere of those who grew uneasy with the aridity of historical criticism in the 1970s and sought to conceive the enterprise of biblical interpretation in fresh ways. One significant shift is that associated with literary criticism. Appreciation of Scripture's literary characteristics is by no means new,[64] but there was an explosion of various literary approaches from the 1970s onwards, which, while diverse, nonetheless shared general agreement that the Bible should be considered primarily as a *literary* document, rather than as a *historical* document. We may use as illustrative examples here the three areas of structuralism, rhetorical criticism and narrative criticism.[65]

*Structuralism* is a philosophical system that draws on anthropology and linguistics as well as literary criticism. Like New Criticism, it focuses on the text as an autonomous object, but seeks to move

---

64. Robert Morgan with John Barton, *Biblical Interpretation* (Oxford: Oxford University Press, 1988), pp. 206–210. David Jasper and Stephen Prickett (eds.), *The Bible and Literature: A Reader* (Oxford: Blackwell, 1999), p. 1, argue that where the Bible has been interpreted apart from other 'secular' literature, biblical criticism has evolved largely independently of other forms of literary interpretation. But throughout most of church history, they hold, the gap between the Bible and literature was not so clearly delimited.

65. See Longman, *Literary Approaches*, and his 'Literary Approaches to Old Testament Study', in David W. Baker and Bill T. Arnold (eds.), *The Face of Old Testament Studies: A Survey of Contemporary Approaches* (Leicester: Apollos, 1999), pp. 97–115.

beyond the surface level to penetrate to the 'deep structure' that a text might share with other texts.[66]

*Rhetorical criticism* compares the rhetorical features of New Testament texts with Graeco-Roman literature, identifying and analysing rhetorical strategies of persuasion.[67] More recently, working from postmodernist assumptions, proponents of the 'New Rhetoric' argue that *all* speech is rhetorical, and functions not just as a form of persuasive argumentation but as a power strategy to enforce certain ideologies. Vernon Robbins has used the metaphor of a tapestry with different textures to call for a 'socio-rhetorical' approach, whose concerns span literary criticism, social-science criticism, rhetorical criticism and ideology.[68]

*Narrative criticism* pays attention to 'story' features such as plot movement, character development, settings, the role of the narrator, and other literary techniques in biblical narratives.[69] Many evangelical scholars have been suspicious of such approaches, especially where the historicity of the biblical account has been called into question. Clearly, rhetorical criticism has a historical element as well as a literary element, and narrative critics, who in early studies often defined the approach in opposition to historical criticism, now regularly acknowledge the possibility and importance of combining 'literary' and 'historical' perspectives. The initial problems conservative scholars had with it are thus giving way to gleaning some of its benefits for interpretation, and many are now careful to note that literary analysis is compatible with high views of the historicity of the text.[70]

---

66. Daniel Patte, 'Structural Criticism', in McKenzie and Haynes, *To Each Its Own Meaning*, pp. 183–200.

67. C. Clifton Black, 'Rhetorical Criticism', in Green, *Hearing the New Testament*, pp. 256–277.

68. Vernon K. Robbins, *Exploring the Texture of Texts: A Guide to Socio-Rhetorical Interpretation* (Harrisburg: Trinity Press International, 1996).

69. Mark Allan Powell, 'Narrative Criticism', in Green, *Hearing the New Testament*, pp. 239–255.

70. In addition to Longman, see Leland Ryken, *Words of Delight: A Literary Introduction to the Bible* (2nd edn.; Grand Rapids: Baker, 1992).

Beyond these approaches, there are two significant areas to explore further.

### The type of text: the importance of the biblical genres

Most of the time, without thinking, we engage a certain gear for a certain type of literature as we read. When we open a newspaper, for example, we treat the section on international news differently from the cartoon page. We read about 'Snoopy' without believing for a moment that there is a real Snoopy (which, however, still comes a shock to some people!). And then, having read about Snoopy, our minds engage a different gear when we start reading the financial pages or the sports section.

This type of thinking is vital to apply to the Bible, because it's a literary library that houses different literary types – poetry, prose, narrative, family trees, court records, fables, proverbs, prophecies, parables, riddles, wisdom reflection, gospel, letter, vision. And different types of literature require different strategies for inter-pretation and application. With John 2, then, we recognize it's gospel narrative, and we don't confuse what it records with what it recommends. The text *records* what Jesus did at a wedding; it doesn't *recommend* that all Christian weddings should go as this one did. The text *describes* Jesus cleansing the temple; it doesn't *prescribe* that we should do as he did. It's much more likely that since this is *gospel* material, its primary task is to proclaim something about *Jesus'* person and work.

John Goldingay has explored some of the implications of the Bible's diverse literary forms for our understanding of the nature of Scripture and the interpretation of Scripture.[71] He considers four models for thinking about Scripture: (1) witness-ing tradition (narrative); (2) authoritative canon (commands in the Torah and elsewhere); (3) inspired word (prophecy); and (4) experienced revelation (psalms, apocalypses, wisdom, letters). In a similar way, Kevin Vanhoozer argues that the literal sense of

---

71. John Goldingay, *Models for Scripture* (Grand Rapids: Eerdmans, 1994); and *Models for Interpretation of Scripture* (Grand Rapids: Eerdmans, 1995).

Scripture is its *literary* sense – the sense the author intended to convey, in and through a particular *literary form*.[72] He uses the analogy of maps:

> Think of the various biblical genres – prophecy, apocalyptic, hymn, narrative, law, etc. – as different kinds of maps. Each map highlights certain features of the world more than others and accomplishes different tasks: informing, warning, encouraging, commanding, assuring, etc. Each genre has its own 'key' and 'scale'. The 'key' explains what a text is about. Just as different maps highlight different aspects of reality (e.g., roads, geological characteristics, historical events), so different literary genres select and attend to some aspects of reality more than others.[73]

The different literary types map the reality of God, the world and humanity in different ways, and yet all do so truly.[74] One corollary of this is that we shouldn't expect a particular type of literature to deliver something it was never intended to deliver, any more than we would expect a street atlas to show rock formations or contour lines. Writers of poetry (say) are interested in *truth*, but it is not the kind of truth that can be captured in a mathematical equation or analysed in a test tube.[75]

For responsible biblical interpretation, then, we must recognize that there are various literary types in the Bible, learn to

---

72. Vanhoozer, *Meaning,* pp. 336–337.

73. Ibid., p. 343.

74. Vanhoozer, 'Language, Literature, Hermeneutics, and Biblical Theology', p. 49 n. 103: 'The biblical narrative maps out divine action in history; biblical law maps out God's will for human behavior; biblical prophecy maps out the privileges and responsibilities of God's covenant people; biblical wisdom maps out how persons are to fit into God's created order, etc.'

75. This is crucial with respect to metaphor and figurative language in Scripture; see D. Brent Sandy, *Plowshares and Pruning Hooks: Rethinking the Language of Biblical Prophecy and Apocalyptic* (Leicester: IVP, 2002).

identify them, become acquainted with various ways of interpreting them, and make sure to 'change gear' as we come across
them.[76]

### The whole of the text: the importance of biblical theology

Another important part of asking what the text says involves
asking what the text *as a whole* says – the complete canon of
Scripture. We sometimes talk of making sure we get 'the big
picture' on an issue where finer details need setting in a larger
framework. In such cases we recognize there is a relationship
between the 'whole' and the 'parts' such that the one illumines the
other. Likewise with Scripture: the Christian faith gives this selection of books a unique relationship with each other, and this has
significant entailments for biblical interpretation.

With the *canonical approach*, especially associated with Brevard
Childs, comes a focus on the final canonical form of the biblical
texts, and a concern to take seriously the role of Scripture in the
church and in Christian formation.[77] Childs holds to the relatively
independent but complementary witness of the Old and New

---

76. Most of the standard textbooks carry long sections on principles appro-
    priate for handling different literary genres: Duvall and Hays, *Grasping
    God's Word*, pp. 217–396; Kaiser and Silva, *Biblical Hermeneutics*, pp.
    69–158; Klein, Blomberg and Hubbard, *Biblical Interpretation*, pp. 259–374;
    McCartney and Clayton, *Let the Reader Understand*, pp. 223–242; Osborne,
    *Hermeneutical Spiral*, pp. 149–260; Stein, *Playing by the Rules*, pp. 73–202;
    Tate, *Biblical Interpretation*, pp. 67–153. In addition, several individual
    books have been devoted to this area: Fee and Stuart, *How to Read the
    Bible*; Marshall D. Johnson, *Making Sense of the Bible: Literary Type as an
    Approach to Understanding* (Grand Rapids: Eerdmans, 2002); Tremper
    Longman III, *Reading the Bible with Heart and Mind* (Colorado Springs:
    NavPress, 1997); Stephen Motyer, *The Bible With Pleasure* (Leicester:
    Crossway, 1997).
77. Charles J. Scalise, *From Scripture to Theology: A Canonical Journey into
    Hermeneutics* (Downers Grove: IVP, 1996); Robert W. Wall, 'Reading the
    New Testament in Canonical Context', in Green, *Hearing the New
    Testament*, pp. 370–393.

Testaments to the 'divine reality' of the text's witness.[78] With a nod to Childs, Christopher Seitz seeks to reconnect the Testaments where they have become disconnected in Christian theology. In his scheme the witness of the Old Testament itself is affirmed, but it is also to be taught within a Christian framework.[79]

In taking the canon into consideration, Vanhoozer borrows the notion of 'thick description' from anthropologists.[80] He notes that texts, like actions, can be described at different levels of complexity:

> One can speak of neural firings, of the movement of an index finger, of pulling a trigger, of assassinating a President – all might be descriptions of the same act, although they work on different explanatory levels. However, the first description is 'thin' when compared to the last. Thin descriptions are the result of using too narrow a context to interpret an intended action.[81]

To confine interpretation to words, history or literary genres is to provide a 'thin description' of Scripture. A 'thick description' requires interpretation at the level of canon, for 'to read the Bible as unified Scripture is not just one interpretative interest among others, but the interpretative strategy that best corresponds to the nature of the text itself, given its divine inspiration'.[82]

The designation increasingly attached to the different facets of this holistic study of the two-testament canon is 'biblical theology'. Although there is no full agreement as to the nature and tasks of biblical theology, there can be little doubt that it is now well and truly on the map of the theological landscape, and that

---

78. Brevard S. Childs, *Biblical Theology of the Old and New Testaments: Theological Reflection on the Christian Bible* (London: SCM, 1992).

79. Christopher R. Seitz, *Word Without End: The Old Testament as Abiding Theological Witness* (Grand Rapids: Eerdmans, 1998).

80. Vanhoozer, 'Exegesis and Hermeneutics', pp. 61–62; *Meaning*, pp. 282, 284–286, 313–314.

81. Vanhoozer, 'Exegesis and Hermeneutics', p. 61.

82. Ibid.

evangelical voices are making significant contributions to the discussion.[83] Biblical theology has a strategic place in Christian interpretation and appropriation of the Bible. It involves reading the Bible as a historically developing collection of documents describing the progressive unfolding of God's purposes of salvation for humanity; it operates with a coherent canon, and seeks to work from individual books out to the canon as a whole, making connections among the various biblical corpora (collections of books, such as wisdom, history etc.), and between the two testaments, with Christ at their heart. Not content with merely describing the theology of biblical books (as some have limited the biblical-theological task), it moves forward to the task of constructing theology for the Christian community and the world today. As such it is intimately related to exegesis, historical theology, systematic theology, and preaching.[84]

There are various facets to the task of biblical theology, then, and we'll explore four of them briefly in the following paragraphs.

*a. The story the Bible tells*
*Metanarrative*, as many now know, is a way of saying 'big story' – a big story not necessarily in the sense of how long it takes to tell, but in terms of how much it tries to explain: an overarching

---

83. E.g. Alexander and Rosner, *Biblical Theology*; Graeme Goldsworthy, *According to Plan: The Unfolding Revelation of God in the Bible* (Leicester: IVP, 1991); Scott J. Hafemann (ed.), *Biblical Theology: Retrospect and Prospect* (Leicester: Apollos, 2002); Charles H. H. Scobie, *The Ways of Our God: An Approach to Biblical Theology* (Grand Rapids: Eerdmans, 2003).

84. Scobie, *Ways of Our God*, p. 8, sees biblical theology as 'a bridge discipline, standing in an intermediate position between the historical study of the Bible and the use of the Bible as authoritative Scripture by the church'. On preaching, see Graeme Goldsworthy, *Preaching the Whole Bible as Christian Scripture: The Application of Biblical Theology to Expository Preaching* (Leicester: IVP, 2000); and Sidney Greidanus, *Preaching Christ from the Old Testament: A Contemporary Hermeneutical Method* (Grand Rapids: Eerdmans, 1999).

story, by which lives are to be ordered. It's not too difficult to see the Bible as such a metanarrative, spanning Genesis to Revelation: a story that begins with God as Creator, that focuses on Israel as the people who will bring God's blessing to the nations, that the New Testament declares has come to its promised fulfilment in the redemption brought about through Christ, the one in whom God's purposes for the universe will be consummated.[85]

This notion of Scripture being a grand story carries a number of significances for our interpretation of it. It enables us to consider individual passages and their place in biblical-theological themes across the entire canon. We understand topics such as God, creation, sin, humanity, law, redemption and mission more fully when we view them in the light of the major plot points on the Bible's storyline, from creation to consummation. Related to this is the importance of locating passages at the right point on the line in the unfolding plan of salvation, of God's dealings with Israel and the church. This is perhaps especially fore-grounded in passages where Paul makes it clear, appealing to Scripture's story-line, that Christians do not live under the Mosaic Law (Romans 4; Galatians 3 – 4), that salvation history has moved on, and that the Law remains authoritative for the Christian only as it has been fulfilled in Christ (Matthew 5:17–48). Moreover, the worldview formed by the story the Bible tells carries implications for belief and behaviour as well as evangelism. As we engage with contemporary culture, we do so on the basis of a Christian world view, shaped by the pages of Scripture – from beginning to end.

---

85. Two introductory treatments of this topic are Philip Greenslade, *A Passion for God's Story: Discovering Your Place in God's Strategic Plan* (Carlisle: Paternoster, 2002); and Vaughan Roberts, *God's Big Picture: Tracing the Story-line of the Bible* (Leicester: IVP, 2003). Both look back to the valuable work of Graeme Goldsworthy, *Gospel and Kingdom: A Christian Interpretation of the Old Testament* (Exeter: Paternoster, 1981).

*b. The literature the Bible contains*

Kevin Vanhoozer has made an important contribution here.[86] He undertakes a biblical theology in terms of the Bible's *literature*, its 'word views', where biblical texts are described not merely at the linguistic level but also at the *literary* level.[87] Some theologians, he claims, have not taken sufficient account of Scripture's 'modes of expression', seeing them as 'wrapping paper to be torn off in one's haste to get to the proposition inside the package'. We should, according to Vanhoozer, allow ourselves to be 'instructed on the way language is used in various language games or literary genres', and note that 'the canon contains a number of such "games" wherein we learn to use concepts such as "God", "sin", and "salvation" correctly'.[88]

If the different genres can be likened to maps (see above), theology can be likened to *cartography*: knowing how to work with maps. Biblical theologians will seek to coordinate the biblical maps with one another, and not reduce the literary diversity to 'sameness':

> No one form of literature – no one map – exhausts all that can be said about God, humanity, and the world. The Christian who is biblically literate – whose thinking, imagination, language, and life is informed by the biblical texts – will have a faith formed by law, wisdom, song, apocalyptic, prophecy, gospel, and doctrine. These literary forms together make up Christian faith and identity. They shape the way we view the world, the way we view God, the way we view ourselves.[89]

---

86. To date, most fully explored in 'From Canon to Concept: "Same" and "Other" in the Relation Between Biblical and Systematic Theology', in *Scottish Bulletin of Evangelical Theology* 12.2 (1994), pp. 96–124. See also Timothy Ward, 'The Diversity and Sufficiency of Scripture', in Paul Helm and Carl R. Trueman (eds.), *The Trustworthiness of God: Perspectives on the Nature of Scripture* (Leicester: Apollos, 2002), pp. 192–218.

87. Vanhoozer, 'Exegesis and Hermeneutics', p. 59.

88. Vanhoozer, 'From Canon to Concept', pp. 101–102.

89. Kevin J. Vanhoozer, 'Mapping Evangelical Theology in a Post-modern World', *Evangelical Review of Theology* 22.1 (1998), pp. 5–27; here p. 15.

Hence, one of the profoundest ways for Christians to engage with contemporary issues is to do so from the perspective of thinking which not only embraces and indwells the entire scriptural story, but which does justice to its different literary voices. A biblical theology of *suffering* will have to allow for the wisdom reflections in Job and Ecclesiastes, for the anguished cries in Lamentations, for prophetic oracles describing vicarious suffering in Isaiah 40 – 55, for expressed hopes in the face of persecution in Daniel and Revelation, as well as for the biblical metanarrative extending from creation (and fall) to consummation (and the eradication of evil and pain). Disputed questions in sexuality will not be satisfactorily answered by gathering mere proof texts, but by an ongoing reading practice broad enough to do justice to the *celebration* of sexuality in the poetry of Song of Songs, to the *circumscribing* of sexuality in the legislation in Leviticus, to the *contemplation* of sexuality in Proverbs – all within the flow of the biblical story stretching from the creation of Adam and Eve to the new creation with the wedding supper of the Lamb and his bride.

### c. The unity-in-diversity the Bible displays

The principle that Scripture must be interpreted by Scripture is based on the assumption that the Bible forms a unity. Not that this view has commanded wide assent in mainstream biblical scholarship: there isn't a biblical *theology* (in the singular), it is argued, only biblical *theologies* (in the plural) that may contradict one another. Walter Brueggemann's *Theology of the Old Testament*, for instance, makes much of the plurivocal quality of the Scriptures, with their claim and counterclaim, testimony and countertestimony.[90] Even if we start from the assumption that Scripture is a unity, we must be careful not to let that assumption blind us to the diversity Scripture does display, and the importance of allowing each corpus and each writing to speak for itself; we must beware lest we twist Scripture into a *uniformity* that does not exist.[91]

---

90. Walter Brueggemann, *Theology of the Old Testament: Testimony, Dispute, Advocacy* (Minneapolis: Fortress, 1997).

91. Craig L. Blomberg, 'The Unity and Diversity of Scripture', in Alexander and Rosner, *Biblical Theology*, pp. 64–72.

It's also important to distinguish between 'unity' and 'centre'. Köstenberger joins others in holding that 'the NT's unity cannot be safeguarded through the projection of a given concept onto the NT as a whole', and that we are best pursuing not a centre, but a cluster of broadly related themes, 'a plurality of integrative NT motifs'.[92] This is the approach Scobie adopts in his *magnum opus* on biblical theology:

> The procedure that seems to offer the most promise and the least risk of distorting the biblical material is that of identifying a limited number of major biblical themes . . . grouping around them associated subthemes, and tracing each theme and subtheme through the OT, then through the NT, following the scheme of proclamation/promise: fulfillment/consummation.[93]

Scobie's own proposal is a multithematic approach structured around four major themes: God's order, God's servant, God's people, and God's way.[94] Many contemporary studies that go under the label of 'biblical theology' employ this sort of approach – tracing themes or trajectories that unite various passages and can be traced through the Bible as a whole.[95] In biblical theology, then, we work with the presupposition that although there is a rich diversity within Scripture, there is still, nonetheless, a profound unity that is demonstrated especially when we consider theological themes throughout both testaments.

---

92. Andreas J. Köstenberger, 'Diversity and Unity in the New Testament', in Hafemann, *Biblical Theology*, pp. 144–158, here p. 154.

93. Scobie, *Ways of Our God*, p. 93.

94. Ibid., pp. 93–99.

95. So a number of the volumes in the 'Overtures to Biblical Theology' series, edited by Walter Brueggemann and published by Fortress; the 'Understanding Biblical Themes' series, edited by Jon L. Berquist and published by Chalice; and the 'New Studies in Biblical Theology' series, edited by D. A. Carson and published by Inter-Varsity Press (Apollos imprint).

## d. The promise the Bible fulfils

The New Testament sounds a note of fulfilment in the coming of Christ, who constitutes the centre of the testaments: the Old Testament prepares the way for him; the New Testament proclaims him. Biblical theology recognizes that the New Testament can be understood only in the light of the Old Testament, and the Old Testament can be understood only in the light of the New Testament.[96] The Christological focal point means the Old Testament is to be interpreted as *Christian* Scripture.

It's thus especially important to consider the use of the Old Testament by the New Testament writers.[97] John cites Old Testament passages repeatedly throughout his Gospel (e.g. 1:23; 2:17; 6:31; 6:45; 7:38; 7:42; 10:34; 12:14–15; 12:38; 12:39–40; 13:18; 15:25; 17:12; 19:24; 19:28; 19:36; 19:37), and alludes to many more passages and themes. That he holds the Old Testament in high regard is hardly debated. What is debated is *how* he uses it. To take two examples from the crucifixion scene, in 19:24 he cites Psalm 22:18, which concerns a righteous sufferer, and in 19:28 he refers to Scripture being fulfilled in Jesus' saying, 'I am thirsty' (with Psalms 69:21 and 22:15 as possible allusions). Even so, they aren't 'prophecies' as such; so how can John say that Jesus 'fulfilled' these texts?

An important key to understanding the New Testament writers' use of the Old Testament is in understanding the presuppositions and methods of interpretation by which they operated.[98] One of the most important of these is the concept of 'typology'. This arises out of the recognition that John does far more than cite Old

---

96. David L. Baker, *Two Testaments, One Bible: A Study of the Theological Relationship Between the Old and New Testaments* (2nd edn.; Leicester: Apollos, 1991).

97. Richard B. Hays and Joel B. Green, 'The Use of the Old Testament by New Testament Writers', in Green, *Hearing the New Testament*, pp. 222–238; Klyne Snodgrass, 'The Use of the Old Testament in the New', in Black and Dockery, *Interpreting the New Testament*, pp. 209–229.

98. E. Earle Ellis, 'How the New Testament Uses the Old', in Marshall, *New Testament Interpretation*, pp. 199–219; especially pp. 209–214; Snodgrass, 'Use of the Old Testament', pp. 214–218.

Testament texts; he shows a deep interest in Old Testament *events* (such as the exodus), and *institutions* (such as the Law, the temple and the feasts), and *persons* (such as Moses). John sees parallels and equivalents to such events, institutions and persons in the life and ministry of Jesus.

Chris Wright points out that although the word 'typology' is generally not familiar to us, the concept is fairly common.[99] A good teacher knows that introducing something new to someone requires working by *analogy* and *correspondence*, to move a person from what is known and familiar to what is unknown and unfamiliar. We sometimes speak of *recapitulation* – going over the same ground again. We are familiar with the notion of a *model* being a scaled-down version of a real thing. Scientists use the concept of *paradigm*, which can be thought of as an accepted pattern of how reality functions, which is used for working out other scientific puzzles. In the world of the law court, we occasionally hear of a *precedent* being set: a judgment made in one case functions as a model or a type in future cases when similar issues are at stake. Even in everyday speech, we sometimes say 'That's just typical!' about somebody's action, when what we mean is that we're not really surprised, because it fits a pattern of behaviour we have come to expect of that person from previous experience.

The use of typology can be detected even within the Old Testament itself; the event of the exodus, for example, becomes a model for later writers to talk about other acts of God's deliverance: God saving his people from Assyria (Isaiah 11:10–16), or bringing the exiles back home from Babylon (throughout Isaiah 40 – 55). The language of Isaiah 40:3 is reused in Malachi 3:1 to talk about a *future* salvation. Then, in the New Testament, it's applied to John the Baptist, who prepares the way for Jesus (John 1:23). And Jesus himself is shown to provide the three exodus gifts of bread, water and light (John 6:35; 7:37–39; 8:12; cf. Psalm 105:39–41). The point is not that the exodus event directly predicted any of these things; the point is that the exodus becomes a

---

99. The following examples are taken from Christopher Wright, *Knowing Jesus Through the Old Testament* (London: HarperCollins, 1992), pp. 111–112.

model (or a 'type') that can be used and reused, *typologically*, by different writers to speak of 'salvation' in a whole range of different contexts.

This typology of promise fulfilment permeates the thinking of Jesus and the early church and is one of the most important presuppositions for their extensive use of the Old Testament. It shows the fulfilment, not just of predictions, but of Old Testament models, history, religion, events, institutions and persons. Luke 24:13–35 is illuminating in this respect (cf. John 5:39, 46–47).[100] The travellers on the road to Emmaus are rebuked not for disbelieving Jesus, but for disbelieving the *prophets* (24:25); and Jesus does not offer them esoteric revelation, but exposition from the *Scriptures* (24:27). The story of Jesus

> needs to be set in a context beyond itself . . . So, as Jesus cannot be understood apart from Jewish Scripture, Jewish Scripture cannot be understood apart from Jesus; what is needed is an interpretation which relates the two – and it is this that Jesus provides.[101]

John 2:19–22 likewise suggests the need to read the Old Testament in the light of the events of salvation. No specific text is cited in 2:19, which raises the question as to which Scripture the disciples believed (2:22); but Psalm 69 is present in the immediate context (2:17; cf. Psalm 69:9). Subsequent events of salvation show that Jesus is the righteous sufferer of Psalm 69, a link made more clear at the cross (John 19:29; cf. Psalm 69:21). So, when we come to the citations of Psalms 22 and 69 in the Johannine crucifixion narrative, these laments of a righteous sufferer fit the Son of God as he suffers and dies on the cross. If David is a suffering servant, Jesus is *the* suffering servant. If David is the son of God, Jesus is *the* son of God. We don't have to see Psalms 22 and 69 as direct messianic prophecies, because they are being used

---

100. R. W. L. Moberly, *The Bible, Theology, and Faith: A Study of Abraham and Jesus* (Cambridge Studies in Christian Doctrine 5; Cambridge: Cambridge University Press, 2000), pp. 45–70.

101. Ibid., p. 51.

*typologically* by John: the psalmist's experience as the king, the Son of God, 'anticipates' the experience of Jesus, *the* king, *the* Son of God. Psalms 22 and 69 find their typological fulfilment in the suffering and subsequent vindication of Jesus. John's use of the Old Testament is thus not by way of 'proof-texting', but is integral to the message of his Gospel, which places Jesus and his mission in the broader context of the story of Israel he fulfils.

## Unlocking the response of the reader

How do readers make sense of texts? This is an area of intense interest, not least because one of the main features of the post-modern climate is the orientation of interpretation to the *reader* rather than the author or the text. Attention here shifts to the 'world in front of the text', and to issues of how far a text con-strains the reader, how free the reader is to impose interpretations on the text, and how the reader interacts with the text. Where his-torical criticism operated with a subject–object distinction between the interpreter (the subject) interpreting the text (the object), 'read-erly' approaches highlight the inevitable subjective dimension of interpretation, where meaning is mediated by my own framework of thought. 'Poststructuralism' has become a broad umbrella term under which a variety of approaches and stances fall, all of which focus on the role of the reader and the impact of texts on readers, and which reject the notion that there is some overarching scheme that corresponds to the meaning of the text.[102]

---

102. A. K. M. Adam, *What is Postmodern Biblical Criticism?* (Guides to Biblical Scholarship; Minneapolis: Fortress, 1995), offers a brief, sympathetic introduction to the area. The Bible and Culture Collective, *The Postmodern Bible* (New Haven: Yale University Press, 1995), provides an encylopedic overview of critical methods. See also A. K. M. Adam (ed.), *Handbook of Postmodern Biblical Interpretation* (St. Louis: Chalice, 2000); and A. K. M. Adam (ed.), *Postmodern Interpretations of the Bible: A Reader* (St. Louis: Chalice, 2001). Evangelical scholars have perhaps been slow to respond to challenges of these approaches, with treatments in some

### The role of the reader: some approaches

In this first section, then, I simply outline and describe, with little comment, some of the main positions on the spectrum of approaches that focus on the role of the reader in interpretation.[103]

#### a. Reading for how the text has been received

A growing number of studies fall under the banner of 'effective history' – the study of the history of a text's 'influences' or 'effects'. As might be expected, the Germans have a word for it – *Wirkungsgeschichte* – and it is enjoying increasing prominence, not least in the most recent work of Anthony Thiselton.[104] It's not just a study of the history of interpretation, but of the history of a text's influence on art, architecture, literature, prayer, hymns, as well as commentaries, lectionaries and liturgy. It is also praised as a way of helping us understand how the 'post-history', or after-life, of the biblical text has shaped our lives, and how this tradition might act as a 'conversation partner' with the contemporary community of faith in the re-actualization of the text.[105] It's little surprise, then, that some hold this out as a potentially

---

of the standard textbooks being reduced to appendices (Klein, Blomberg and Hubbard, *Biblical Interpretation*, pp. 438–443, 450–457; McCartney and Clayton, *Let the Reader Understand*, pp. 296–300; Osborne, *Hermeneutical Spiral*, pp. 366–396; cf. Tate, *Biblical Interpretation*, pp. 157–194, 214–233). Thiselton (*New Horizons*) and Vanhoozer (*Meaning*) are among the main exceptions, who engage with postmodern thinkers throughout their major works on hermeneutics.

103. See Edgar V. McKnight, 'Reader-Response Criticism', in McKenzie and Haynes, *To Each Its Own Meaning*, pp. 230–252; Thiselton, *New Horizons*, pp. 515–555; Vanhoozer, *First Theology*, pp. 236–256.

104. Anthony C. Thiselton, 'Communicative Action and Promise in Interdisciplinary, Biblical, and Theological Hermeneutics', in Roger Lundin, Clarence Walhout and Anthony C. Thiselton, *The Promise of Hermeneutics* (Grand Rapids: Eerdmans, 1999), pp. 133–239; especially pp. 191–208.

105. Ibid., p. 195.

fruitful area for dialogue between biblical scholars and theologians.[106]

## b. Reading to get involved

Some approaches to 'reader-response criticism' explore the way the text calls for the reader to respond. In literary theory this is most closely associated with Wolfgang Iser, who notes that texts contain 'gaps' the reader has to fill, thus becoming involved in the 'act of reading'.[107] Anyone who has enjoyed a good novel or film will be familiar with the notion of being drawn into the story, of having to negotiate the twists and turns of the plot. In a similar way, readers may discover that Jesus' enigmatic reply to his mother in John 2:4 forces them to ask questions, the answers to which might have to be put on hold until (for instance) it's made more clear what Jesus' 'hour' is.

Clearly, then, this approach works best with more open-ended texts such as narratives, and is frequently combined with narrative-critical studies of the Gospels. Mark Allan Powell has produced one such work, offering a case study of the visit of the magi in Matthew 2:1–12.[108] He's particularly interested in identifying the responses of real readers to the text and comparing these with what appear to be the *expected* responses to the narrative, looking at how the readers presupposed by the narrative are expected to read, and what they are expected to know and believe.

## c. Reading from where I stand

A whole range of ideological approaches point out that all readers of

---

106. Markus Bockmuehl, '"To Be Or Not To Be": The Possible Futures of New Testament Scholarship', *Scottish Journal of Theology* 51.3 (1998), pp. 271–306; at pp. 295–298.

107. Wolfgang Iser, *The Implied Reader: Patterns of Communication in Prose Fiction from Bunyan to Beckett* (Baltimore: Johns Hopkins University Press, 1974); and *The Act of Reading: A Theory of Aesthetic Response* (Baltimore: Johns Hopkins University Press, 1978).

108. Mark Allan Powell, *Chasing the Eastern Star: Adventures in Reader-Response Criticism* (Louisville: Westminster/John Knox, 2001).

all texts bring their prejudices with them to the act of reading, and seek to read texts from the perspective of particular agendas. So, if I am a feminist or a vegetarian or a pacifist or a homosexual, goes the argument, it might be important for me to reflect on what the text has to say or does not have to say about those issues. For instance, a reader of John's Gospel with *feminist* interests may pay considerable attention to the role of Jesus' mother, the Samaritan woman at the well, and Mary and Martha, to see what the Gospel has to say explicitly or implicitly about gender issues, whether the text adopts a male-centred stance or undermines that stance in some way. Hence, 'ideological criticism' (to use a label increasingly attached to this broad set of concerns) might highlight how the texts themselves have been shaped by particular dominant ideologies as well as considering the role of readers' own social and political agendas.[109] What links these various approaches is an emphasis on the interpreter's 'social location', which is made explicit, is seen as a benefit, and becomes a major feature in interpretation.[110]

Liberationist hermeneutics offers perhaps the classic example of 'reading from where I stand'. Associated especially with Latin American theologians, its starting point for reading the Bible is the experience of the poor and oppressed, alongside a commitment to social transformation.[111] Feminists, like liberationists,

---

109. Adam, *What is Postmodern Biblical Criticism?* pp. 45–60; Bible and Culture Collective, *Postmodern Bible*, pp. 272–308; David J. A. Clines, *Interested Parties: The Ideology of Writers and Readers of the Hebrew Bible* (Journal for the Study of the Old Testament Supplement Series 205; Gender, Culture, Theory 1; Sheffield: Sheffield Academic Press, 1995); Tina Pippin, 'Ideology, Ideological Criticism, and the Bible', *Currents in Research: Biblical Studies* 4 (1996), pp. 51–78.

110. Brian K. Blount, *Cultural Interpretation: Reorienting New Testament Criticism* (Minneapolis: Fortress, 1995); Fernando F. Segovia and Mary Ann Tolbert (eds.), *Reading from this Place*. Vol. 1: *Social Location and Biblical Interpretation in the United States* (Minneapolis: Fortress, 1995); and *Reading from this Place*. Vol. 2: *Social Location and Biblical Interpretation in Global Perspective* (Minneapolis: Fortress, 1995).

111. Tim Gorringe, 'Political Readings of Scripture', in Barton, *Cambridge*

have drawn on a variety of interpretive procedures, including historical-critical and social-scientific approaches (e.g. in reconstructing the lives of women in ancient Israel and the early church) and literary methods (e.g. seeing how narrative texts represent female characters). Feminist hermeneutics also represents a spectrum of approaches, from those who start with an affirmation of the authority of the biblical text, operate with a 'hermeneutic of trust', and look for ways in which texts might bring hope and affirmation to contemporary women, right through to those whose authority is the oppressed experience of women, who operate with a 'hermeneutic of suspicion', critique Scripture and seek to expose the patriarchal elements in it.[112] A growing area related to liberationist hermeneutics is *postcolonial criticism*, which works from the experiences of nations where colonizers' interpretations of Scripture have held sway, and where, in response, different ethnic communities – Native Americans, Hispanics, Asian-Americans – self-consciously develop their own traditions of interpretation.[113]

One corollary of these various studies has been the call for biblical scholars to practise an 'ethics of reading' – in the sense of allowing 'ordinary readings' or 'grassroots' readings equal access to the table, in terms of evaluating the values that emerge from

---

*Companion to Biblical Interpretation*, pp. 67–80; Fernando F. Segovia, 'Reading the Bible Ideologically: Socioeconomic Criticism', in McKenzie and Haynes, *To Each Its Own Meaning*, pp. 283–306; Thiselton, *New Horizons*, pp. 410–430.

112. Bible and Culture Collective, *Postmodern Bible*, pp. 225–271; Danna Nolan Fewell, 'Reading the Bible Ideologically: Feminist Criticism', in McKenzie and Haynes, *To Each Its Own Meaning*, pp. 268–282; Anne Loades, 'Feminist Interpretation', in Barton, *Cambridge Companion to Biblical Interpretation*, pp. 81–94; Sandra M. Schneiders, 'Feminist Hermeneutics', in Green, *Hearing the New Testament*, pp. 349–369; Thiselton, *New Horizons*, pp. 430–462.

113. Fernando F. Segovia, *Decolonizing Biblical Studies: A View from the Margins* (Maryknoll: Orbis, 2000); R. S. Sugirtharajah, *Postcolonial Criticism and Biblical Interpretation* (Oxford: Oxford University Press, 2002).

readings of texts, and in taking responsibility for the model of interpretation used and the consequences of adopting it.[114]

### d. Reading from the perspective of my life story
Using the labels 'autobiographical biblical criticism' or 'personal voice criticism', this is related to the previous type, but is particularly concerned with reading biblical passages from the perspective of the interpreter's own life story, looking at the impact of their autobiography on the interpretation of texts.[115]

### e. Reading according to my community
It's become fashionable in the current intellectual climate to say that what matters is how the particular *community* to which I belong reads the text. The critic Stanley Fish is most closely associated with this perspective.[116] According to Fish, 'the reader's response is not to the meaning, it is the meaning'.[117] The text exercises minimal constraints on the reader. Fish does not hold that readers can make a text mean anything; it is rather that understanding is achieved within the confines of an 'interpretive community', which determines what texts mean. Readers do not discover meaning, but construct it.

The most frequently cited illustration of this is related in his essay 'How to Recognize a Poem When You See One'.[118] Fish describes how a list of names of scholars in linguistics and literary

---

114. Daniel Patte, *Ethics of Biblical Interpretation: A Reevaluation* (Louisville: Westminster/John Knox, 1995); Elizabeth Schüssler Fiorenza, *Rhetoric and Ethic: The Politics of Biblical Studies* (Minneapolis: Fortress, 1999).

115. Ingrid Rosa Kitzberger (ed.), *The Personal Voice in Biblical Interpretation* (London: Routledge, 1999).

116. In his later work, and particularly as represented in the collection of essays gathered together in *Is There a Text in This Class? The Authority of Interpretive Communities* (Cambridge: Harvard University Press, 1980).

117. Fish, *Is There a Text in This Class?* p. 3.

118. Ibid., pp. 322–337.

theory from one class was left on the board when the next group of students filed in. He told them it was a religious poem of the kind they had been studying in that class on seventeenth-century religious poetry, and they were able to work through the 'poem' (the list of names), make links with biblical passages, and establish coherence. For Fish, this shows that meaning is not a property of the text, still less of an author's intention, but is *constructed*, and dependent on the interpretive community to which readers belong, in which they are socialized, and according to the literary and cultural values they have assimilated.

Stanley Hauerwas has appealed to Fish in his treatment of Scripture. The Bible has been appropriated by individuals and academics, says Hauerwas, and is frequently read through the nation's agenda, whereas it is meant to be read and appropriated in the context of discipleship and the believing community.[119] For Hauerwas, Scripture belongs to the community of faith, and interpretation is determined by the practices of the community that reads it. Stephen Fowl is likewise concerned to emphasize the role of the Christian community in hermeneutics, where 'theological convictions, ecclesial practices, and communal and social concerns should *shape and be shaped by* biblical interpretation'.[120] In this context Fowl argues for 'underdetermined' interpretation, which rejects the assumption that texts have determinate 'meaning', and which holds that a variety of interpretive aims, interests and practices of interpretive communities result in diverse interpretations.[121]

---

119. Stanley Hauerwas, *Unleashing the Scripture: Freeing the Bible from Captivity to America* (Nashville: Abingdon, 1993).

120. Stephen E. Fowl, *Engaging Scripture: A Model for Theological Interpretation* (Challenges in Contemporary Theology; Oxford: Blackwell, 1998), p. 60; his italics.

121. Fowl, *Engaging Scripture*, pp. 32–61; and 'The Role of Authorial Intention in the Theological Interpretation of Scripture', in Green and Turner, *Between Two Horizons*, pp. 71–87, where Fowl defends a 'chastened notion of authorial intention', and rejects the claim 'that an author's meaning is "the meaning" of a text' (p. 73).

*f. Reading to undo the text*

This brings us to *deconstruction*, arguably the flagship of post-structuralism, with Jacques Derrida the captain on board.[122] Deconstruction involves

> a way of reading that involves both discovering the incompleteness of the text and finding a fresh, if transient, insight made possible by the 'free play' or indeterminacy of the text.[123]

As in structuralism, language is seen as a system of signs, but *post*-structuralism shows how a signifier refers to another signifier, which refers to another signifier, and so on in endless deferral. As Adam explains:

> In the language that deconstruction appropriates from structural linguistics, deconstruction questions the supposed connection between the 'signifier' (the word, or gesture, or image, or symbol, or sound) and the 'signified' (the meaning of the word/gesture/image/symbol/sound). Deconstruction involves showing that there is no necessary connection between signifier and signified.[124]

Derrida doesn't deny intentional meaning, but argues that understanding authorial intention may generate contradictions at points where the text opens itself to a reading that evades the intention of its author. Hence, deconstruction frequently involves a close reading of texts to uncover the tensions within the text, the ways in which texts undermine what they purport to say. It shows how 'meaning' is constantly deferred, how texts undo established hierarchies, are unable to sustain a single interpretation, and that the possibility of fixing a final meaning is presumptuous and a claim to power. Some deconstructionists, therefore, offer readings that make explicit what is hidden or marginalized in the text.

---

122. Bible and Culture Collective, *Postmodern Bible*, pp. 119–148.

123. William A. Beardslee, 'Poststructuralist Criticism', in McKenzie and Haynes, *To Each Its Own Meaning*, pp. 253–267; here p. 253.

124. Adam, *What is Postmodern Biblical Criticism?*, pp. 27–28.

Difficult to define, it's perhaps best to see deconstruction in action, and the work of Stephen Moore on John 4 offers one striking example.[125] The Samaritan woman comes to the well to draw *literal* water, but Jesus speaks to her of *spiritual* water (the irony of which, interpreters frequently assume, the woman has no inkling). Jesus longs for the woman to desire the water he can give, and only so will *his* thirst be quenched. But when the themes of thirst and drinking occur again at the crucifixion, the two levels of meaning – the literal and symbolic – that had been held apart in the well episode now collapse. Jesus says, 'I thirst' (19:28) – not for spiritual water, but for literal water! Not only does Jesus, the source of spiritual water, thirst for real water, but when he has drunk, he gives up his *spirit* (19:30)! So, the opposition between the literal and the symbolic water of John 4 is overthrown. The earthly water we thought was superseded in chapter 4 is reinstated in chapter 19, where the flow of living water (cf. 19:34; 7:37–39) is shown to depend on literal water! Jesus separates literal water and figurative water when he talks of the Samaritan woman's need; she, on the other hand, sees the two as inseparable. Hey presto, says the deconstructionist, the woman was right after all, and Jesus was wrong!

### g. Reading for the 'play' of texts

This position moves from the close reading of texts by deconstructionists to a free-playing reading of the text. The first volume in an intriguing series from Sheffield Academic Press – 'Playing the Texts' (which should give some idea of what to expect!) was an interdisciplinary dialogue between fantasy theory (and literature) and biblical texts, looking at how some biblical texts can be read as fantastic literature, by utilizing aspects of theory normally applied to fantasy literature and, in turn, at the

---

125. Stephen D. Moore, 'Are there Impurities in the Living Water that the Johannine Jesus Dispenses? Deconstruction, Feminism, and the Samaritan Woman', *Biblical Interpretation* 1.2 (1993), pp. 207–227; and Stephen D. Moore, *Poststructuralism and the New Testament: Derrida and Foucault at the Foot of the Cross* (Minneapolis: Fortress, 1994), pp. 43–64.

influence of the Bible on contemporary cultural 'texts' (e.g. literature and cinema).[126]

In these approaches, cultural studies and biblical studies encounter each other, and work in the intersection of the two disciplines is growing.[127] Much of it self-consciously sets aside past scholarship, as well as theological concerns, or shows how much so-called disinterested scholarship is itself ideological. The offerings are diverse, with some analysing the place of the Bible in culture, and others looking at the impact of ancient and contemporary culture on the interpretation of the Bible. There are few theoretical studies; most offer a postmodern 'play' between biblical texts and facets of contemporary culture from the visual arts, music, literature, TV, science fiction, politics, newspapers, pornography and film, leading to (to cite some examples) juxtapositions of pornography and Song of Songs, manna and McDonald's, Ezekiel and Axl Rose, and Rahab (Joshua 2) and Walt Disney's *Pocahontas*.

### The role of the reader: some reflections

It should be clear from what I've said about the author and the text, that I disagree with the notion that texts have no stable meaning, and that radical pluralism in readings is something to be pursued as a good thing in and of itself. The danger of highlighting the radical end of the spectrum is that we could be tempted to rubbish all 'reader' approaches to biblical texts. In fact, although there are some things to be aware of, there may also be some

---

126. George Aichele and Tina Pippin (eds.), *The Monstrous and the Unspeakable: The Bible as Fantastic Literature* (Playing the Texts 1; Sheffield: Sheffield Academic Press, 1997).

127. George Aichele (ed.), *Culture, Entertainment and the Bible* (Journal for the Study of the Old Testament Supplement Series 309; Sheffield: Sheffield Academic Press, 2000); Roland Boer, *Knockin' on Heaven's Door: The Bible and Popular Culture* (Biblical Limits; London: Routledge, 1999); J. Cheryl Exum and Stephen D. Moore (eds.), *Biblical Studies/Cultural Studies: The Third Sheffield Colloquium* (Journal for the Study of the Old Testament Supplement Series 266; Gender, Culture, Theory 7; Sheffield: Sheffield Academic Press, 1998).

genuine challenges to our reading practice. Even deconstruction helps address the pride that thinks all ambiguity can be banished from the text, and that its meaning can be captured exhaustively.[128] Evangelicals have always been concerned with the impact of biblical texts on readers, and in this area, as in so many others, we must make sure to keep hold of the baby in our attempts to get rid of the bath water. In this section, then, we reflect on how we might tread with care through this potential minefield.

### a. Reading with humility

We have too often wrongly assumed that we are neutral thinkers whose experience and tradition never clouds our judgment. We need to remember that we are finite, that we are sinners, and that our minds require ongoing transformation. We need to read with humility. Moreover, some of the questions I ask of the text are a reflection of who I am. Maybe someone from Africa or Eastern Europe would ask a different set of questions. Maybe a person of the opposite sex would approach it differently. Maybe someone without a degree in theology would have a different perspective. So, we'll need to be humble when it comes to learning from others. Above all, we need humility with respect to the text. These approaches do a service wherever they remind us of the need to *submit* to the text as readers, and not merely to subject it to scrutiny, walk away and wash our hands like a doctor after examining a patient. Readers do not have the ability to discern everything absolutely and without error. But we are not required to attain perfectly infallible interpretations; we are called to appropriate humility.

### b. Reading in a spiral

Traditional views of hermeneutics have assumed a subject–object relationship between the interpreter and the text, where the subject (the interpreter) is able to set aside personal interests and use principles to interpret the object (the text) accurately. Some of these 'reader' approaches break down this subject–object distinction. The reader when he or she approaches the text, it is said,

---

128. Vanhoozer, *First Theology*, p. 247.

brings a certain amount of baggage with them, so that even the questions the reader asks of the text reflect the limitations imposed by their baggage. But the questions the reader asks shape the responses that come back from the text. And those responses, in turn, reshape the reader, so that in the next round, the questions addressed to the text are slightly different, and generate a fresh series of responses. In this way, a *hermeneutical circle* is set up. For some exponents, real and objective meaning is denied. A text has many meanings, none of them objectively true, and all of them valid according to their effect on the reader.

Of course, if we followed this line logically, we wouldn't be able to communicate anything at all to anyone at all. Most of us are aware that while language is *sometimes* ambiguous, it still works extremely well most of the time. Hence, more sophisticated exponents argue that we are not going round and round a vicious circle, so much as travelling round a virtuous spiral. We read the Bible and engage with it; we read again, and our understanding improves. We re-read, and our focus is further adjusted more accurately than it was the previous time – and so on. We can get closer and closer to the meaning of the text until we grasp it *truly*, even if not exhaustively. We recognize we bring things to the text, but we continually let the text stand over us, correcting our misconceptions of it, while we are transformed more into line with it.[129] Grant Osborne has adopted this model, recognizing the dynamic interaction between text, community, context and reader.[130] An increasing number of scholars in critical theory as well as biblical hermeneutics have refused the either-or antithesis sometimes assumed between absolute objectivism and rampant subjectivism. We don't have to claim *absolute* knowledge. But nor do we have to despair and conclude that knowledge is *anarchic*. Interpretation is not *absolute* or *anarchic*, but it may still be *adequate* – adequate for the purposes of understanding appropriately and responding appropriately.[131]

129. Klein, Blomberg and Hubbard, *Biblical Interpretation*, pp. 113–114.
130. Osborne, *Hermeneutical Spiral*, p. 324.
131. Vanhoozer, *Meaning*, pp. 139–140.

## c. Reading for the two horizons

The issue of the relationship between the text and the reader is sometimes addressed in terms of 'horizons'. In basic terms, this model recognizes that the biblical text stands in a given 'horizon', and that the contemporary interpreter stands in a given 'horizon'. For understanding to take place, the two sets of variables, from the past and the present, must be brought into relation with one another, the goal being the *fusion* of the two horizons.[132] The language of 'horizons' is most closely associated with Hans-Georg Gadamer, and Thiselton has utilized the model in such a way that he is able to affirm the author's intended meaning *and* to recognize that the interpreter's own horizon influences meaning:

> The hermeneutical goal is that of a steady progress towards a fusion of horizons. But this is to be achieved in such a way that the particularity of each horizon is fully taken into account and respected.[133]

Gadamer is sometimes associated with relativistic approaches to interpretation, though there is some dispute about this.[134] But he was certainly concerned to question the claim that scientific method *alone* is necessary for truth, and argues that 'prejudice' and tradition are important in providing presuppositions for understanding. No less than Rudolf Bultmann argued that it was impossible to interpret the Bible without presuppositions.[135] Even theologically conservative scholars have offered an account of apologetics where presuppositions play a crucial role. Many text-

---

132. Thiselton, *Two Horizons*, pp. xix, 11.

133. Ibid., p. 445.

134. Bartholomew, *Reading Ecclesiastes*, pp. 19–21, 204–205; Bruce B. Miller II, 'Hans-Georg Gadamer and Evangelical Hermeneutics', in Michael Bauman and David Hall (eds.), *Evangelical Hermeneutics: Selected Essays from the 1994 Evangelical Theological Society Convention* (Camp Hill: Christian Publications, 1995), pp. 213–232.

135. Rudolf Bultmann, 'Is Exegesis Without Presuppositions Possible?' in *Existence and Faith: Shorter Writings of Rudolf Bultmann*, ed. Schubert M. Ogden (London: Collins, 1960), pp. 289–296.

books on hermeneutics devote substantial sections to exploring a distinctively Christian 'preunderstanding' in matters related to faith and knowledge, creation and sin, the nature of God and Scripture.[136] Moreover, we should be willing to have our preunderstanding altered. If it remains unalterable, then our interpretation will only confirm our existing views.

Hence, we become aware of the complexity of our own horizons, and engage in serious self-searching on what it is in our horizon that might be imposed wrongly on the text. At the same time, we recognize that there is a distance between ourselves and the text, and we allow for that distance, respecting the *distinctiveness* of the horizon of the text as against the distinctiveness of our own horizon. We seek to determine the intention of the author as expressed in the text, and make efforts to understand the horizon of the text in order to avoid the danger of reading our own horizon of understanding into that of the text. Then we relate the horizon of the text to the issues of our own horizon of understanding. We discover that texts open up new horizons for readers. They can bring about change; they engage with readers 'in ways which can productively transform horizons', such that 'the very process of reading may lead to a re-ranking of expectations, assumptions, and goals which readers initially bring to texts'.[137]

### d. Reading as a progressive experience

Above all, on these models, we recognize that reading and understanding is a *progressive* experience. Personal testimony often illustrates this best. One of the first books I was given as a young Christian was a semi-popular commentary on Paul's letter to the Romans. I devoured it, and when I got to the end, I understood Romans! In reality, of course, my knowledge of the argument of the letter was meagre; but one can't become a Christian without

---

136. Duvall and Hays, *Grasping God's Word*, pp. 85–94; Klein, Blomberg and Hubbard, *Biblical Interpretation*, pp. 81–116; McCartney and Clayton, *Let the Reader Understand*, pp. 5–77; Poythress, *God-Centered Biblical Interpretation*, pp. 13–68; Shillington, *Reading the Sacred Text*, pp. 11–26.

137. Thiselton, *New Horizons*, p. 8.

*some* understanding of what Paul writes there about what it means to be a sinner who deserves judgment, but who has been made right with God through faith on the basis of Christ's work on the cross. So, I *did* understand Romans and I did so *truly*. But then a few years later, I attended some Bible studies on Romans, and realized there was *more* to know. And then much later I went to Bible college, and studied Romans again (in the Greek text!) and I learned some more. Most recently of all, my job requires me to get to grips with current scholarship on Paul's relationship to Judaism, and his theology of covenant and justification, which drives me back to Romans again . . . and again. I'm now more aware of what I *don't* know, perhaps, but I could understand Romans even as a young Christian, with no knowledge of Greek and no inkling of hermeneutical principles, and I could understand it *truly*.

### e. Reading and intellectual virtues

Recent work on epistemology has explored the link between intellect and virtue.[138] It holds that the practice of moral virtues such as wisdom, honesty, foresight, understanding, discernment, truthfulness, perseverance and studiousness are just as important to knowledge as brain power! Just as there are intellectual *virtues*, so there are intellectual *vices* – folly, obtuseness, laziness, gullibility, dishonesty, wilful *naïveté*. They too affect our ability to understand. Indeed, so far as Scripture is concerned, wisdom relates to character formation more than our IQ and how many degrees we've earned. Moreover, the cultivation of intellectual virtues is not a momentary action, but a lifelong venture; issues surrounding reading and understanding need to be viewed from a *lifetime* perspective. We should also recognize that we belong to communities of faith which can encourage and reinforce virtuous behaviour to provide a check against self-deception.

### f. Reading ethically

What are the qualities that make for a good reader of the Bible? They are, according to Vanhoozer, *ethical* qualities that include rec-

---

138. W. Jay Wood, *Epistemology: Becoming Intellectually Virtuous* (Contours of Christian Philosophy; Leicester: Apollos, 1998).

ognition of the 'other' (the author in the case of interpretation), the humility and hard work required to listen attentively, and the wisdom to understand the complex ways the author's meaning relates to and challenges my world.[139] This 'ethics of reading', unlike that which we encountered earlier, is not about readers standing over texts, suspicious of texts, and exposing them. Rather, this 'ethics' respects persons whose communicative actions are embodied in texts; it holds that texts may not be manipulated by readers as those who have no rights; it allows itself to be exposed to the scrutiny of the text.

Along similar lines, Thiselton has made an important distinction between *socio-pragmatic* approaches and *socio-critical* approaches. In the first case, interpreters come to the text looking only to have their own ideas affirmed and validated. In the latter case, readers are open to having their agendas *critiqued* by Scripture.

> if there cannot be any critique from outside of a community, *hermeneutics serves only to affirm its corporate self, its structures, and its corporate values. It can use texts only by the same ploy as that which oppressors and oppressive power-structures use, namely in the service of its own interests.*[140]

We can appreciate the importance of communities of faith for biblical interpretation, as Hauerwas and Fowl have emphasized, but reading must nevertheless not be a projection of our community's aspirations (still less an individual's) on to the text. We need to enquire whether the reading is mandated by the text itself or chosen and adopted by the interpretive community, perhaps to suit its own ends. The traditions and lifestyle of communities can be challenged by texts, and need to be when the community falls into error and sin. The role for interpretive communities is in developing interpretive virtues that, in turn, enable us to be more virtuous readers.[141]

---

139. Vanhoozer, *Meaning*, pp. 367–452.
140. Thiselton, *New Horizons*, pp. 6–7; his italics.
141. Vanhoozer, *First Theology*, pp. 275–308.

## g. Reading as performance

The notion that there is no true understanding of texts apart from lived obedience in conformity to texts has been a part of much recent reflection in biblical hermeneutics, with particular attention being paid to the age-old analogy of 'performance'.

Nicholas Lash avers that 'for different kinds of text, different kinds of activity count as the fundamental form of their interpretation', and that 'there are at least some texts that only begin to deliver their meaning in so far as they are "brought into play" through interpretive performance'.[142] N. T. Wright uses the analogy of an unfinished Shakespeare play whose missing fifth act is 'performed' by the church, the actors who immerse themselves in the story of the first four acts (Creation – Fall – Israel – Jesus) and who work out a fifth act for themselves on the basis of what's gone before.[143] Similarly, Frances Young makes the point that the relationship between the text and the interpreter can be understood by analogy with the relationship between a musical score and a musician who performs the score.[144] Stephen Barton calls for a reading practice that will bring the reading of Scripture into the process of community formation, worship and mission, and will place responsibility on the community to read and perform the biblical text in ways that are transforming and life-giving.[145]

These reflections on interpretation as performance are crucial, providing God himself is accorded his due role in the drama. Michael Scott Horton draws on the analogy of drama and performance, but makes it clear that the divine role is not merely that of the playwright, much less that of a spectator in the audience. Not only is he the main actor in the drama, the central

---

142. Nicholas Lash, 'Performing the Scriptures', in *Theology on the Way to Emmaus* (London: SCM, 1986), pp. 37–46; here pp. 40, 42.

143. Wright, *New Testament and People of God*, pp. 139–143.

144. Frances M. Young, *The Art of Performance: Towards a Theology of Holy Scripture* (London: Darton, Longman & Todd, 1990).

145. Stephen C. Barton, 'New Testament Interpretation as Performance', *Scottish Journal of Theology* 52.2 (1999), pp. 179–208.

character on stage, but he also has the most significant speaking part.[146]

## Concluding reflections

In many respects, our task has been modest: to survey that area of biblical studies which deals with the interpretation of, and critical reflection on the interpretation of, biblical texts. We have sought to paint in broad brush strokes some of the issues involved in considering the relationship between author, text, and reader, and have called for an integrated approach which does justice to the distinctive features of each of those facets in interpretation. Throughout, we have attempted to describe the main contours of biblical hermeneutics rather than engage at length with specific biblical texts. In that sense, our task has been preliminary as well as modest. Not content with mere *survey*, students of Scripture will seek to *study*, to present themselves to God as workers who do not need to be ashamed and who correctly handle the Word of truth (2 Tim. 2:15). Such handling, as our final reflections seek to suggest, is a lifelong venture and leads to ongoing transformation.

### *Reading for life, not crises*
When it comes to interpreting the Bible, one senses little appreciation for it until a 'crisis' comes along. Shall we ordain women? Can we condone same-sex relationships? Who does Palestine belong to? What about world poverty? Will the temple be rebuilt? Is there

---

146. Michael S. Horton, *Covenant and Eschatology: The Divine Drama* (Louisville: Westminster/John Knox, 2002), p. 121. For further reflections on 'performance' in theology and biblical interpretation, see Kevin J. Vanhoozer, 'The Voice and the Actor: A Dramatic Proposal about the Ministry and Minstrelsy of Theology', in John G. Stackhouse, Jr (ed.), *Evangelical Futures: A Conversation on Theological Method* (Leicester: Apollos, 2000), pp. 61–106, more fully developed in his *The Drama of Doctrine: A Canonical-Linguistic Approach to Theology* (Louisville: Westminster/John Knox, 2003).

a hell, what's it like, who's going there, and for how long? The problem is that the practice of interpretation is made to address these 'crisis' issues of seeming great relevance and is then put away until the next issue raises its critical, fascinating or ugly head. The best antidote is to have good reading practice already in place.

Crisis interpretation assumes that the Bible should be a (preferably numbered) list of propositions that start with the triune nature of God and end with whether we should eat mince pies before or after the Christmas carol service, taking in nuclear weapons, vegetarianism and cloning along the way. Not that the Bible might not tackle those topics at some level, but it doesn't do so in the abstract; it does so in a series of different types of documents, all of which are engaged with particular people in specific contexts, set within a storyline stretching from creation to consummation – which informs its various stages along the way as well as its significance for us who are incorporated by the divine author into its narrative sweep.

### Reading for transformation, not information

This too is vital. We have sometimes been guilty of imagining the sole purpose of Scripture is to provide *information*. Psalm 19 (vv. 7–8) reminds us it's a word that *transforms* us:

> The Law of the LORD is perfect,
>     reviving the soul.
> The statutes of the LORD are trustworthy,
>     making wise the simple.
> The precepts of the LORD are right,
>     giving joy to the heart.
> The commands of the LORD are radiant,
>     giving light to the eyes.

That's written by someone who not only reads the Word of God, but who loves it and who lives it, and who expects to be changed by it.

Throughout the psalm it's a *life-transforming* word. Ultimately, that's what the best biblical interpretation is all about – because it's based finally in God's self-disclosure, and it's rooted in an ongoing relationship with him. It's Scripture that has the priority on our understanding of God and the world. Every time we're tempted to orient our lives by the *Financial Times*, the football results, or the latest film, we need to come back again to Scripture and be transformed by it. Hence, handling the Bible with integrity is as much a way of *life* as a way of reading. Following the Word entails *embodying* the Word. Practical interpretation is ultimately the way we live our lives each day as believing individuals and as believing communities, shaped by the Spirit of God, constantly seeking to be conformed to his Word, who meditate on it day and night, and who hide it in our hearts that we might not sin against him.

© Antony Billington, 2003.

## 4. FOR THE BIBLE TELLS ME SO? THE ROLES OF FAITH AND EVIDENCE IN BELIEVING THE BIBLE

### David Gibson

*David Gibson is a postgraduate theological student at King's College, London. He has a degree in theology from Nottingham University and was formerly a Staff Worker with the Religious and Theological Studies Fellowship.*

### Introduction

'Why do you believe that the Bible is the Word of God? How can you persuade me that it's true?'

It had been a difficult first term at university for Jo. A committed Christian, she was facing a real challenge with her theology and religious studies degree. Her A level in RS had been taught by a Christian teacher who was able to explain things sympathetically and give guidance from a biblical point of view. But at university it was different. Few, if any, of the lecturers seemed to share her Christian faith and some were openly quite hostile to any form of conservative belief about the Bible. Jo was faced with a constant barrage of critical theories about the biblical texts and intimidating bibliographies of titles written by eminent professors, none of whom seemed to believe what she believed. Towards the end of the term she tried to explain her evangelical convictions to Alex, another first-year student on her course, who seemed happy to accept everything they were being taught. But Alex's questions at the end of their discussion left her struggling: 'Why do you believe that the Bible is the Word of God? How can you persuade me that it's true?'

How should Jo respond to these questions?

This chapter attempts to outline some of the issues that need to be addressed in constructing a theology of belief in the Bible. What is it that convinces us that the Bible is God's Word – is it faith, or evidence about the Bible's reliability and truthfulness, or some combination of the two? Also, on what basis and using which method can we seek to persuade others of the divine origin of the Bible – by presenting evidence for the Bible's reliability, or pointing them to Christ, or some combination of the two?

Here I will be arguing for a form of presuppositionalism over against a more evidentialist approach, but this will be unpacked in terms that are more theological than philosophical.[1] This is not to deny the value of these terms, as in most Christian thought they rest on clear theological understandings about what they mean and where their value comes from.[2] However, I wish to outline an approach to the truth of the Bible that does not start with the merit or demerits of certain terms used in apologetics but that starts by working outwards from the biblical data.

The chapter aims to develop an explicitly theological approach to the Bible – by this I mean that *the Bible itself tells us why it is we believe the Bible to be God's Word* and this fact has to be embedded in all our thinking about the complex relationship between faith and evidence. The progression of argument will inevitably lead us to consider what is involved in both presuppositionalism and evidentialism, and to consider briefly how the argument bears on what

---

1. *Presuppositionalism* is a position which holds that there are certain primary beliefs or truths that must be presupposed when approaching all other articles of knowledge; *Evidentialism* is a position which requires that evidence or reasons are necessary to hold belief rationally.

2. See the discussion in D. A. Carson, *The Gagging of God* (Leicester: Apollos, 1996), pp. 95–96, 184–189. Here various approaches to apologetics are discussed within the context of the fresh challenges created by postmodernism.

has become known as 'Reformed epistemology'.[3] We will also reflect briefly on the suggestion that Jo should not even try to provide an answer to Alex's questions, as the questions themselves are misguided – it is belief in Christ, not the Bible, that is the really important matter.


## The priority of the gospel and the testimony of the Spirit

We can get straight to the heart of the issue by considering a number of biblical texts that point us towards a theological approach to the Bible:

> At that time Jesus said, 'I praise you, Father, Lord of heaven and earth, because you have hidden these things from the wise and the learned, and revealed them to little children.' (Matthew 11:25)

> Simon Peter answered, 'You are the Christ, the Son of the living God.' Jesus replied, 'Blessed are you, Simon son of Jonah, for this was not revealed to you by man, but by my Father in heaven.' (Matthew 16:16–17)

> In reply Jesus declared, 'I tell you the truth, no-one can see the kingdom of God unless he is born again.' (John 3:3)

> We have not received the spirit of the world but the Spirit who is from God, that we may understand what God has freely given us. This is what we speak, not in words taught us by human wisdom but in words taught by the Spirit, expressing spiritual truths in spiritual words. The man without the Spirit does not accept the things that come from the Spirit of God, for they are foolishness to him, and he cannot understand them, because they are spiritually discerned. (1 Corinthians 2:12–14)

---

3. See R. Rauser, *Let Reason Be Your Guide? A Brief Introduction to Reformed Epistemology* (Leicester: Religious and Theological Studies Fellowship Monographs, 2001).

The god of this age has blinded the minds of unbelievers, so that they cannot see the light of the gospel of the glory of Christ, who is the image of God. For we do not preach ourselves, but Jesus Christ as Lord, and ourselves as your servants for Jesus' sake. For God, who said, 'Let light shine out of darkness,' made his light shine in our hearts to give us the light of the knowledge of the glory of God in the face of Christ. (2 Corinthians 4:4–6)

But when God, who set me apart from birth and called me by his grace, was pleased to reveal his Son in me so that I might preach him among the Gentiles, I did not consult any man . . . (Galatians 1:15–16)

So I tell you this, and insist on it in the Lord, that you must no longer live as the Gentiles do, in the futility of their thinking. They are darkened in their understanding and separated from the life of God because of the ignorance that is in them due to the hardening of their hearts. (Ephesians 4:17–18)

For we know, brothers loved by God, that he has chosen you, because our gospel came to you not simply with words, but also with power, with the Holy Spirit and with deep conviction. (1 Thessalonians 1:4–5)

But you have an anointing from the Holy One, and all of you know the truth . . . As for you, the anointing you received from him remains in you, and you do not need anyone to teach you. But as his anointing teaches you about all things and as that anointing is real, not counterfeit – just as it has taught you, remain in him. (1 John 2:20, 27)

This is the one who came by water and blood – Jesus Christ. He did not come by water only, but by water and blood. And it is the Spirit who testifies, because the Spirit is the truth. For there are three that testify: the Spirit, the water and the blood; and the three are in agreement. We accept man's testimony, but God's testimony is greater because it is the testimony of God, which he has given about his Son. Anyone who believes in the Son of God has this testimony in his heart. Anyone who does not believe God has made him out to be a liar because he has not believed the testimony God has given about his Son. (1 John 5:6–10)

It could be argued that none of these texts relates directly to the issue of how we come to believe the Bible, but they do impinge directly on two theological issues: first, how we come to perceive spiritual truth; and, further, how we come to embrace it for what it truly is – the testimony about Christ and his gospel. These texts make it clear that the human mind is incapable of seeing and embracing spiritual truth without the working of the Holy Spirit; he removes innate blindness and illuminates the mind to grasp the truth of the gospel. It is the Holy Spirit who gives birth to faith and it is then faith that grasps hold of the spiritual truths held out in the gospel. Faith recognizes Christ for who he claims to be, grasps the meaning of the cross, sees the light of the gospel of the glory of Christ and therefore believes the words that communicate these truths to be true words.

My thesis here can be simply stated: *through the work of the Holy Spirit in illuminating the mind to the truths of the gospel, the Bible is accepted as true through faith.* We come to accept the truthfulness of the Bible because we have first had our minds enlightened to see the truth of the Gospel, which we embrace by faith. This faith enables us to see that the words of the Bible purport to be God's words and to grasp that God's words are true words. J. I. Packer explains this further:

> Having disclosed himself objectively in history, in His incarnate Son, and in His written scriptural Word, God now enlightens men subjectively in experience, so that they apprehend His self-disclosure for what it is. Thus he causes them to know Him and his end in revelation is achieved . . . Historic Protestantism has regularly described this part of the Spirit's ministry as His witness to divine truth. It is a healing of spiritual faculties, a restoring to man of a permanent receptiveness towards divine things, a giving and sustaining of power to recognize and receive divine utterances for what they are. It is given in conjunction with the hearing or reading of such utterances, and the immediate fruit of it is an inescapable awareness of their divine origin and authority.[4]

---

4. J. I. Packer, *'Fundamentalism' and the Word of God* (London: IVF, 1958), pp. 118–119.

This position is known historically as the 'internal testimony of the Spirit' and is found classically in John Calvin. In context, Calvin was rejecting the idea that faith in the truth of Scripture rested on the authority of the church, yet his central argument is relevant to our discussion here. His words are worth quoting substantially:

> They who strive to build up firm faith in Scripture through disputation are doing things backwards . . . even if anyone clears God's Sacred Word from man's evil speaking, he will not at once imprint upon their hearts that certainty that piety requires. Since for unbelieving men religion seems to stand by opinion alone, they, in order not to believe anything foolishly or lightly, both wish, and demand rational proof that Moses and the prophets spoke divinely. But I reply: the testimony of the Spirit is more excellent than all reason. For as God alone is a fit witness of himself in his Word, so also the Word will not find acceptance in men's hearts before it is sealed by the inward testimony of the Spirit. The same Spirit, therefore, who has spoken through the mouths of the prophets must penetrate into our hearts to persuade us that they faithfully proclaimed what had been divinely commanded . . . Some good folk are annoyed that a clear proof is not ready at hand when the impious, unpunished, murmur against God's Word. As if the Spirit were not called both 'seal' and 'guarantee' (2 Cor. 1:22) for confirming the faith of the godly; because until he illumines their minds, they ever waver among many doubts!
>
> Let this point therefore stand: that those whom the Holy Spirit has inwardly taught truly rest upon Scripture, and that the Scripture indeed is self-authenticated; hence it is not right to subject it to proof and reasoning . . . Therefore, illumined by his power, we believe neither by our own nor by anyone else's judgment that Scripture is from God; but above human judgment we affirm with utter certainty (just as if we were gazing upon the majesty of God himself) that it has flowed to us from the very mouth of God by the ministry of men. We seek no proofs, no marks of genuineness upon which our judgment may lean; but we subject our judgment and wit to it as a thing far beyond any guesswork![5]

---

5. J. Calvin, *Institutes of the Christian Religion*, 1.7.4, 5 (tr. F. L. Battles; Philadelphia: Westminster, 1960), pp. 79–80.

Two points follow from this. First, it is clear that Calvin establishes a distinct difference between 'inspiration' and 'internal testimony'. Inspiration is bound up with the very nature of Scripture and is what guarantees the conclusion that 'the prophets spoke divinely'; it therefore also guarantees that the Scriptures are by definition authoritative. The internal testimony work of the Spirit is what enables us to perceive that Scripture is authoritative. This distinction is very important to bear in mind given that in much modern theology, particularly in the Barthian tradition,[6] the internal testimony of the Spirit replaces the traditional concept of inspiration and is regarded as the decisive factor in making Scripture authoritative.[7]

Second, an argument for the truth of the Bible following this position holds that the truthfulness of the Bible is an article of faith – it is not something we come to by empirical discovery. In much the same way as one cannot prove the existence of God, given that it is a belief one holds through faith, so likewise one cannot conclusively prove the full truthfulness and divine origin of the Bible. On what ground should articles of faith be believed? Packer states that Scripture answers this question by

> resolving the ground of faith, formally, into the veracity of God and, materially, into the divine origin of the propositions put forward for belief. The proper basis for believing is, on the one hand, the acknowledgment that God speaks only truth and, on the other, the recognition of what is proposed as something which He Himself has said. Articles of faith are just truths for which God is perceived to have vouched.[8]

In other words, if Scripture declares that God is a God of truth

---

6. See G. W. Bromiley, 'The Authority of Scripture in Karl Barth', in
   D. A. Carson and J. D. Woodbridge (eds.), *Hermeneutics, Authority and Canon* (Carlisle: Paternoster/Grand Rapids: Baker, 1986),
   pp. 275–294.
7. See J. Frame, 'The Spirit and the Scriptures', in Carson and Woodbridge,
   *Hermeneutics, Authority and Canon*, p. 222.
8. *'Fundamentalism'*, p. 117.

who speaks only truth, and if Scripture claims that it is the actual words of that God, then that is the ground of our believing the Bible to be true. This is a belief we come to by faith because our belief in the God who spoke the Bible's words is by faith. Accepting the doctrine *of* Scripture's truthfulness and authority is akin to accepting other doctrines *in* Scripture. As Packer states:

> All scriptural affirmations are in fact divine utterances, and are through the Spirit apprehended as such by faith. But among the affirmations of Scripture is the biblical doctrine of Scripture which we have surveyed; and one effect of the Spirit's witnessing is to make men bow to this doctrine. The case is just the same as with any other article of faith . . . Just as the Spirit teaches all Christians to receive as authoritative articles of faith the doctrines which the Scriptures assert, so He teaches them to regard as an authoritative source of doctrine the Scriptures which assert them.[9]

Although it goes beyond the scope of our discussion here, this approach necessarily impacts on other aspects of the doctrine of Scripture such as the inerrancy and infallibility of Scripture. Believing that the Bible is completely truthful and without error are likewise truths based on the trustworthiness of God and are again not aspects of the Bible we can empirically set out to prove decisively.[10] They may be demonstrable and rationally justifiable but, because the Bible itself claims to be truthful and reliable,[11] we come to the Bible with an *a prioi* belief in its perfections, rather than seeking to

---

9. Ibid., pp. 119, 121.

10. See P. Helm, 'The Perfect Trustworthiness of God', in P. Helm and C. R. Trueman (eds.), *The Trustworthiness of God: Perspectives on the Nature of Scripture* (Leicester: Apollos, 2002), pp. 237–252.

11. See Wayne Grudem, 'Scripture's Self-Attestation and the Problem of Formulating a Doctrine of Scripture', in D. A. Carson and J. D. Woodbridge (eds.), *Scripture and Truth* (Grand Rapids: Baker, 1983), pp. 19–59.

prove it *a posteriori* from each successive text.[12]

To sum up thus far: we come to believe in the truthfulness and divine origin of the Bible through the internal testimony of the Spirit – the Spirit performs this work in our hearts as he opens our eyes to the glory of the gospel and brings us to faith in Christ.[13] Scripture itself witnesses that it is from God directly and that all that it says is to be received as his Word. These are evident facts we are incapable of seeing without the Spirit's illumination, but which, through his work, we come to hold by conviction. To concur with Packer again:

> The effect of this witness is thus the self-authentication of Scripture to the Christian's conscience. We conclude that where there is faith in Christ, and the Bible is known and read at all, there also, more or less explicit, is faith in Scripture as God's written Word.[14]

However, this is not the end of the matter when it comes to the issue of how we seek to persuade others of the divine origin of the Bible.

### External and internal justification

It has become common to talk about two sorts of defence for the Bible, two patterns of justification for the Bible being of divine

---

12. It should be noted that this viewpoint says only that we believe in advance the *truthfulness* of the text before we come to it, not the *meaning* of the text. It does not invalidate historical-grammatical exegesis and interpretation. See J. I. Packer, *God Has Spoken: Revelation and the Bible* (London: Hodder & Stoughton, 1965), p. 105.

13. See further L. Berkhof, *Introductory Volume to Systematic Theology* (Grand Rapids: Eerdmans, 1932), pp. 182–185, who states, 'We should bear in mind that the particular work of the Holy Spirit described by this name does not stand by itself, but is connected with the whole work of the Holy Spirit in the application of the redemption wrought in Christ.'

14. *'Fundamentalism'*, p. 120.

origin. Here the work of Paul Helm is extremely helpful.[15] Helm distinguishes between *external justification* – the view that the Bible can only be said to be of divine origin if it meets certain criteria established independently of it; and *internal justification* – the view that the Bible ought to be believed to be of divine origin on its own evidence.[16]

At first glance the thought of external justification is appealing – it would seem to offer non-arbitrary and generally accepted grounds for concluding that the Bible is the Word of God. However, there are at least three main reasons why we must deem external justification to be highly problematic. Helm outlines these as:

1. Externalism assumes that there is some obvious, unquestionable test or criterion of what is appropriate for a divine revelation, or that there is some *a priori* standard of reasonableness that the Scriptures must meet. But who is to decide what this standard is?[17]
2. Accepting an external criterion as proof of the Bible's divine origin is necessarily compromising – it makes the authority of the Bible and of God dependent on other matters external to the Bible. Acceptance of the Bible as God's revelation is made to depend on other non-revealed matters.
3. Even at its best, externalism can only offer the probability that the Bible is God's Word – and this is not the kind of foundation on which Christian belief about the Scriptures is based.[18]

---

15. P. Helm, 'Faith, Evidence and the Scriptures', in Carson and Woodbridge, *Scripture and Truth*, pp. 303–320; idem, *The Divine Revelation* (London: Marshall, Morgan & Scott, 1982), especially pp. 71–88.
16. *Divine Revelation*, p. 73. Helm argues that though it is possible to combine these two positions, between them they exhaust the possible patterns of justification.
17. See Helm's extended discussion of the externalist views of Archibald Alexander (1772–1851), the influential Princeton theologian, in 'Faith, Evidence', pp. 305–306, and also of Locke and reason in *Divine Revelation*, pp. 73–78.
18. *Divine Revelation*, pp. 78–79.

These problems with externalism lead us conversely into the area of internal justification and it is this position that I want to examine more closely. It is important to see that, if all the above arguments function negatively against externalism, the second argument above functions as a positive endorsement of internalism. Further, it is vital to see that this argument is not merely a form of philosophical logic, but actually expresses some important theological truths about God, about Christ and about the words they speak.

Hebrews 6:13 states that 'When God made his promise to Abraham, since there was no-one greater for him to swear by, he swore by himself . . .' This shows the principle that the validating source of something is always the higher and final authority; in this instance, when God himself wants to validate his words, he offers himself as validation for those words, since there is no higher authority. The same is true of Christ's words in John 8:14: 'Even if I testify on my own behalf, my testimony is valid, for I know where I came from and where I am going.'

The point here is that, as Robert L. Reymond states, 'Jesus validated his claims by appealing to his knowledge of himself', exactly the same principle as in Hebrews 6:13.[19] It is this, and not primarily logic, that demands that nothing external to God's words can validate God's words. If the Bible is God's Word, then it is a Word that is necessarily authoritative. This is not because of any proof that can be offered about it, but because it was God who spoke it. Primarily such biblical data lead to the conviction that the Bible is necessarily self-authenticating, self-evidencing, self-attesting and self-validating. They lead to Calvin's phrase, which we have already considered: 'God alone is a fit witness of himself in his Word'.

## The problem of circularity

This view, of course, raises the problem of whether such an

---

19. R. L. Reymond, *A New Systematic Theology of the Christian Faith* (Nashville: Thomas Nelson, 1998), p. 80.

approach to the Bible is based on a circular argument – it uses the Bible to validate the Bible! Some of the most thoughtful work in this area has been done by John Frame in his work *The Doctrine of the Knowledge of God*. On this issue he states:

> Criticism [of circularity] is effective only when the critic can suggest a better way. But there is no alternative to circularity. First, allegiance to our Lord demands that we be loyal to Him, even when we are seeking to justify our assertions about Him. We cannot abandon our covenant commitment to escape the charge of circularity. Second, no system can escape circularity because all systems – non-Christian as well as Christian – are based on presuppositions that control their epistemologies, argumentation and use of evidence. Thus a rationalist can prove the primacy of reason only by using a rational argument. An empiricist can prove the primacy of sense-experience only by some kind of appeal to sense-experience . . .[20]

Frame also points out that circularity is only justifiable when arguing for the ultimate criterion in any system of thought; such reasoning is not a carte blanche for circularity at all points in all types of argument. But perhaps the most important point here is Frame's distinction between 'narrow' and 'broad' circularity.

A statement such as 'The Bible is the Word of God because it is the Word of God' is an example of 'narrow circularity'. Statements such as 'Scripture is the Word of God because in Exodus, Deuteronomy and elsewhere God indicates his desire to rule his people by a written text; because in 2 Timothy 3:16 and in 2 Peter 1:21 the Old Testament is identified with that covenantal constitution; because Jesus appointed the apostles to write authoritative words' – these are examples of more 'broad circularity' because this type of argument offers us more data.[21]

We should note, however, that even this type of 'broad' circularity is closely related to the more 'narrow' type of statement, as

---

20. J. Frame, *The Doctrine of the Knowledge of God* (Phillipsburg: Presbyterian & Reformed, 1987), p. 130.
21. Ibid., p. 131.

both are what we might call testimony evidence. That is, in different ways they are both built on what God himself has said or testified about the Bible. The circle could then be broadened beyond this to include other internal evidence, such as the coherence or unity of Scripture and so forth; we will look at arguments like this shortly.

Very importantly, Frame argues that the circle can be broadened even more to include extrabiblical data: 'The Bible is the Word of God because archaeology, history, and philosophy verify its teachings.' However, Frame wishes to stress that these extrabiblical fields are not to be used in a value-neutral way, but only by presupposing that they are Christian sciences – the argument is still actually circular because we would be using archaeology, history and philosophy that presuppose the biblical world view.[22] We will come back to this issue of extrabiblical data later; here we must pause to consider the relationship between the above examples of narrow and broad circularity and what we have seen earlier about the internal testimony of the Spirit.

I propose that statements of the narrowly circular sort, such as 'The Bible is the Word of God because it is the Word of God' should be abandoned. They may be logically defensible, but it can be argued that it is not this sort of conviction that the testimony of the Spirit brings about. Rather, it is better to say that 'The Bible is the Word of God because it says it is the Word of God.' This may seem a very subtle distinction, but it changes the matter entirely. With the latter statement, belief in the Bible is grounded in something that, by faith, we believe God has said; as we have seen, that grounds our faith in the Bible in the veracity of God. Further, the Spirit's work of testifying to the Scriptures must be understood as that work which opens our minds to see all that Scripture evidences about itself and which we would not otherwise see.

The work of the Spirit does not lead us to have the conviction that the Bible is the Word of God without any reasons whatsoever, as if it were a kind of 'holy brainwashing'. This is what

---

22. Ibid.

could lead to the statement 'The Bible is the Word of God because it is the Word of God.' Frame makes the point that the work of the Spirit is not in conflict with a rationality defined by a Christian epistemology. He states that sin

> keeps us from acknowledging warranted conclusions, rational conclusions. The work of the Spirit is to remove those effects of sin, to overcome their resistance. The Spirit does not whisper to us special reasons that are not otherwise available . . .

Rather, we should understand the work of the Holy Spirit as causing us to see the reasons that are available, the internal evidence for the Bible being the Word of God.[23] That evidence may be as 'narrow' as God's own word about the Scriptures ('The Bible is the Word of God because it says it is' – testimony evidence). Or it may be as 'broad' as the many other internal evidences that can be given – we might refer to these as material evidences.

Historically, the various internal evidences for the Bible's divine origin have been variously expressed; perhaps one of the most famous is the Westminster Confession of Faith, which suggests that the ways by which the Bible evidences itself to be the Word of God are

> the heavenliness of the matter, the efficacy of the doctrine, the majesty of the style, the purpose of the whole (which is to give all glory to God), the full disclosure it makes of the only way of man's salvation, the many other incomparable excellencies, and the entire perfection thereof.[24]

These are the ways in which Scripture witnesses to us about its divine origin. We are incapable of seeing them without the witness of the Spirit – or, more precisely, incapable of seeing them as marks of divinity without the Spirit. Calvin outlines a similar argument and yet states very explicitly that such internal evidences are not primarily what make us sure about the Bible:

---

23. Frame, 'Spirit and the Scriptures', p. 232.
24. Westminster Confession of Faith, 1.5.

once we have embraced [Scripture] devoutly as its dignity deserves, and
have recognized it to be above the common sort of things, those
arguments – not strong enough before to engraft and fix the certainty of
Scripture in our minds – become very useful aids.[25]

In the terms of our discussion here, what makes us certain of
the Bible as the Word of God? It is the Spirit's testimony to the
'narrow' or foundational, internal testimony evidence that depends
on the character of God and the word he speaks, together with the
Spirit's testimony to the 'broad' or aiding, internal material evidence, as outlined in Calvin and the Westminster Confession.

## Two questions and an illustration

To help us see the force of this argument about 'narrow' and
'broad' forms of internal evidence, it is helpful to make a distinction between two questions and it is vital to see that they should
not necessarily be answered in the same way:

1. Why do you believe the Bible is the Word of God?
2. What evidence is there for believing that the Bible is the Word
   of God?

To see that these questions are different, consider the following
illustration. If you were to ask me why I believe my wife loves me,
I might reply either that I just know she does or that I know it
because she says she does. Neither would be an inadequate answer
and neither would call into question the reality of my wife's love,
even though I have not given any substantial or material evidence
beyond the testimony of her own word.

However, if you were then to ask me what material evidence
there is that my wife loves me, I could happily list any number of
ways in which by attitude, action, word and gesture my wife dem-
onstrates that she loves me. But am I wrong not to base my belief

---

25. *Institutes*, 1.8.1, 82.

in her love on the material evidence? Certainly not – we might want to suggest that, if there were no material evidence what-soever, my belief in her love could be questioned. But that is not the same thing as saying that the ground of my belief in her love is the material evidence. In the sphere of human relations there is a 'knowing and being known' that does not formally depend on the material evidence for that knowledge; there is, so to speak, a sense in which 'we just know' that something is true, not for no reason whatsoever, but because of the reality of the relationship.

The reason why we believe that the Bible is the Word of God is not in the first instance because of all the material evidence for the Bible being the Word of God. We might answer this question first by stating that we know the Bible is the Word of God because the Holy Spirit has opened our eyes to grasp by faith that it is true; or that because of faith we accept that the Bible is the Word of God because God says it is. This is internal, testimony evidence of the narrower kind outlined above. It is sufficient to warrant certainty, because the Spirit's work has brought us into a relationship with the living God whereby we are sure, by faith, that certain articles of faith are true.

This argument is similar to that advanced by one of the pro-ponents of Reformed epistemology, Alvin Plantinga,[26] in that he suggests that Christians are warranted in their Christian belief by a three-stage process: by reading Scripture, being led by the Holy Spirit, and then receiving faith from the Holy Spirit. As people read the Bible, they receive the internal testimony of the Spirit and can pronounce in faith, 'Yes, that's right, that's the truth of the matter; this is indeed the word of the Lord.'[27] However, con-trary to Plantinga et al.,[28] that does not mean that it is invalid to

26. A. Plantinga, *Warranted Christian Belief* (New York: Oxford University Press, 2000). See also his 'Reason and Belief in God', in A. Plantinga and N. Wolterstorff (eds.), *Faith and Rationality: Reason and Belief in God* (Notre Dame: University of Notre Dame Press, 1983).

27. Quoted in Rauser, *Let Reason Be Your Guide?* p. 41.

28. See particularly the criticism of George Mavrodes, outlined in Frame, about Plantinga and Wolterstorff's devaluing of positive apologetics, as

speak of other positive reasons in the form of material evidence for the Bible being the Word of God. We must make the distinction between the ground of our faith in the Bible and the evidence for the Bible. The ground of our faith is explicitly theological: it is based on the gospel, the work of the Spirit, the testimony of God, and yet this faith is accompanied by material evidence.[29]

## Extrabiblical evidence

So far I have left more or less untouched the issue of extrabiblical evidence and its relationship to how we come to believe in the Bible. This is a complex area that poses many sophisticated epistemological problems. However, following Frame, I suggest that because Christianity contains propositional claims about God's acts in history and because those claims are true, then God has left his fingerprints in our world. Two important points follow.

First, the Christian evidential argument can never be merely evidential.[30] We should notice the presupposition in the preceding sentence, which means that we work outwards from the truth about God and the Bible to historical matters, rather than trying to evaluate neutrally all the data in history that will somehow lead us to God. I suggest it cannot be otherwise, given what we have seen about human blindness and the necessary work of the Spirit. Christian handling of evidence must always start from Christian presuppositions about the framework of interpretation for that evidence. Consider the issue of the resurrection of Jesus; here Frame is worth quoting in full:

---

well as Frame's own observations in 'The New Reformed Epistemology' (Appendix I), *Doctrine of the Knowledge of God*, pp. 391ff.

29. See also the excellent brief treatment of Reformed epistemology in D. A. Carson and J. D. Woodbridge, *Letters Along the Way: A Novel of the Christian Life* (Wheaton: Crossway, 1993), pp. 149–157.

30. Frame, *Doctrine of the Knowledge of God*, p. 143.

In 1 Corinthians 15, the Resurrection is presented in the context of Old and New Testament Theology; it is not presented merely by using 'inductive evidence' apart from a theological framework of meaning. To be sure, Paul appeals to witnesses to establish the fact of the Resurrection (vv 3–14) but even that is presented as part of Paul's authoritative apostolic instruction (v 3). The point is not so much that the Corinthians could verify the Resurrection for themselves by consulting the witnesses, though that is true and that fact does confirm what he says. Paul's point is rather that the testimony to the Resurrection was part of the apostolic preaching and is therefore to be accepted as part of that apostolic testimony. After making that point, Paul then gives an additional reason why the Resurrection ought to be believed: if it is denied, the whole doctrinal content of Christianity must also be denied (vv 12–19). Paul then goes on to compare Christ with the Old Testament figure of Adam and Christ's redemption with the Old Testament description of man's sinful condition (vv 20–22). Following that, Paul presents an even more theological discussion of the role that the Resurrection plays in the organism of revelation. Clearly, then, the Resurrection is no 'brute fact' and the grounds for believing it are not 'purely empirical' or 'purely inductive.' Empirical considerations, such as witnesses, play a role but the crucial point is that the Resurrection is central to the presuppositional revelation: we cannot consistently presuppose Christ if we deny the Resurrection.[31]

This is relevant to our discussion because it is an example of how truths in Scripture are understood on the basis of scriptural pre-suppositions. I suggest that the same is exactly true of truths *about* Scripture.

To return to the illustration about my wife's love for me, if you were to ask me what material evidence there is that my wife loves me, I might reply by saying that she buys me theological books for my birthday. However, in many people's presuppositional frame-work (including my wife's!), buying theological books as a birthday present could be regarded as evidence of my wife not loving me! It could in fact be evidence for all sorts of things – for instance, that

---

31. Ibid., pp. 146–147.

she regards me as a heretic and in need of some orthodox teaching. Other people might regard a romantic meal or some new clothes as the proper evidence of love. The point here is to show that books count as evidence of love only within the presuppositional framework of our particular relationship and, even then, strictly speaking, only within my presuppositional framework. Presuppositions control how we interpret evidence and this means the Christian apologist cannot regard the presentation of evidence as a blank cheque that, when cashed, guarantees belief in the Bible. V. Philips Long makes the same point in his discussion of archaeology, a discipline often relied on either to prove or disprove the reliability of biblical history. He shows that the material remains unearthed by archaeology do not in fact *speak* at all, but *must be interpreted* on some basis: once the researcher begins to analyse the evidence,

> theoretical concerns begin to transform the archaeological evidence
> into an historical account. In this sense archaeological evidence, despite
> its brute factuality, is no more objective than any other type of
> evidence.[32]

The second thing to note here arises from a passage such as Romans 1. This outlines how the evidence about God in nature is 'clearly seen' and so leaves sinners 'without excuse' (Romans 1:20). Although the passage raises a host of questions to do with general revelation and common grace,[33] it is important to realize that Paul's argument here is that the apprehension of God's revelation of himself in creation has become marred by our sin – we are guilty of suppressing the truth we are presented with (Romans 1:18). This means that we must understand the Christian presenta-

---

32. V. Philips Long, *The Art of Biblical History* (Leicester: Apollos, 1994), p. 144, quoting F. Brandfon, 'The Limits of Evidence: Archaeology and Objectivity', *Maarar* 4/1 (1987), p. 30.

33. On the question of how these issues relate to the Bible see A. N. S. Lane, 'Sola Scriptura? Making Sense of a Post-Reformation Slogan', in P. E. Satterthwaite and D. F. Wright (eds.), *A Pathway into the Holy Scripture* (Grand Rapids: Eerdmans, 1994), pp. 297–327.

tion of evidence, whether for the Bible or anything else of apologetic interest, to be a presentation of moral obligation. That is to say, as Frame states, the evidence

> rightly *obligates* consent. A believing response to this revelation is not merely optional; it is required . . . Thus the evidential argument is *demonstrative*, not merely probable.[34]

This is an important point, as it highlights that the essential apologetic task is not to achieve intellectual assent after all the evidence has been presented, but to call for faith and repentance. This is also another possible criticism of Reformed epistemology – it is concerned to establish epistemic rights, what we may believe, but says little about epistemic obligations, what we should believe.[35]

### 'Classical apologetics' and Christ and the Bible

Before I come to some concluding reflections it will be helpful to consider an approach to the truth of the Bible known as 'classical apologetics' and to compare this with the influential work of John Wenham. Both schools of thought lead us to the vital issue of the role that Christ's view of the Bible should have in our discussion.

The classical apologetics line, as represented by thinkers such as R. C. Sproul, John Gerstner and Arthur Lindsley,[36] seeks to prove the divine origin of the Bible by taking as the starting premise the Bible's general historical reliability. The argument runs as follows:

*Premise 1:* The Bible is a basically trustworthy document.

---

34. *Doctrine of the Knowledge of God*, p. 142.
35. See Carson, *Gagging of God*, p. 188, and Frame, *Doctrine of the Knowledge of God*, p. 384.
36. R. C. Sproul, John Gerstner and Arthur Lindsley, *Classical Apologetics* (Grand Rapids: Zondervan, 1984).

*Premise 2:* On the basis of this (generally) reliable document we have sufficient evidence to believe confidently that Jesus is the Son of God.

*Premise 3:* Jesus Christ, being the Son of God, is an infallible authority.

*Premise 4:* Jesus Christ teaches that the Bible is more than generally trustworthy: it is the very Word of God.

*Premise 5:* The Word, in that it comes from God, is utterly trustworthy because God is utterly trustworthy.

*Conclusion:* On the basis of the infallible authority of Christ, the Church believes the Bible to be utterly trustworthy, infallible and authoritative.[37]

This argument is important because it introduces the concept that Christ's teaching about the Bible is vital for our doctrine of Scripture. However, this route of getting to Christ's teaching is significantly flawed and should be rejected as an apologetic device. R. L. Reymond states the case:

> I do not believe the progression is a valid argument in that the conclusion declares more than the original premise will allow. If one approaches these issues without Christian presuppositions, one can only conclude at best that the Bible is probably, or even possibly, God's Word.[38]

Similarly, John Frame adds:

> The [proponents of this view] overestimate, I think, the current scholarly consensus on the reliability of the Gospels. They assume that almost every NT scholar will concede that the Gospels are 'generally reliable.' I doubt it.[39]

---

37. R. C. Sproul, *Reason to Believe* (Grand Rapids: Zondervan, 1982), pp. 30–31.

38. *New Systematic Theology*, pp. 74–75.

39. J. Frame, 'Van Til and the Ligonier Apologetic', *Westminster Theological Journal* 47 (1985), p. 297.

Some scholars, of course, have argued well for the historical reliability of the Gospels and my argument does not mean to deny the validity of the historical-critical method in itself.[40] Rather, my point here is to show that even this method of arguing for belief in the Bible simply locates the heart of the argument in the historical arena, and historical study cannot be allowed either to hold belief in the Bible hostage until all the evidence is in, or to expect to conduct its business entirely free of presuppositional interference. The classical apologetics position falls foul of accepting a supposedly 'neutral' approach to history and evidence, as if presuppositions can all somehow be set aside and the data be evaluated entirely free from interfering frameworks of interpretation for that history and evidence. From a more theological point of view, it is vital to note that the Christian does not believe that the Bible is God's Word simply because Jesus taught that it was. The fact that Jesus did teach this (Matthew 4:4, 7, 10; 19:4–5; 22:29; Luke 16:17; John 10:35; 16:12–14) is sometimes outlined among Christians as the primary reason why we believe the Bible is God's Word, but this is not so. The issue must be decided further back than that – as we have seen, it is decided formally by the truthfulness of God and materially by the divine origin of the words.[41]

If Christians state that the reason they believe the Bible is authoritative is because Jesus said so, and unbelievers respond by asking how they know Jesus actually said the things those Gospel passages report, how would they respond? By arguing that there is good evidence that those passages are historical, as do Sproul et al.? But at the very least this would be exposing that the real reason why the believer believes the Bible is not because of Jesus' teaching, but because they hold that it is generally historically reliable.

It is very helpful to compare this sort of reasoning about Christ and the Scriptures with the argument of John Wenham in his

---

40. See, e.g., Craig L. Blomberg, *The Historical Reliability of the Gospels* (Downers Grove: IVP, 1987), especially pp. 234–254.

41. See Packer, *'Fundamentalism'*, p. 117.

seminal work *Christ and the Bible*.[42] It could be argued that Wenham is unclear about the starting point for his argument – he seems to be similar to the classical apologists with statements such as:

> if the Gospels are substantially true, we are justified in regarding as historical those features in them which are often repeated and which are found in a variety of Gospel strata.[43]

However, this would be an unfair representation, as for Wenham it seems clear that how we come to believe that the Gospels are substantially true is actually a matter of faith. Consider the following lengthy quotation:

> [This argument] starts by accepting as valid the characteristic Christian experience of conversion. A convert from a non-Christian religion or from modern secular society seldom arrives at the decisive moment of faith with a view of biblical inspiration already formulated in his mind. His quest is a wrestling with the Christ portrayed in the New Testament and witnessed to by Christians. As he progresses in his search the Gospels seem to him more and more to have the ring of truth. At last he comes to the moment when he says, 'Lord, I believe.' He has arrived at faith with a conviction about the basic truth of the New Testament witness to Christ, but without necessarily any clear beliefs about the truth or falsity of many of the details or about the status of the Bible as a whole. God has become real to him in Christ through the external witness of the gospel and the internal witness of the Holy Spirit. In conversion he has made the discovery that God, made known in Jesus Christ, is the centre and starting-point of all true knowledge. Growth in the knowledge of things of God (which includes progress in theological understanding) *comes by holding fast to the centre and by working outwards from there* (emphasis added). There is a progression: God; God revealing himself; God revealing himself supremely in Christ; Christ teaching the truth of Scripture; finally,

---

42. J. Wenham, *Christ and the Bible* (3rd edn.; Guildford: Eagle, 1993). First published in 1972.

43. Ibid., p. 13.

with Scripture as a guide, the Christian exploring the apparently limitless jungle which makes up the world of phenomena.[44]

Wenham's argument here is important as it helps us to make the distinction between faith in Christ through the gospel and faith in Christ's teaching about the Bible. The distinction here is not between two different faiths, but between the logical order of progression whereby we come to accept that the Bible is true. That is to say, it is saving faith in Christ that first of all gives conviction about the truth of Christ; and it is through this saving faith that the Holy Spirit is at work to bring conviction about the truth of the biblical witness to Christ. This is not an inadequate answer to the question of why we believe the Bible but, as we have seen in the illustration about my relationship with my wife, it does not have to be the end of the matter.

It can lead us to our next position – faith in Christ's teaching about the Bible. Christ's teaching about the Scriptures forms part of the material evidence for the divine origin of the Bible, but it is not the sole or even foundational reason why we believe the Bible. Jesus' teaching about the Scriptures shows us that the presupposition we have arrived at because of the work of the Spirit through the gospel, testifying to the veracity and character of God, is a correct presupposition to have. Before we even come to look at Jesus' teaching about the Bible we can be confident that those words that tell us what Jesus' teaching is, are true and authoritative words.

This helps us to know how to respond to our unbelieving friends who ask how we know Jesus actually said the things those Gospel passages report. In the very first instance it is because of our conversion, because of faith, the gospel and the work of the Spirit. We believe that Jesus said the things the Bible claims he said because we believe *in* Jesus, we believe that the gospel is true and that the work of the Spirit is a reality in our experience.

At this point it is worth commenting on the alternative viewpoint I mentioned at the start, namely that the whole issue of arguing for belief in the truthfulness of the Bible is beside the point

---

44. Ibid., p. 14.

and obscures the fact that we are called to trust in Christ, not the Bible. This point is well taken if it is meant to highlight the dangers of bibliolatry and exalting the Bible above Christ. However, in much recent theology this viewpoint is expressed as a way of wanting to sit loose to some of the tricky issues about the full truthfulness and reliability of the Bible. It locates the authority of the Bible not in the fact of God speaking but in the person of Jesus Christ.[45] This position should be resisted for a couple of reasons.

First, this position does not go far enough in pressing home its own fundamental premise that the key issue with the Bible is to point us to faith in Christ through the gospel. Once we take this as our starting point we are bound then to ask what believing the gospel of Christ actually means. Peter Jensen explains:

> The key consequence of accepting the gospel is, therefore, that Jesus
> Christ becomes our Lord, exercising the authority of his kingdom in our
> lives. From the gospel, we can see both what the nature of his authority
> must be and also the means by which he exerts it. The instrument of his
> authority is the word . . .[46]

This means that the Bible itself cannot be simply a witness to the authority of Christ without any inherent authority itself. It is the word of the Sovereign Lord. It is the means by which he exercises his sovereign rule over us. The words of the Bible carry the authority of the author. As Jensen shows, this is something we accept in everyday life as in the receiving of a letter from a good friend. We do not ignore the letter and say to our friend, 'I did not believe your words because they were not you.' On the contrary, as we treat the words so we treat the author of the words.[47]

---

45. See, e.g., Francis Watson, *Text and Truth: Redefining Biblical Theology*
    (Edinburgh: T. & T. Clark, 1997), p. 1; John Barton, *People of the Book? The
    Authority of the Bible in Christianity* (London: SPCK, 1988), p. 83.

46. Peter Jensen, *The Revelation of God* (Leicester: IVP, 2002), p. 153. Jensen
    develops this by demonstrating the covenantal nature of Scripture and
    showing how this is God's instrument for ruling the covenant people.

47. Ibid., p. 165.

Furthermore, it could be added that at the very least the lordship of Christ obligates us to accept his own teaching about the Bible as being authoritative and trustworthy in its entirety.

A second criticism is that this position actually works with an illogical divide between the particular words of the Bible that tell us about Christ and the Bible's own theological claim that all its words are God's words. Not far beneath the surface here is discomfort with the traditional understanding of inspiration, perhaps due to a mistaken belief that regarding the whole of Scripture as the breathed-out words of God leads to a flattening of the diversity of the Bible and interpretive ignorance of its different literary genres. However, Timothy Ward has recently argued extremely cogently that, first, the traditional understanding of inspiration is more than equal to these criticisms and, second, that the primacy of Christ in the biblical revelation can actually only be secured by a robust belief in the sufficiency of the whole canon of Scripture to testify about him. As he states:

> If 'Jesus Christ' is set up as the sole unquestionable principle of the self-interpretation of Scripture, the 'centre' in the light of which other parts of Scripture are judged not to witness truly to him, to fall short of his gospel . . . then the 'Jesus Christ' in terms of whom we read Scripture will be a Jesus Christ whose identity is formed for us only partly by Scripture – probably by those parts which most appeal to us.[48]

## Conclusion

I am now in a position to offer a few reflections on some of the issues raised at the start of this chapter, and will draw the various strands of my argument together in the following four points:

1. It should be obvious by now that a coherent theology of belief in the Bible means that we do not have just a solitary argument

---

48. T. Ward, *Word and Supplement: Speech Acts, Biblical Texts, and the Sufficiency of Scripture* (Oxford: Oxford University Press, 2002), p. 292.

for why we believe what we believe about the Bible. The issue facing us is not whether evidence has any role in our belief, or whether we must think only of the gospel and the work of the Spirit. Rather, the real challenge we face is to understand the theological relationship between matters such as the gospel, faith, internal and external evidence. It will be helpful to try to tease out a little of what the systematic relationship between these topics actually means.

2.  This chapter has suggested that the foundational issue at stake here is actually the Christian gospel – the truth about Jesus Christ, our sin-blinded perception of reality, and our need of salvation from the wrath to come. In grasping the truth of the Bible, the work of the Spirit is paramount to enable us to embrace spiritual truths.

    This means that as we think about discrete topics such as why we believe in the Bible, our starting point must be to operate with the gospel as rationale and presupposition in all our thinking. The same is true in other matters of Christian belief, for example in giving a reason for the Christian world view on suffering, or other religions. At the heart of Christian thinking is belief in the gospel and how this affects all areas of epistemology and theological reflection. This essentially means that the discipline of apologetics, for instance, cannot afford to see itself as anything other than contextual evangelism. To return to Jo and Alex at the start of this chapter, Alex's questions should actually be grasped as an opportunity to share the truth of the gospel as it pertains to belief in the Bible. For Jo to pretend that she believes because she understands and knows simply because of hard evidence, is to deny the reality that she knows because she has first believed – and her belief in Christ needs to be brought to bear on all the different issues related to belief in the Bible.

3.  Further, to develop the issue of apologetics a little, what we have seen in this chapter means that the use of evidence for the Bible needs to be married to a solid understanding of how presuppositions function in arguing for biblical truth. It demands a creative apologetic that does not use evidence as the foundation or trump card in the armoury. We have no 'brute' or

'plain' facts that are somehow incontrovertible evidence for the truth of the Bible.

Therefore, most importantly, we should exercise care in using evidence as the proof of biblical truth. Christian apologists may well find a role in their argument for stating, for instance, that archaeology shows that Gallio was the proconsul of Achaia as Acts 18:12 says. But it is incompatible with Christian belief about the Bible to give the impression that such archaeology is vital to our faith or somehow gives the Bible a reliability it did not have before the discovery was made. In short, what we are arguing for here is the integrity in apologetic presentation that our presuppositions demand – we must be prepared to argue that our belief in the Bible is not based on all the evidence for the Bible.

4. It follows closely from this that a theological understanding of evidentialism means that any presentation of evidence to do with revelation must be coupled with a presentation of the moral obligation that such evidence warrants. We are prone to think that the gospel calls for faith and repentance, while all the evidence for the Bible calls for only aroused interest or intellectual credibility. However, on Paul's example in Acts 17:30, people's ignorance in grasping both evidence and the meaning of that evidence is a culpable act of moral rebellion that leaves them facing God's judgment. The Christian use of revelatory evidence cannot be 'look and decide for yourself', but 'look and repent.'

Taken together, then, these points mean that Christian belief in the Bible rests on a number of different factors, all of which exist in a clear theological relationship to each other. The starting point of our faith in Christ means that our confidence is placed firmly in the gospel and the work of the Spirit. Through these means we are able to experience the 'utter certainty' about the Bible that Calvin described, 'just as if we were gazing upon the majesty of God himself'. This gospel presupposition and rationale embraces the Bible's truthfulness and reliability because of God's truthfulness, because the Bible's words are God's words, and because Jesus himself regarded the Bible in this way. It works out from here to see all the internal evidence that the Scriptures are from God himself, and its examination of all the external evidence is coupled with the gospel presupposition that God has actually given us all the evidence we need to know that he is there and to believe in him.

## Suggested Further Reading

Calvin, J., *Institutes of the Christian Religion* (tr. F. L. Battles; Philadelphia: Westminster, 1960).

Carson, D. A., *The Gagging of God* (Leicester: Apollos, 1996).

Carson D. A., and J. D. Woodbridge (eds.), *Hermeneutics, Authority and Canon* (Carlisle: Paternoster/Grand Rapids: Baker, 1986).

Carson, D. A., and J. D. Woodbridge (eds.), *Scripture and Truth* (Grand Rapids: Baker, 1983).

Frame, J., *Apologetics to the Glory of God: An Introduction* (Phillipsburg: Presbyterian & Reformed, 1994).

Frame, J., *The Doctrine of the Knowledge of God* (Phillipsburg: Presbyterian & Reformed, 1987).

Helm, P., *The Divine Revelation* (London: Marshall, Morgan & Scott, 1982).

Helm P., and C. R. Trueman (eds.), *The Trustworthiness of God: Perspectives on the Nature of Scripture* (Leicester: Apollos, 2002).

Jensen, P., *The Revelation of God* (Leicester: IVP, 2002).

Long, V. Philips, *The Art of Biblical History* (Leicester: Apollos, 1994).

Packer, J. I., *'Fundamentalism' and the Word of God* (London: IVF, 1958).

Packer, J. I., *God Has Spoken: Revelation and the Bible* (London: Hodder & Stoughton, 1965).

Rauser, R., *Let Reason Be Your Guide? A Brief Introduction to Reformed Epistemology* (Leicester: Religious and Theological Studies Fellowship Monographs, 2001).

Ward, T., *Word and Supplement: Speech Acts, Biblical Texts, and the Sufficiency of Scripture* (Oxford: Oxford University Press, 2002).

Wenham, J., *Christ and the Bible* (3rd edn.; Guildford: Eagle, 1993). First published in 1972.